Study Guide

Pamela Park-Curry

The Ohio State University

Sociology
for the
Twenty-First Century

SECOND EDITION

Tim J. Curry
Robert M. Jiobu
Kent Schwirian

The Ohio State University

PRENTICE HALL, *Upper Saddle River, New Jersey 07458*

© 1999 by PRENTICE-HALL, INC.
Simon & Schuster / A Viacom Company
Upper Saddle River, New Jersey 07458

10 9 8 7 6 5 4 3

ISBN 0-13-0-13-095655-4

Printed in the United States of America

Table of Contents

PREFACE

I love sociology.

I can vividly remember my first sociology course in college – you might say it was "love at first insight." I remember being fascinated as every topic we studied had real life applications. Each concept (and there were many) was an explanation of a part of social reality that together, by the end of the quarter, led to an increased understanding of social interaction and social structure. I was an "undecided" major when I began the course, a sociology major when I finished.

I know from teaching sociology that many of you are taking this course to fulfill a college requirement while some of you are taking it as an elective. A few of you might also be exploring courses in search of a major. No matter what your reason, I believe that sociology will contain information that will benefit you throughout your life.

Most of you will be starting your careers, your families, and living the majority of your life in the twenty-first century. The increasing pace of technological innovation will present a challenge to you. You will be living in a future that will require you to know how to access vast quantities of rapidly changing information as well as to be able to critically assess that information. Curry, Jiobu, and Schwirian recognized this. They designed Sociology in the Twenty-First Century to help you understand the world in which you live, how it has developed in the past century, and where it is going in the future. By the end of this course, you should have a better understanding of the sociological causes, consequences, and interpretations of this social change. The integration of web resources throughout the book will help you develop your ability to access information quickly and efficiently on almost any topic. Each and every chapter will have information and insights that will be part of your world now and in the future.

Because I feel that the ideas and perspectives in Sociology in the Twenty-First Century will benefit you, I designed this study guide to help you master the basic concepts of the book. One of the most effective methods is to use this guide at the beginning and the end of each chapter. When you are about to read a chapter, read over the chapter outline in the study guide as a preview to the textbook. Briefly scan the topics and concepts that will be included in the textbook chapter. Then carefully read the chapter in the textbook. You will note that all the key concepts are included in the study guide but that the textbook elaborates upon them explaining them fully in a sociological context. In particular, note the tables, charts, and boxes in the textbook paying attention to the concepts and ideas being illustrated. Take some time to review the critical questions contained throughout the chapter. Many of the critical questions ask you to reflect on personal experiences and observations. Finally, take the self-test questions in the study guide. If you encounter problems, the page number where the information is found is in the answer key.

I believe that one of the joys of sociology is simply being able to see how sociological concepts and ideas apply to you, your family, your work environment, your community, your country and the world. I sincerely hope that this study guide is useful to you and that you enjoy your sociology course.

Pamela Park-Curry, Ph.D.

Chapter 1

What is Sociology?

THE SOCIOLOGICAL VIEWPOINT
> *Definition of Sociology: science, social structure, social interaction and social change*

THE ORIGINS OF SOCIOLOGY AND THREE CENTRAL FIGURES:
KARL MARX, EMILE DURKHEIM, AND MAX WEBER
> *Karl Marx*
> *Emile Durkheim*
> *Max Weber*
> *Marx, Durkheim, and Weber Compared*

PERSPECTIVES WITHIN SOCIOLOGY
> *Functionalism – the Functionalist Perspective*
> *Conflict Theory – the Conflict Perspective*

RESEARCH METHODS
> *Qualitative Methods*
> *Quantitative Methods*
> *Quantitative and Qualitative Methods Compared*
> *Ethics and Research*

ADDITIONALLY
> *Harriet Martineau*
> *Critical Thinking*
> *Time-line of Twenty-First Century American Sociology*
> *Sociology for the Twenty-First Century*

CRITICAL QUESTIONS
> *Sociological perspective*
> *Alienation, anomie, rationality*
> *Functionalism and conflict theory*
> *Interview research methods*

SELF TEST QUESTIONS/ANSWERS

CHAPTER SUMMARY and KEY TERMS

The Sociological Viewpoint

The story on page 1 is used to illustrate the sociological viewpoint. That is, the perspective from which you view the world is influenced by your position in it. This may include your social class, sex, race, profession and/or family background. The sociological viewpoint focuses on the social setting of behavior, the social interaction among the parties involved and the change through time in social structure and social interaction.

Sociology	**Sociology** is defined as the scientific study of social structure and social interaction and of the factors making for change in social structure and social interaction. Scientific means that sociological knowledge is based on the principles of science where evidence is gathered through observation and experimentation.
Social structure	**Social structure** is made of the relatively permanent components of our social environment. Even though all members of a society contribute to the social structure, it is larger than any single individual. This is because individuals are constantly entering and exiting the social structure. We may influence the social structure very little at birth, a great deal during adulthood and little again during old age. Social structure imposes order and stability on social life. It also may constrict our behavior. Sociologists seek to understand how social structure is created, how it changes, and how it affects our lives.
Social interaction	Actions toward and reactions from other individuals constitute social interaction. **Social interaction** may take place with someone who is not even physically present, as in an imaginary conversation. Sociologists study the nature of social interaction and how relationships can positively or negatively affect our lives.
Social change	Even though social life and structure are relatively stable, they are in a constant process of change. Individuals' lives change over the course of their lives. Societies may change due to a natural catastrophe, war, a population explosion or a new invention.

The Origins of Sociology and Three Central Figures: Karl Marx, Emile Durkheim, and Max Weber

Sociology developed more than 100 years ago as the result of intellectuals' attempts to explain changes taking place in traditional societies. In Europe, the Industrial Revolution was creating profound and permanent changes.

August Comte	August Comte is credited as the father of sociology. He believed that sociology was a science and referred to it as "positive philosophy." Comte proposed that sociologists should study two things: why society changes and why it does not.
Karl Marx	German philosopher Karl Marx is well known for his book, *The Communist Manifesto*. Like Martineau, Marx believed that social scientists should try to improve society. His personal goal was to free workers (the proletariat) from oppression and poverty that he felt they suffered as the result of industrialization. He proposed revolution as the only route to freedom. Marx predicted that this would happen as follows: factory owners (the bourgeoisie) decrease the workers' over time pay in order to make a higher profit; the workers, living in misery, realize that their only hope is to unite and overthrow the owners; the workers revolt, finally, take over the factories, establish a new government and a single class society, and abolish the private ownership of property.
Alienation	Marx thought that capitalism's focus on profit resulted in humans being treated like machines. This transformed work from something meaningful to something meaningless. It resulted in **alienation**, a situation in which workers were estranged from their social worlds and felt that life was meaningless.

Emile Durkheim	French social scientist Emile Durkheim was the first person to hold the title of professor of education and sociology. Durkheim focused on what holds society together. He distinguished two types of solidarity (cohesiveness).
Mechanical solidarity	Members of traditional societies are very similar to each other. They participate in the same social life within the same culture and thus share almost identical values. The society is small, the division of labor simple and the level of technology low. Durkheim referred to this as **mechanical solidarity**.
Organic solidarity	Industrial societies, on the other hand, are large and have a complex division of labor. Members of these societies come into contact with many strangers on a daily basis. While members share some values, they disagree on many others. Due to their differences, Durkheim pointed out, people in industrial societies are interdependent. They rely on each other for specialized knowledge and skills. Durkheim termed this **organic solidarity**. The word organic refers to the idea that each part in an industrial society functions like a part of the body. Due to the interdependence of parts, an injury to one part will affect all others.
Anomie	Finally, Durkheim noticed that rapid changes which sometimes occur in industrial societies produce a situation in which norms become unclear or disappear. He termed this situation of uncertainty **anomie** and identified it as the cause of many social problems including suicide.
Max Weber	German scholar Max Weber had an enormous impact on the development of sociology. While attaching Marx's ideas, Weber actually arrived at related conclusion about life under industrial capitalism.
Rationalism	Max Weber contributed the idea of **rationalization** to sociology. This is the replacement of traditional thinking with thinking that emphasizes deliberate calculation, efficiency, self-control, and effectiveness in the accomplishment of specific goals. Weber felt that rationalization and industrialization occurred simultaneously. He believed that rationalization increased efficiency within society but warned that cold calculation could not replace the warmth of close social ties.

Perspectives within Sociology

Within sociology there are two major viewpoints or perspectives. The **functionalist viewpoint** stems from the work of Durkheim while the **conflict viewpoint** stems from the work of Karl Marx

Functionalism	**Functionalism** or the functionalist viewpoint argues that parts of a society work together to maintain the cohesion of the system. This cohesion is the result of consensus and common values shared by members of the society. The theory assumes that a failure in one aspect of the system will negatively affect the others. Functionalist theory assumes that components of society work to maintain equilibrium, or balance, which permits the whole society to operate smoothly. However, events such as war can upset the equilibrium.
Functions	**Functions** are actions that positively affect the social system.
Dysfunctions	**Dysfunctions** are actions that negatively affect the social system.
Manifest functions	**Manifest functions** are those whose consequences are intended. For example, a manifest function of higher education is to obtain critical thinking skills necessary to acquire a fulfilling job.
Latent functions	**Latent functions** are those whose consequences are not intended. For example, a latent function of higher education is that colleges and universities serve as marriage markets. Chances are very good that you will marry someone you meet at college. However, this was probably not the intention of the founders of your school.

Conflict theory   Contrary to the functionalist viewpoint or perspective, the conflict viewpoint or **conflict theory** proposes that society is held together by **social power**—the ability to control the behavior of others against their will. This theory originated in the thinking of Marx. Conflict theorists believe that social power allows some groups to dominate others. This results in the constant potential for conflict between the haves and the have nots. Conflict may take place between individuals, groups of individuals, or organizations. This theory sees social change as a regular feature of social life as subordinate groups will strive to change their positions. Conflict theorists propose that conflict actually holds society together by serving the dominant group and by creating shifting alliances among special interest groups.

Research Methods

Research methods are divided into two types: qualitative and quantitative. The type of method used depends upon the type of inquiry.

Qualitative methods   **Qualitative methods** are designed to gain the subjective understanding, interpretation, and meaning of social behavior. Qualitative researchers use three basic techniques: historical analysis, interviews and life histories, and participant observation.

Historical analysis   **Historical analysis** is often based on old letters, diaries, and baptismal records. This type of analysis is useful because it provides both detailed information and the broad societal context. Inaccurate or incomplete records may bias historical analyses.

Interviews   Interviews and life histories help answer questions about meaning, symbolism, or some other aspect of social life which is difficult to record numerically. In the **structured interview**, the researcher asks the respondent a series of questions and records the answers by writing or tape recording them. Similarly, the **life history** involves a long interview or series of interviews through which the researcher attempts to discover essential features or turning points in the respondent's life. Usually the initial questions are general. As the interview progresses the researcher will gently prod the respondent to fill in the details.

Participant observation   Researchers will conduct **participant observation** to gain very detailed and sometimes intimate knowledge of a person or group. This technique involves the researcher's actual participation and recording of events.

Quantitative methods   **Quantitative methods** rely heavily on statistical and mathematical techniques to study social behavior. The survey and controlled experiment are two popular methods of quantitative analysis.

Survey   The **survey** is probably the most widely used method for gathering data. They may be administered in person, over the telephone, or through the mail. For a survey to be scientific, it must be directed at a population.

Population   **Population** refers to any group the researcher is studying such as all college freshmen or residents of a particular city.

Sample   Since it is often impossible to survey every member of a population, researchers **sample** a small number of cases and use them to represent the entire population. Researchers attempt to obtain a representative sample rather than a large sample. A **representative sample** of the United States, for example, would include about the same proportion of Hispanics, African Americans, women, etc. as the whole nation. If done successfully, this results in a sample which mirrors the population. As a result, researchers can be confident that their conclusions from the sample are generalizeable to the whole population. The most accurate method for assuring generalizeability is to use **random sampling**. In this technique, everyone in the population has an equal chance of being selected as a respondent.

Experiment   An **experiment** is a method of researching the relationship between two or more variables in controlled conditions. The first stage of an experiment is the pre-test in which a sample is selected and surveyed to dismiss any which, for one reason or another, are not appropriate for the study. In the second stage the researcher randomly divided the participants (called subjects) into two groups. The **experimental group** receives the "treatment" while the **control group** does not. The third stage occurs after the treatment has been given and involves a post-test of all of the subjects to assess the effect of the treatment. Sociologists rarely use controlled experiments because it does not allow the study of social behavior under natural conditions.

Concern for **ethics** in research developed after World War II. In several cases, the good intentions of researchers resulted in severe emotional distress of subjects. In response, the American Sociological Association has prepared a set of guidelines to protect people involved in research. Under these guidelines the respondents must remain completely anonymous and may quit whenever they wish. They must be informed of the researcher's institutional affiliation and the purpose of the research. All academic research supported by the federal government must be reviewed by a Human Subjects committee which guards the civil rights and well-being of the participants.

Additionally:

Harriet Martineau Harriet Martineau translated and edited Comte's work to make it available to a wider audience. She believed that when scientific laws governing human behavior were understood, they could be used to create a better world. In her best-known work, *Society in America*, Martineau concluded that social strains result when people behave in ways that are contrary to their core values. Over time, such strains cause social change. Her ideas have carried through to modern strain theory (see Chapter 3).

Critical thinking Pages 6 and 7 discuss critical thinking which is reflective skepticism about a given subject matter. Throughout the book you will be challenged to think critically about society from a sociological viewpoint.

Time Line of Early Twentieth Century American Sociology While Marx, Durkheim and Weber are highlighted in the text, be sure to look at the American sociologists of the early twentieth century and how Sumner, Ward, Dubois, Small, Park and Adams build on the theories of the European sociologists but shaped their theories to fit American social problems such as massive immigration, rapid industrialization, and urbanization. One can see why sociology became a discipline concerned with the scientific method, social structure, social interaction and social change.

Sociology and the Twenty-First Century The title of the textbook is <u>Sociology for the Twenty-First Century</u> and chapters will include a discussion on the future. One of the core elements of the definition of sociology is social change. Change is continually taking place in all parts of society and such change sill have implications for the future of society and our future as individuals. One way to look at this social change is to examine trends carefully within the context of critical thinking.

Critical Questions:

CQ: (page 5)   How does the sociological approach differ from that of the psychologist and the economist? Do the different viewpoints of these disciplines enhance or contradict each other?

Refer to the discussion on critical thinking on page 6 of your textbook. Remember that critical thinking is reflective skepticism about a given subject. To answer this question, first list the ideas and subjects that each discipline emphasizes. (Hint: think about the topics you would find in introductory sociology, psychology, and economics textbooks). Now list what each leaves out. What, if anything, does this tell you about the way each discipline views human behavior? Is one discipline more concerned about interpersonal relationships than the others? How about economic differences among members of a society? Are these perspectives in opposition to each other? If so, what components can be gleaned from each? If not, how might we put them together to paint a more complete picture of human behavior?

CQ: (page 15)   Can you supply examples of the problems of alienation, anomie, and imprisonment in the iron cage of rationality from your own life? Do these terms have meaning to today's college students?

In order to answer this question, you must understand the key terms. Refer back to your textbook and write the definitions of alienation, anomie, and iron cage of rationality. Remember that each of these terms represents societal conditions, not individual feelings. The authors state that alienation produces the feeling that life is meaningless. What feelings might be generated by the situation of anomie? How would you feel under such conditions? Think back to your first term at college. Did either alienation or anomie apply to the conditions in which the new freshmen class found themselves? Did you experience any of the feelings associated with alienation or anomie? What were the sources of your feelings? How long did it take for those feelings to change? What were Weber's assumptions about the iron cage of rationality? What do you think college life would be without rationality? Would universities exist? Are your experiences with alienation, anomie, and the iron cage of rationality based more on conditions of the whole society or on a smaller sub-set of society, such as your college or university?

CQ: (page 18)   How would a functionalist and a social conflict theorist differ in their interpretation of the enslavement of Africans for the plantation system of the American South.

Review the basic assumptions of Durkheim (page 16) and how contemporary functionalists view the way systems in society work. What was the manifest function of slavery? How did slavery function to maintain the equilibrium of the American South? Looking closely but still from a functionalist perspective, what were dysfunctions of the practice and what proved to be latent functions? What term would conflict theorists apply to their interpretation of slavery? What group was dominant in the South? What group was dominated? What were major historical events that illustrate the dynamics of social change that conflict theorists say is a regular function of social life?

CQ: (page 20)   Do you think the sex of the interviewer might influence the kind of information sought in the interview? Would a young man be as likely as a young woman to ask the same questions of an elderly woman? Why or why not?

What are the assumptions about social interaction between people of the opposite sex? About the young and old? Imagine yourself as the research subject in a face-to-face interview. What topics would be easier for you to discuss man-to-man or woman-to-woman? Can you think of any topics that might be easier to discuss with an interviewer of the opposite sex? Would you feel differently if the interviewee was much older than you? If so, how? What implications does this have for social science research? What other characteristics might influence survey research? Generate some hypotheses regarding the effect of interviewer/interviewee interaction on the types of questions asked and the types of answers that may be given.

Self Test Questions
Multiple Choice

1. Which is NOT of concern to sociology?
    a. social structure
    b. social interaction
    c. sociological point of view
    d. all of the above are of concern to sociology

2. The relatively permanent components of our social environment which impose order and predictability are known as:
    a. social change
    b. social structure
    c. social interaction
    d. sociological imagination

3. The term "natural sociologist" refers to the idea that:
   a. sociologists study social interaction with the same methods that natural scientists study the natural world
   b. sociologists are concerned with natural causal ordering
   c. each of us practices sociology informally to make sense of our world
   d. none of the above

4. Which is NOT a component of critical thinking?
   a. identifying the issue or assertion
   b. determining whether key terms are clearly defined
   c. disagreeing with existing assertions
   d. generating new assertions

5. Which sociologist contributed the idea that social strains emerge when people behave in ways that conflict with their core values?
   a. Karl Mark
   b. Emile Durkheim
   c. Max Weber
   d. Harriet Martineau

6. According to Marx, which of the following is the potential product of repetition, monotony, lack of meaning, and lack of control in the workplace?
   a. mechanical solidarity
   b. alienation
   c. anomie
   d. verstehen

7. In small farming villages the division of labor is simple and the residents have identical values. This is an example of:
   a. mechanical solidarity
   b. anomie
   c. organic solidarity
   d. verstehen

8. A situation in which societal norms are in conflict or entirely missing is known as:
   a. alienation
   b. anomie
   c. dysfunction
   d. hostile

9. Kim is a nuclear physicist who lives in a complex industrial society. When her car breaks down she seeks the help of a mechanic and when she is sick she visits the doctor. What links Kim to the other members of her society?
   a. mechanical solidarity
   b. anomie
   c. organic solidarity
   d. verstehen

10. The replacement of traditional-mindedness with thinking based on self-control, efficiency, and deliberate calculation is:
    a. rationalization
    b. industrialization
    c. bureaucratization
    d. politicization

11. Which sociologist emphasized the role in modern society of rationalization—the replacement of traditional modes of thinking with modes stressing deliberate calculation, efficiency, and self-control?
    a. Emile Durkheim
    b. August Comte
    c. Max Weber
    d. Karl Marx

12. Which group of theorists would argue that, like an organism, components of a social system work together for the cohesion of the whole system?
    a. interactionists
    b. functionalists
    c. conflict theorists
    d. Marxists

13. Professor Singh assigned a group project to his Introductory Sociology class. As a result of the interaction within a work group, two students met, began dating, and eventually married. This is an example of:
    a. mechanical solidarity
    b. latent consequences
    c. organic solidarity
    d. manifest consequences

14. Which viewpoint stresses the ideas of power and dominance?
    a. interactionism
    b. functionalism
    c. structuralism
    d. conflict theory

15. Qualitative research techniques are designed to attain which of the following?
    a. subjective understanding of behavior
    b. interpretation of behavior
    c. meaning of social behavior
    d. all of the above

16. The assertions that whites have historically used their domination over nonwhites to gain benefits at the expense of nonwhites and that men have historically used their domination over women to gain benefits at the expense of women reflect which sociological viewpoint?
    a. conflict
    b. interactionist
    c. functionalist
    d. organic

17. The ability to get others to conform to one's wishes even against their own desires is called:
   a. muscle
   b. coercion
   c. social power
   d. social control

18. In the context of a research project, any group the researcher is studying is referred to as the:
   a. sample
   b. cases
   c. population
   d. subjects

19. In which of the following sampling techniques does everyone in the population have an equal chance of selection?
   a. random
   b. representative
   c. controlled
   d. selected

20. Dr. Brown designs an experiment to test the effect of taking a women's studies class on attitudes toward women. He divides participants into two groups, one that takes the class and one that does not. The group that takes the class is called:
   a. the random sample
   b. the control group
   c. the representative group
   d. the experimental group

21. The Literary Digest poll predicted incorrectly that in the 1936 election the Republican candidate for president would beat the Democratic candidate. The cause of this error was:
   a. its sample of respondents was biased
   b. it asked the wrong questions
   c. it had a faulty control group
   d. there was a computer glitch in the analysis

22. A sample which mirrors the characteristics of the population from which it comes is a:
   a. uniform sample
   b. representative sample
   c. random sample
   d. purposive sample

True - False

T	F	1. Sociology's emphasis on answering logical questions with evidence obtained from experiments and systematic observation defines sociology as a science.
T	F	2. In order for social interaction to occur, the actors must be in close physical proximity to each other.
T	F	3. Critical thinking involves studying a subject skeptically.
T	F	4. Weber is known as the father of sociology.
T	F	5. Alienation describes a situation in which one feels estranged from his/her social world and feels that life is meaningless.

T	F	6. Dysfunctions are actions which have negative consequences for the social system.
T	F	7. Research techniques of participant observation, interviewing, and historical analysis are used in qualitative analysis.
T	F	8. Quantitative analysis relies heavily on statistical and mathematical techniques.
T	F	9. If constructed correctly, random samples will yield representative samples.
T	F	10. In an experiment, the group to whom the experimental stimulus is administered is called the stimulus group.
T	F	11. A sample is any group a researcher is studying.
T	F	12. Quantitative analysis is often the best way to describe and explain both behavior and its context.

Self Test Answers

Multiple Choice

1. d (3)	6. b (12)	11. c (13)	16. a (17)	21. a (23)
2. b (4)	7. a (12)	12. b (16)	17. c (17)	22. b (22)
3. c (5)	8. b (13)	13. b (16)	18. c (21)	
4. c (6)	9. c (13)	14. d (17)	19. a (22)	
5. d (9)	10. a (13)	15. d (19)	20. d (23)	

True - False

1. T (3)	4. F (8)	7. T (19)	10. F (23)
2. F (4)	5. T (13)	8. T (21)	11. F (22)
3. T (6)	6. T (16)	9. T (22)	12. F (21)

NOTES FOR FUTURE STUDY AND REVIEW:

Chapter 2

Culture, Society, and Social Change

CULTURE AND SOCIETY
> *Values and Norms*
> *Symbols and Language*
> *Ethnocentrism and Cultural Relativity*

TYPES OF SOCIETIES
> *Hunting and Gathering*
> *Horticultural and Pastoral*
> *Agrarian*
> *Industrial*
> *Postindustrial*
> *Transitional*

THE GREAT SOCIAL TRANSFORMATION
> *Communal Relationships*
> *Associational Relationships*
> *The Great Social Transformation and This Text*

THEORIES OF CHANGE AND DEVELOPMENT
> *Social Change and the Credit Card*
> *Social Evolution*
> *Functionalism and Social Evolution*
> *Modernization Theory*
> *Conflict Theory and Change: World Systems*

CATALYSTS FOR CHANGE
> *Human Agency: Individual and Collective*
> *Revolution and War*
> *Cultural Processes*
> *Population*
> *Natural Catastrophes*
> *Technology*

CULTURE, SOCIETY AND SOCIAL CHANGE IN THE TWENTY-FIRST CENTURY

CRITICAL QUESTIONS
> *Culture and Society*
> *Types of Societies*
> *Great Social Transformation*
> *Theories of Change and Development*

SELF TEST QUESTIONS/ANSWERS

CHAPTER SUMMARY and KEY TERMS

Culture and Society

The stories of the Kwakiutl Indians and the Jigalong people illustrate that different types of physical environments will yield different cultures. The Kwakiutl Indians lived in an area of abundant natural resources. The people were so rich with these resources that they could develop and sustain a cultural tradition, the potlatch ceremony, in which goods were destroyed to increase the destroyer's prestige. The Jigalong, on the other hand, lived in the arid western Australian desert. Natural resources, such as water, were scarce. Thus the Jigalong developed elaborate supernatural rituals to influence rainfall.

Often one hears the terms **culture** and **society** used interchangeably but in this sociological context, they have different meanings. Culture is reserved for the products created by human (both material and nonmaterial) while society is reserved for the entity that divides humankind into a particular kind of groups. In this way, the phrase *cultural diversity* refers to the many distinct cultures that exist within a large, heterogeneous society, for example, the culture of African Americans in the United States.

Culture	**Culture** is the mutually shared products, knowledge, and beliefs of a human group or society. It is divided into two types: material culture and nonmaterial culture. *Material culture* consists of the physical objects used by people to accomplish goals. Examples include tools and machinery used in construction and computers used to analyze mathematical problems. *Nonmaterial culture* consists of values, art, language, worldviews, and other symbolic representations of the social and physical world. Examples include fairy tales, complex legal codes, music, and knowledge.
Society	All human groupings must live within a given territory. Groupings that obey a central authority (a government) and share a common culture are called a **society**. It is society that provides us with an overarching social structure.
Cultural universals	**Cultural universals** are the cultural solutions to broad problems which all societies face. For example, all people eventually die. Therefore each culture must develop ways to deal with death. Other cultural universals include reproduction, rearing children, survival, maintaining societal order, and answering questions of human origin. If you look closely at the chapter headings of many of the chapters in the text, you will note that each chapter looks at the way cultures have developed social structures and social interactions to deal with broad problems that must be addressed in order for the culture to survive.
Values	**Values** are the preferences people share about what is good or bad, right or wrong, desirable or undesirable. They give us general guidelines for behavior. These values influence behavior, emotion, and thought. American values include equality, democracy, hard work, and achievement.
Norms	**Norms** are specific expectations about how people behave in a given situation. They provide us with a set of behavioral guidelines that we can draw on in certain situations. Violating norms leads to social discomfort. For instance, if your instructor came to class wearing a bright orange wig, the students would probably experience a level of discomfort. Some may feel embarrassed for the professor, some may make jokes, and others may query the professor about his or her choice of hair color. Regardless of the reaction, the situation would not go unnoticed. Norms are divided into several types, depending on their level of perceived seriousness.
Folkways	Norms concerning relatively unimportant matters are called **folkways**. The wig-wearing professor is an example of a folkway. Punishment for violating a folkway is not very severe. It may include stares, snickers, or laughter, but nothing physically damaging.

Mores	**Mores** are norms concerning very serious matters. Mores frequently involve the welfare and continued existence of the society. Examples of mores include expectations of not killing other human beings and not stealing from them. Punishments for violating mores can be very serious.
Taboos	**Taboos** are norms about things that are so serious as to be almost beyond comprehension. In American culture, eating another human or having sexual relations with animals constitute taboos. Violating taboos results in extreme punishment and ostracism.

Two very important parts of culture are the **symbols** and **language** of the culture. Language is so important that when a language disappears so does the accumulated experience of the culture that produced it.

Symbols	Communication often takes place through **symbols**, or representations that stand for something else. Almost anything can be a symbol. Some symbols represent important cultural values. In the United States, for example, balancing scales represents justice and the bald eagle represents freedom.
Language	**Language** is the most powerful and complex symbol. It consists of words that are symbols standing for ideas or objects, and rules for combining words into longer, more complex ideas. The Sapir-Whorf hypothesis states that language is so important that it may actually shape our perception of the world. The idea is that we have little choice but to interpret the world in terms of the words and grammar of our native language.

The fact that most of us are raised in one culture and only begin to encounter other cultures once our own values, norms, language and symbols are well established has consequences for how we view our own culture and how we view other cultures.

Ethnocentrism	Most people are born and raised in one culture. Often they understand little about other cultures. Sometimes this leads people to view other cultures with a mixture of curiosity, accepting, and loathing. These mixed feelings form the basis for **ethnocentrism** the tendency to judge other cultures by the standards of their own culture. In essence, ethnocentrism is the belief that our culture is superior to all other cultures.
Cultural relativism	**Cultural relativism** is the opposite of ethnocentrism. The view of cultural relativism recognizes that each culture is unique and valid. This view started in Anthropology in the early 1900s.
Multiculturalism	**Multiculturalism** is closely related to cultural relativism. One goal of multiculturalism is to incorporate other cultural viewpoints into the curriculum. This includes teaching from the viewpoint of minority groups rather than from a purely Euro-centric perspective. Multiculturalism began in education in the 1960s but has only recently gained popularity.

Types of Societies

No two societies are identical. They differ in geographic location, proximity to competing societies, level of technology, and environmental resources. These are among the differences that shape a society and determine its **mode of subsistence** -- the way a society obtains the basic materials necessary to sustain itself. The mode of subsistence is probably the most basic feature of a society. It strongly influences the economy, social organization, political structure, and social life. Due to this importance, sociologists use it to divide societies into the following types.

Hunting and gathering	**Hunting and gathering** societies obtain sustenance by hunting animals and gathering nuts, berries, and other wild plants. Kinship ties hold hunting and gathering societies together. Labor is divided on the basis of sex and age. Members of theses societies spend only about three hours each day obtaining sustenance. Hunting and gathering societies are small (50 to 100 people) and nomadic. Only a few thousand hunters and gathers are left in the world.

Horticultural and pastoral	In **horticultural societies**, sustenance is primarily obtained from the cultivation of domestic plants. It was made possible by the invention of the hoe. Horticulture is like gardening on a large scale. Horticultural societies are less nomadic than hunting and gathering societies, but they must move occasionally when the soil becomes depleted. Many horticultural societies use slash and burn agriculture which quickly depletes the soil. Members of these societies develop relatively permanent housing and they form large groups. Horticulture is more productive than hunting and gathering. **Pastoral societies** derive most of their sustenance from grazing domestic animals. *Nomads* are pastoralists who follow their herds as the migrate from place to place. These societies usually produce more food than their populations can immediately consume. This creates a surplus which becomes the source of wealth and inequality.
Agrarian	The invention of the plow about 6,000 years ago allowed farmers to harness animal labor. This led to the development of **agrarian** societies. Productivity was further improved with irrigation and fertilization technologies. Agrarian societies are even more efficient in obtaining sustenance than horticultural societies. Thus agrarian societies could support more people in more permanent settlements. This led to the development of cities. They were also highly stratified as the nobility class owned the land.
Industrial	**Industrial societies** rely on technology and mechanization as the main source of sustenance. They institutionalize innovation by investing in research and education to promote technological advances. This creates a snowball effect as new technologies facilitates communication between people which leads to more innovations.
Postindustrial	**Postindustrial societies** are based primarily on the creation and transmittal of specialized knowledge. Examples include law, medicine, education, finance, and real estate. You can think of a postindustrial society as one whose jobs consist mainly of those in the service sector. Education is an important factor in helping a society move from industrial to postindustrial. It takes many more years of education to become a doctor than to become a factory worker. The United States was the first country to become postindustrial. Today, more than half of the jobs in the United States are in the service sector. Japan, Australia, New Zealand, and most of Western Europe are other examples of postindustrial societies.
Transitional	Most countries of the world do not fit neatly into one of the above types. Most are in transition from one form to the next; usually from agrarian to industrial. Thus we call these **transitional societies**. Most people in transitional societies earn their subsistence as peasant farmers.

The Great Social Transformation

Obviously life in an agrarian society will be different from life in an industrial society. Social scientists have used various terms to describe these differences. The authors of your text have chosen communal and association societies. Whereas the above typology was based on mode of subsistence, this type is based on the resulting characteristics. These include the closeness of relationships, division of labor, level of technology, contact with other societies, and social organization.

Communal	**Communal societies** are characterized by rich personal relationships. The main social units are the family, kin, and community. Think of the United States before the Civil War as an example. Many people of this era lived with extended families. They were often born and raised in the same town which enabled them to know all of the residents well. In addition to close personal relationships, other characteristics of communal societies include a limited division of labor, an economy based on nearby commodities, a low level of technology, nonbureaucratic political institutions, limited social stratification, rich ceremonial life, and limited contact with other societies. Finally, life in communal society tends to be less complex, less diverse, more traditional, and more personal than life in associational societies. Hunting and gathering, horticultural, and agrarian societies are largely communal.

Associational   In contrast, **associational societies** are highly impersonal and the main social units are organizations, corporations, and bureaucracies. Think of the United States today as an example. We deal with many strangers on a daily basis. We cannot possibly become friends with everyone in our cities. Rather than knowing many people as friends, we know many people as casual acquaintances. Often we deal with such people based on the role they play rather than solely on their personalities. For example, we may go to the same doctor for several years but think of him or her in the role of doctor rather than as an individual. Family, kin, and community remain important in associational societies. However, other large-scale social units are also prominent, if not dominant. Aside from the impersonal nature of relationships, associational societies have a complex division of labor, an economy based on manufacturing and related activities, a high level of technology, complex and bureaucratic political institutions, a complex stratification system with a large middle class, a value of rationality, and a connection with a global network of societies. In comparison with communal societies, life is more complex, more diverse, less traditional, and more impersonal. Industrial and postindustrial societies are associational.

GST   The **GST (Great Social Transformation)** is the shift of societies from communal to associational relationships. This transformation is profound and affects all aspects of life. Therefore, the authors will relate it to the subject matter of each chapter.

Theories of Change and Development

As we look at the varieties of societies from hunting and gathering to post-industrial and as we note that there is a change from communal to associational, societies are constantly undergoing change. Remember that one of the core elements of the definition of sociology is *social change* The concept of **cultural lag** is introduced and then the four theoretical perspectives on change and development: *evolutionary theory, functionalism, modernization, and world systems.*

Cultural lag   Though we now take credit cards for granted, they are actually a relatively new phenomenon. The first credit card appeared in 1950. The next card was introduced eight years later. Today , thousands of organizations offer them. We can now use credit cards to buy groceries, take vacations, and finance our education. However, the ease of obtaining and using credit cards has caused financial problems for some members of our society. Sociologists believe that one reason is that developments in credit card technology outpaced developments in values, norms, and ideologies regarding their proper use. This is known as **cultural lag**. Specifically, cultural lag occurs when material culture changes more rapidly than nonmaterial culture.

Theories of Change   *Evolutionary theories* assert that societies are shaped by the forces of social evolution. They are based on the work of Charles Darwin. These theories state that human society begins as a simple entity (like hunting and gathering) and evolves into a complex society (industrial). They also propose that social competition selects the fittest society for survival. Evolutionary theorist believe that all societies follow the same path to development. This is known as a unilinear path. However, these beliefs are no longer accepted. Critics point out that social evolutionary theorists were extremely ethnocentric. They used the theory to justify the domination of Western whites and to label as inferior the "backward" societies of Africa and Asia.

As presented in Chapter 1, *functionalist theory* attempts to explain how social systems achieve and remain in equilibrium. Change upsets balance and therefore presented a problem to early functionalist theory. In response, Talcott Parsons updated the theory by incorporating the idea of social evolution. According to Parsons, change simply moves the equilibrium from one state to another. He introduced the concept of *differentiation*—the division of a single social unit into units that are independent but related to each other. Unlike early evolutionary theorists, contemporary theorists argue that societal development is multilineal. That is, it occurs in different ways in different societies. The incorporation of evolution into functionalist theory has several problems. First, the perspective explains why societies remain in equilibrium but not why they change. Second, it does not take into account political actions and choice. Finally, the analogy between biological and social evolution breaks down as humans have the ability to choose their futures while animals do not.

According to *modernization theory*, traditional societies will eventually take on the characteristics of an industrial society. Manufacturing and related activities will become the means of subsistence, cities and governments will develop and grow, income inequality will increase, and literacy and democracy will spread. In short, modernization theorists believe that all societies will eventually converge on a single type similar to the United States. Modernization occurs largely through technology passed from "modern" societies to traditional societies. The theory assumes that the benefits of industrialization outweigh the problems. This assumption is debatable based on the work of Marx, Weber, and Durkheim. Modernization theory also assumes that the histories of all nations will mirror those of industrialized nations such as the United States. This is not true as countries have different resources available to them which will affect their development.

Conflict theorists assume that change is universal and ongoing and that power is an essential part of life. Over the past 20 years these assumptions have been incorporated into a general explanation of change and development called *world systems theory*. According the this theory, all nations are part of a world system. The system includes core nations, those that are highly industrialized and powerful; periphery nations, which are dependent upon core nations; and semi-periphery nations, which are closely tied to the core nation and therefore receive more benefits than periphery nations. The world system has been established over the past 200 years in an effort to colonize Africa, Asia, and South America. Most of the world system was established through military force.

Catalysts for Change

Because change is such a fundamental process, sociologists look at the causes and sources of change. A *catalyst for change* is a cause or source of change. Many catalysts for change fall outside the scope of any one theory. There are six main catalysts for change: human agency, ideology, revolution/war, cultural processes, natural catastrophes, population, and technology.

Human agency **Human agency**, the activities of individuals or groups aimed at attaining a goal or end, is one of these catalysts. Sociologists recognize that people influence world events. However, they prefer explanations of change which are based on social forces embedded in society. Sociologists propose that humans direct change but do not create it.

Ideology **Ideology** is an important part of human agency. These are the beliefs that support and justify a particular social arrangement.

Invention **Invention** is one type of cultural process which involves combining known cultural elements in a novel manner to produce a new product. This is particularly important in industrial and postindustrial societies.

Discovery **Discovery** is another type of cultural process which occurs when someone suddenly notices something that has not been noticed before. Inventions and discoveries that are too radical for current ways of thinking are usually rejected.

Diffusion **Diffusion** is the cultural process where a cultural element from one group or society is transmitted to another. When a cultural element diffuses it is often modified to meet the needs of the receiving society.

Shifts in *population* often trigger massive social changes. Those who study population, demographers, are interested in birth, mortality, and migration. Social change may also be triggered by *natural catastrophes* such as floods and earthquakes. Disaster research is a small but significant area of sociology. It is devoted to the study of social factors associated with a disaster. Finally, *technological changes* also result in social change.

Culture, Society, and Social Change in the Twenty-First Century

One profound change that is occurring as cultures and societies are impacted by change from all types of catalysts is the homogenizing of culture. Local differences are being replaced by a standard culture that comes from the major urban centers of industrial nations. This process of cultural homogenization is also being created by multinational organizations which view the entire world as their marketplace and no particular nation as their home. This process of cultural homogenization will continue as technology and change causes the world to become a smaller place.

Critical Questions

CQ: (page 37)   Suppose you were describing American culture to a recently arrived exchange student from Moscow University. Where would you begin, and what would you tell him or her about life in your city?

Hint: in order to teach someone from another society about life in the United States, it is helpful to inform yourself about the visitor's society. This will give you a point of departure for discussion and comparison. In the case of a Russian student, it is important that you have at least a basic understanding of communist and capitalist economic systems. You should also contextualize yourself with a brief history and current events of the visitor's society. Now you can compare and contrast life in your city with life in Moscow in an informed manner.

CQ: (page 43)   Was the United States ever an agrarian society? When? What aspects of our agrarian heritage are still evident in our culture? For instance, how are our agrarian roots evident in the song "American the Beautiful"?

Think of much of the content of early American history including the urge to move West and obtain land, the conflicts between the Native American Indians and the settlers, the need for slaves, as well as the myths and stories that are part of our past. Are you or your relatives from a rural area where farmland has been "in the family" for generations?

CQ: (page 46)   What does the concept "communal" mean to you? Which relationships of yours are primarily communal and which are primarily associational?

Write your answer to the first question. Now review the key terms communal, associational, and Great Social Transformation (GST). Which of your relationships fit the definition of communal most closely? Which do you identify as associational? Would the people you list agree with you? Do you have any relationships that are difficult to categorize as either communal or associational? (Remember that these categories represent ideal types rather than discrete categories. This means that some relationships may contain features of both communal and associational relationships). Do you have more communal or more associational relationships? Which would you miss most if they disappeared from your life? Given the society in which you live, is it possible to live without communal and/or associational relationships? How would your lifestyle have to change if you wanted to live without communal relationships? How would it change if you wanted to live without associational relationships? Are the answers to these questions different for members of traditional societies? It would be very informative to discuss these questions with the international students in your class and compare their responses with your own.

CQ: (page 51   Is change and development always a good thing? How would a modernization theorist respond to that question? A world systems theorist?

Write four to five sentences to answer this question. Now review your response and write the assumptions you brought to your answer. What do you consider good? For whom do you consider good-the whole society, dominant groups, minority groups, yourself? What are the benefits of living in a traditional society? What are the problems? Do you think people of different social categories answer this question in the same manner?

In answering how modernization and world systems theorists would answer this question, you must first review the key terms modernization theory and world systems theory? What are the assumptions of each theory? How does your response fit these ideas? Are you a modernization or a world systems theorist?

CQ: (page 57)   One reason that change is continuous in contemporary society is that we have a large cultural warehouse of items to use in creating new arrangements. Can you think of any new and improved inventions or discoveries that were really a combination of existing cultural elements?

Technology as a catalyst for change is going to be key to thinking of answers to this: combining computer technology with needs and advances in medicine, communication, transportation, finance, and manufacturing; applying technology to arts areas, music, photography, entertainment and sports areas. What new arrangements have come about due to the world wide web? Students taking this sociology course will be among those who "create new arrangements" to meet the needs of the twenty-first century.

Self Test Questions
Multiple Choice

1. The mutually shared products, knowledge, and beliefs of a human group or society is known as:
    a. potlatch
    b. culture
    c. norms
    d. values

2. Computer software is an example of:
    a. material culture
    b. norms
    c. nonmaterial culture
    d. values

3. The knowledge of how to use computers is an example of:
    a. material culture
    b. norms
    c. nonmaterial culture
    d. values

4. Within a large and socially heterogeneous society such as the United States, there are many distinct cultures. The term that describes this situation is:
    a. cultural diversity
    b. cultural plurality
    c. cultural universality
    d. multiculturalism

5. Cultural solutions to broad problems faced by many cultures is known as:
    a. material culture
    b. folkways
    c. cultural diversity
    d. cultural universals

6. Most Americans share the idea that adult citizens should be free to vote on the political candidate of their choice. This is a/an:
    a. value
    b. folkway
    c. taboo
    d. attitude

7. Jack wore one blue sock and one orange sock yesterday. He violated a:
   a. taboo
   b. more
   c. cultural universal
   d. folkway

8. In the United States the bald eagle is an example of a/an:
   a. symbol
   b. expression
   c. value
   d. nonmaterial culture

9. The tendency to judge another culture by the standards of your own culture is:
   a. ethnocentrism
   b. cultural relativity
   c. symbolic representation
   d. multiculturalism

10. Through time within a society:
    a. the content of values remains the same
    b. the content of values may change even though their outward form remains the same.
    c. the outward form of values may change even though their content remains the same.
    d. the content of values and their outward form remain the same.

11. Which term describes the view that each culture is unique and valid?
    a. ethnocentrism
    b. cultural relativity
    c. symbolic representation
    d. multiculturalism

12. Which is the goal of multiculturalism?
    a. to incorporate the minority point of view into the curriculum
    b. to produce a more complete picture of society
    c. to create greater tolerance for diversity
    d. all of the above are goals of multiculturalism

13. Agrarian societies:
    a. were made possible by the invention of the plow
    b. were characterized by the emergence of cities
    c. had enough wealth to support toolmakers, administrators, and other nonagricultural specialists
    d. all of the above

14. Industrial societies:
    a. rely on technology and mechanization as the main source of sustenance
    b. institutionalize innovation
    c. often invest heavily in defense technology
    d. all of the above

15. The type of society whose mode of subsistence is the creation and transmittal of specialized knowledge is:
    a. horticultural
    b. agrarian
    c. industrial
    d. postindustrial

16. Societies characterized by close personal relationships whose main social units consist of family, kin, and community are:
    a. industrial
    b. postindustrial
    c. communal
    d. associational

17. Which is NOT a characteristic of communal societies?
    a. rich ceremonial life
    b. low level of technology
    c. formalized relationships
    d. limited division of labor

18. Which is most characteristic of associational societies?
    a. complex stratification
    b. rationality is valued
    c. life is complex and diverse
    d. all of the above are characteristics of associational societies

19. Often advances in medical technology outpaces developments in values and norms related to their use. This is an example of:
    a. material culture
    b. culture lag
    c. culture shock
    d. nonmaterial culture

20. What sociological perspective has integrated aspects of social evolution theory into its discussion of change emphasizing the tendencies for societies to achieve and remain in equilibrium?
    a. functionalist
    b. conflict theory
    c. post-modernist
    d. world systems

21. Which theory of social change argues that traditional societies will eventually take on the characteristics of industrial societies?
    a. cyclical
    b. social evolution
    c. modernization
    d. world systems

22. What type of catalyst for change was illustrated by President Johnson's ordering of American troops into Vietnam?
    a. human agency
    b. revolution and war
    c. cultural processes
    d. natural catastrophes

23. The diffusion of technology and the actions of multinational corporations are contributing to the:
    a. impoverishment of small societies
    b. homogenization of cultures
    c. development of a pluralistic world system
    d. political revolutions in the core nations

True - False

T	F	
T	F	1. The Kwakiutl Indian's cultural practice of potlatch was unrelated to their physical environment.
T	F	2. Norms concerning relatively unimportant matters are called folkways.
T	F	3. The sanctions for violation of taboos are generally more severe than the sanctions for violation of mores.
T	F	4. Language is the most powerful and complex type of symbol.
T	F	5. Viewing a society as vulgar and immoral for eating dog is an example of cultural relativity.
T	F	6. In horticultural societies the mode of subsistence is large-scale gardening.
T	F	7. Most of the world's population lives in industrial societies.
T	F	8. Japan is an associational society.
T	F	9. In the United States, people tend to have more communal relationships than associational relationships.
T	F	10. The term The Great Social Transformation (GST) refers to the profound change in social relationships from communal to associational brought about by industrialization, urbanization, bureaucratization, rationalization, and globalization.
T	F	11. The idea that societies move from communal to associational is consistent with evolutionary theory.
T	F	12. The idea that societies move from communal to associational is consistent with modernization theory.
T	F	13. The United Kingdom is an example of a core nation.
T	F	14. According to world systems theory, nations that are highly industrialized and powerful, and that control the world system are called modernized.
T	F	15. Noticing that something has not been noticed before is called diffusion.

Self Test Answers

Multiple Choice

1. b (32)	6. a (33)	11. b (36)	16. c (44)	21. c (50)
2. a (32)	7. d (34)	12. d (36)	17. c (46)	22. a (53)
3. c (32)	8. a (35)	13. d (40)	18. d (46)	23. b (57)
4. a (33)	9. a (36)	14. d (40)	19. b (48)	
5. d (33)	10. b (33)	15. d (41)	20. a (49)	

True - False

1. F (31)	6. T (39)	11. T (48)
2. T (34)	7. F (42)	12. T (50)
3. T (34)	8. T (45)	13. T (51)
4. T (35)	9. F (44)	14. F (51)
5. F (36)	10. T (43)	15. F (54)

NOTES FOR FUTURE STUDY AND REVIEW:

Chapter 3

Socialization and Deviance

THE GREAT SOCIAL TRANSFORMATION AND SOCIALIZATION

SOCIALIZATION AND THE LIFE COURSE
> *Socialization and Stages of the Life Course*
> *Agents of Socialization*

SOCIALIZATION AND THE SELF
> *Cooley: The Looking Glass Self*
> *Mead: Role Taking*
> *Blumer: The Symbolic Interactionist Perspective*

MORAL SOCIALIZATION
> *Jean Piaget and Lawrence Kohlberg*
> *Carol Gilligan: Morality and Gender*

DEVIANCE AND CRIME
> *The Great Social Transformation and Deviance and Crime*
> *Crime*
> *Amount of Crime*
> *Explanations for Deviance and Crime*

SOCIALIZATION AND DEVIANCE IN THE TWENTY-FIRST CENTURY

CRITICAL QUESTIONS
> *Mass Media and Socialization*
> *Self Concept and The Looking Glass Self*
> *Facing a Moral Dilemma*

SELF TEST QUESTIONS/ANSWERS

CHAPTER SUMMARY AND KEY TERMS

The Great Social Transformation and Socialization

Socialization is a complex task for any society, however, as societies shift from communal to associational, the process of successfully socializing all members of the society becomes more difficult. In communal societies virtually all member of the society receive much the same socialization from people who have strong personal ties to the person being socialized. In associational societies, much of socialization is taught by someone other than a family member and not all members of an associational society receive the same socialization experience. Additionally, in associational societies, a substantial number of people do not receive sufficient socialization to become responsible members of society.

Socialization and the Life Course

The authors begin the discussion of socialization by defining the types of socialization and dividing the life course into four stages: childhood, adolescence, adulthood, and old and very old age. They then discuss the processes of socialization specific to each stage.

Socialization	**Socialization** is the process by which people learn the skills, knowledge, norms, and values of their society and by which they develop their social identity.
Primary socialization	**Primary socialization** occurs in the early stages of life. It stresses the basic knowledge and values of the society.
Secondary socialization	**Secondary socialization** emphasizes synthesis, creativity, logic, emotional control, and advanced knowledge as well as reality and practicality.
Life course	Socialization is an important part of our **life course**—the stages into which our life span is divided, such as adolescence or middle age. Socialization occurs at each of these stages.

Childhood is romanticized as a time of playful innocence. Thus children are often shielded from exposure to sex, death, alcohol, and violence. Elementary aspects of formal learning are complete by the end of childhood.

Adolescence did not become a separate stage in the life course until industrialization created a surplus of workers. Adolescents are subject to a mix of norms regarding freedom and obedience. For example, 18 year olds are old enough to serve in the military but not to drink alcohol. Margaret Mead studied the lives of adolescent girls in Samoa in 1925. She found that Samoan girls were free of the turbulence and conflict experienced by American girls because Samoan society treated sexual matters in an open manner while America did not. A new stage of the life cycle, youth, may be emerging. This would occur between adolescence and adulthood.

Adulthood occurs between the mid-twenties and mid-sixties. This is the time for putting learning into practice. During early adulthood, until age 40, people break away from their parents, establish their own households, and assume responsibility for their well-being. This stage can be very different for women and men as many women leave the labor force between the ages of 25 and 35 to raise children. Careers peak during middle ages (40-60). During this period people also begin to emphasize closeness and compassionate relationships.

Old and very old age involve a withdrawal from long-held roles and adjustment into new ones. Health becomes more important during this period. The very old stage is relatively new. It has resulted from the increasing numbers of people living into their eighties.

Agents of socialization	**Agents of socialization** are the individuals, groups, organizations, and institutions that provide substantial amounts of socialization during the life course. The most important are family, school, peer groups, and mass media.

The *family* is the most important agent of socialization. The family form differs among societies but its functions are the same. These include socializing children, teaching children physical and intellectual skills, and giving children a social location in society.

The *school* is the agent of socialization responsible for teaching children cognitive skills such as reading, writing, and math. The school is usually a child's first experience with a formal agent of socialization. The school regards children as students who are expected to meet objective standards and abide by rules. Schools also reinforce the values of society. For example, in the United States children learn to compete for rewards.

The *peer group* consists of friends who are about the same age and have about the same social status. They are very influential in shaping children's values and behaviors. The peer group's influence increased with age and peaks during the teen years.

The term *mass media* refers to communications that are disseminated to large audiences without direct feedback or other interpersonal contacts between senders and receivers. Mass media includes television, films, radio, newspapers, and books. Television is by far the most dominant agent of socialization among the media. Many people worry that children will be socialized into a make-believe world as a result of watching television. Another concern is that viewing violence on television will cause children to become violent.

Socialization and the Self

The agents of socialization all have an impact on our socialization. But what is the process by which the socialization actually takes place? How do we develop into the person each of us becomes? Several theories are introduced. One important theoretical perspective introduced in this section is **symbolic interactionism.**

Self	Over the life course, humans develop a sense of **self**: a perception of being a distinct personality with a unique identity.
Looking glass self	**Charles Horton Cooley** developed the idea of the **looking glass self**-the process through which we imaginatively assume the reactions of other people. This occurs in three stages: First, *you form an image of the way you appear to other people.* This includes physical characteristics, personality, and intelligence. Second, *you imagine how other people judge this image of you.* Finally, *you respond to the imagined reactions of others.* This will effect your self-esteem.
Role taking	**George Herbert Mead** stated that socialization begins in childhood and continues over our lifetime. As children play, they learn **role taking**: assuming the role of another person and then judging themselves from the viewpoint of that other person. Children eventually distinguish these roles. They begin by taking the role of *specific others*. This includes individuals who are important to them such as parents, teachers, or peers. As they mature, children begin to take the role of the *generalized other*. This is an abstract entity, such as school, the community, and eventually society as a whole. The ability to take the role of the generalized other occurs in three stages: The *imitation* stage occurs up to about age three. In this stage children do not have an independent identity and are incapable of taking any roles. They simply imitate the behavior of others. The *play* stage lasts from about ages three to six. Here children spend a great deal of time pretending to be someone else by taking the role of specific others. The *game* stage occurs after age six. Now the children play at activities requiring complex behaviors determined by what other children do. These games contain rules. Thus children must know their own role as well as the roles of others.
Symbolic interaction	**Herbert Blumer** studied under Mead. He broadened Mead's approach to form a general theory called **symbolic interaction**. This theory assumes that social life is possible only because humans can communicate through symbols with language as the most important symbol. Because we interpret the world through symbols, and because we can stand back and think of ourselves as

objects, human behavior is ultimately subjective and leads to the conclusion that *"if we define situations as real, they are real in their consequences."*.

Role model   With its emphasis on subjectivity and meaning, symbolic interaction is especially useful for understanding socialization. We build meanings by observing what other people do and by imitating them. A **role model** then becomes a person who serves as an especially important reference point for our thoughts and behavior as we follow his or her example.

Symbolic interactionism is a third sociological theoretical perspective that when added to the functionalist and conflict perspectives will be used throughout the text to analyze social structures and social interaction. Note the table on page 73 for a comparison of how each perspectives views society and the key concepts and processes of each perspective.

Moral Socialization

We know from Chapter 1 that each culture has a complex set of values and norms. What is the process by which people acquire the sense of right or wrong of the culture? This is an important part of the socialization process and has been conceptualized as taking place in stages as we mature.

Moral   By **moral socialization** we mean the way people come to acquire a sense of right and wrong.
socialization   **Jean Piaget** is probably the best-known scholar in this area. Piaget would relate "moral dilemmas," little stories that revolve around an ethically ambiguous situation, to children and ask them to discuss the behavior of each character. Piaget concluded that morality develops in two stages.
The *heteronomous stage* lasts until age 12. Here children accept rules laid down by adults.
In the second, *autonomic stage*, children learn that rules may be flexible. They learn what they can get away with while still remaining within the parameters of the rules.

Lawrence Kohlberg expanded on Piaget's work by reading older people a story and asking them to discuss it. In the story, a woman is dying of cancer which can be cured by an expensive drug. Her husband raises half of the money and tries to negotiate a deal with the druggist. When the druggist won't give him the medicine, the husband steals it. In talking with people, Kohlberg concludes that morality develops over three stages:
In the *preconventional stage* people obey laws and social expectations only to avoid punishments or to gain benefits. Most children under nine and some adolescents fall into this category.
In the *conventional stage*, people incorporate societal rules and expectations into their own value system. They obey rules not only to win approval or gain rewards, but also because they feel obligated to do the right thing. Many adolescents and most adults fall into this category.
The *postconventional stage* is the highest stage of moral development. Here, people use broad ethical principles to guide their behavior. This includes respect for human dignity and equality. People usually do not reach this stage before age 20 and some never reach it at all.

Carol Gilligan argues that Piaget and Kohlberg defined morality from a masculine point of view and assumed that the moral reasoning of women was inferior to that of men. Gilligan argues that men define morality in terms of justice in which the goal is to reach a decision that can be judged as either right or wrong while women define it in terms of the responsibility of not hurting people.

Deviance and Crime

It is obvious as we look around, as we read the newspapers, and as we listen to the news that not everyone learns the values and norms to the same extent. There is much variation in behavior and sociologists have looked at the nature and processes of deviance and crime.

Deviance   Technically, **deviance** is any violation of a widely held norm. In practice, most deviance is ignored, mildly punished, regarded as amusing, or even supported. One example is wearing blue jeans to a formal banquet. However, serious violations of norms result in more severe punishments. The determination of what is and is not considered deviant in society is relative. In essence, it is socially constructed. The definition of an act as deviant may change over time or place.

Social controls

Deviance has the potential of disrupting social life. Therefore every society develops methods of controlling it. **Social controls** are mechanisms that monitor behavior and penalize the violations of norms. These vary from a mild scolding, such as "Don't do that!" to execution by the state. Social controls are divided into two types:

Internal controls are seated within the individual and are learned through socialization. This occurs when individuals come to love non-deviant behavior and dislike deviant behavior. *Sociopaths* are people who commit murder or serial killings over a long period of time. Such people have no internal controls.

External controls rely on societal mechanisms to prevent deviance. Examples include the police, the Internal Revenue Service, and the family.

GST and deviance

Deviance changes as societies progress through the GST. Deviance is low in communal societies because internal controls are strong. People learn the cultural traditions and cannot conceive of disobeying them. Communal societies also have fewer rules and laws than do associational societies. However, punishment for deviance that does occur in communal societies is swift, harsh, and to the point. Associational societies are far more complex and diverse. Thus they require many more rules and laws. Because these societies are impersonal, tradition is not adequate to prevent deviance. Therefore, associational societies have developed elaborate legal and criminal justice systems which hold individuals responsible for their crimes. Fines and incarceration are standard forms of punishment in associational societies. Because associational societies are characterized by many types of organizations, deviance can also take place in organizations. This is called *white-collar crime* or *organizational deviance.*

Laws

Communities formulate **laws** which are a body of rules governing the affairs of that community and which are enforced by the political authority, usually the state.

Crimes

Crimes are acts that have been declared illegal by that authority. The authority in an industrial society might be the formal government or tribal elders in a traditional society. All types of societies criminalize acts that severely upset societal order and that cannot be easily controlled through internal controls. Criminalization often depends upon who is in power. Not all deviant acts are crimes and not all crimes are deviant acts. The Federal Bureau of Investigation (FBI) gathers crime information from local police departments and reports the data to the public. The data are useful but not perfect. Police departments are not always accurate or cooperative. However the largest error in data comes from the underreporting of crimes by victims. Only about half of all crimes are reported to the police.

Stigma

Serious crimes may go unreported if the crime involves a **stigma**, or social marker that brings shame on a person. For example, some people are reluctant to report that they have been raped for fear of being stigmatized. Data show that police solve only about 66% of all homicides. Most sociologists believe that the United States is one of the most crime-ridden societies in the world. Major urban centers such as New York, Chicago, and Houston have more homicides in one year than Great Britain and Japan have in a decade. Fear of crime has increased dramatically, making it a leading social issue of the mid-1990s.

Theories of deviance and crime

Several sociological theories have been developed to explain the occurrence of deviance and crime: Included are cultural transmission theory, labeling theory, strain theory, and social bond theory.

Cultural transmission theory states that deviance is learned through socialization. Clifford Shaw and Henry McKay set the foundation for the theory. They studied Chicago and found that even though different ethnic groups had inhabited certain neighborhoods over time, the crime rates in those neighborhoods remained high. Deviance became part of the culture of these neighborhoods. Shaw and McKay assumed that socialization into deviance was taking place. Edwin Sutherland picked up on this line of reasoning. He suggested the concept *differential association*: people learn conformity or deviance from the people with whom they associate. This theory is useful but fails to address two issues. First, most youths that encounter deviant cultures do not become deviant and most people who live in high crime areas do not become criminals. Second, it does not explain how a particular culture becomes defined as deviant.

Labeling   *Labeling theory* fills in some of the gaps of cultural transmission theory. **Labeling** is the process through which a definition is attached to an individual. The theory studies how the labels are applied, the consequences for the labeled individual, and the power of some people to attach labels. According to these theorists, deviance resides not in the act itself, but in the reactions of other people to a behavior. Labels create deviance in this order: a person is labeled, other people begin to treat them as deviant and refuse to help or support them, the person internalized the label and begins to seek the company of people in a similar situation, and the process becomes a self-fulfilling prophecy. Labeling theory explains how deviance can be created through social interaction. But it does not account for crimes of passion and it ignores the possibility that some people consciously choose to engage in deviant behavior.

Strain theory   Robert Merton built upon Durkheim's idea of anomie , the condition in which norms and values are weak, in serious conflict, or absent, to develop his **strain theory**. Merton argued that during an anomic situation, a structural strain develops between the culturally prescribed goals of the social system and the socially approved means of attaining goals. This strain produces large amounts of deviance. Merton stated that individuals respond to strain in the following five ways, only the first of which in not deviant.
- **Conformity** is the response in which the individual accepts both the goals and the socially accepted means of achieving them. People who attend college with the hopes of obtaining a well-paying job which will enable them to buy a nice house and car are conformists.
- In the response of **innovation** the individual accepts the goals of society but rejects the socially approved means and uses deviance to obtain the goals. Members of organized crime are considered innovators as they accept society's goals of material success but use deviant methods of acquiring their wealth.
- Those who respond with **ritualism** have no interest in the conventional goals of society. However, ritualists go through the motions by following the prescribed rules. Merton used the cautious and compulsive bureaucrat as an example.
- **Retreatism** consists of rejecting both the means and goals of society without replacing them with anything that society regards as worthwhile. Some retreatists use drugs to withdraw while others live as hermits in isolated areas.
- Individuals who respond with **rebellion** reject both the goals and means of society but replace them with new goals and means. For example, a rebel might reject education as a means of obtaining wealth and turn instead to meditation to achieve inner peace.

Demographics is important in the study of crime. About half of the people arrested for violent crime and two-thirds of the people arrested for property crime are aged 16-25. As a result, the crime rate rises and falls in proportion to changes in the number of people in this age category. Gender is also relevant to crime. Men constitute about 90% of people arrested for violent crimes and about 75% of people arrested for property crimes.

Socialization and Deviancy in the Twenty-First Century

The pace of socialization will probably quicken in the future. Less time will be devoted to teaching specific knowledge and more time will be spent teaching students how to learn on their own. People will have multiple careers and education will become a lifelong process Culture lags between the introduction of a new technology and the development of deviant behavior associated with that technology could become a major issue. With more people working in the service sector, white collar crime will probably increase.

Critical Questions

CQ: (page 69)   Many critics feel that the mass media, particularly television, offers little to enhance a child's primary socialization. Do you agree? Which shows currently on television do you think are positive socialization experiences for children? Which are negative? What about the commercials?

Before answering this question, you must distinguish between what is good and bad for children. What assumptions did you make? What is the desired behavior for children? What assumptions do you have about the link between what kids watch on television and their behavior, attitudes, and values? One way to collect knowledge is through observation. Watch a few television shows including the commercials. Make notes on the content. How do these programs and commercials socialize children? Besides consumerism, what types of messages are they sending children? Do they contain gender or racial stereotypes?

CQ: (page 73)   From a sociological viewpoint, could your self-concept exist apart from the reactions of other people? How does your unique sense of self reflect the various experiences you have had in groups, such as your family, religious groups, sports teams, and the like?

Define the key terms sociological viewpoint and self. How does Cooley's concept of looking-glass self fit into this question? Family, religious groups, and sports teams are all agents of socialization. Which have had the greatest influence on your sense of self? Why? Have you rejected any of the direction given to you by these agents? Which played a larger role in the formation of your self-concept, personal choice or socialization? Are they separable?

CQ: (page 76)   Have you ever faced a moral dilemma? If so, how did you resolve it? Did you consider the reactions of others or did you rely on preset rules? Or did you find some other way?

What was the dilemma? What were the possible outcomes? What were the pros and cons of each potential choice? What choice did you make? Why? What were the reactions of others to your choice? To the outcome of the situation? Did this affect your sense of self? Do you regret your choice? In retrospect, what would you have done differently? How does your dilemma and your choice fit Kohlberg's and Gilligan's research? Was your choice consistent with Gilligan's conclusion about the different conceptions of morality between females and males?

Self Test Questions
Multiple Choice

1. The stages into which our life span is divided such as adolescence or middle age is called:
    a. life line
    b. seasons of life
    c. life course
    d. life stages

2. Which type of socialization emphasizes, among other things, synthesis, creativity, logic, and emotional control?
    a. education
    b. school
    c. secondary socialization
    d. primary socialization

3. Which of the following is true of childhood?
    a. it is a period romanticized as a time of playful innocence
    b. by its end, the elementary aspects of formal learning have been completed
    c. ethnicity, race, and class make a difference in the course of childhood
    d. all of the above are aspects of childhood

4. Adolescence became a separate stage of the life course in American society:
    a. when World War II required a decision be reached about the draft age
    b. when in the nineteenth century the forces of industrialization created a surplus of workers
    c. because in the 1950s Dr. Spock argued that the developmental tasks of the teenager were different from those of the subteens
    d. because of local laws requiring mandatory education until the age of 16 years

5. Which of the following is NOT true of adulthood in the United States?
    a. the pace of learning quickens in adulthood in comparison to that in adolescence and childhood
    b. most people find it a satisfying time of life
    c. it occurs from the mid-twenties through the mid-sixties
    d. the willingness to help others increases in this stage

6. Usually a child's first experience with a formal agent of socialization takes place in the:
    a. family
    b. school
    c. mass media
    d. peer group

7. Which agent of socialization becomes more important during adolescence and less important during adulthood?
    a. family
    b. school
    c. mass media
    d. peer group

8. The term that describes the way you think other people see you is:
    a. looking-glass self
    b. role-taking
    c. game stage
    d. conventional stage

9. According to Mead, which of the following is an example of the generalized other?
    a. brother
    b. teacher
    c. supervisor
    d. peer group

10. In which of Mead's stages do children play at activities requiring multiple roles and complex behaviors determined by what other children do?
    a. play
    b. imitation
    c. game
    d. postconventional

11. Symbolic interaction theory stresses the importance of:
    a. our innate biological constitution as a source of motivation for our behavior
    b. symbols and meanings in relationships and social interactions
    c. human behavior as objective rather than subjective
    d. symbols which are grounded in our biology

12. In which of Piaget's stages of moral development does a child simply accept the rules as set by adults?
    a. heteronomous
    b. preconventional
    c. autonomic
    d. postconventional

13. According to Kohlberg, a person who is concerned for the environment and the rights of animals has reached which stage of development?
    a. heteronomous
    b. preconventional
    c. autonomic
    d. postconventional

14. In studying the moral development of men and women, Carol Gilligan argues:
    a. women approach morality as an obligation to exercise care, to satisfy needs, and to avoid hurting people
    b. women and men approach morality from different perspectives
    c. men view morality as governed by preset rules and laws
    d. Carol Gilligan argues all of the above are true

15. Any violation of a widely held norm is called:
    a. crime
    b. deviance
    c. degeneracy
    d. none of the above

16. Which type of social controls are learned through socialization and are seated within the individual?
    a. internal controls
    b. self controls
    c. external controls
    d. significant other controls

17. Punishments for norm violations in communal societies are often:
    a. mild and aimed at restoring group harmony
    b. deferred until the violator has an opportunity to make restitution
    c. based on an ancient system of formal laws and social controls
    d. swift, harsh, and to the point

18. American society is:
    a. one of the most crime-ridden countries in the world
    b. one of the least crime-ridden countries in the world
    c. about average in crime for a large society
    d. about average for crime in an associational society

19. Which is NOT a reason why crime underreported in the United States?
    a. a few police departments will not cooperate with the FBI in order to compile accurate crime data
    b. people are reluctant to report minor crimes such as the theft of a backpack
    c. some victims are reluctant to report a crime if they think they will be stigmatized
    d. all of the above are reasons why crime is underreported in the United States

20. Which of the following is NOT a part of differential association theory?
    a. deviant behavior is learned through interaction with others especially small intimate groups
    b. people acquire techniques, motives, attitudes for deviant behavior from generalized others
    c an individual learns definitions which are favorable or unfavorable to prevailing norms
    d. a person who has frequent, intense contact will be influenced more than if they had infrequent contacts of limited duration

21. Which theory argues that if people define a person as deviant that person may internalize the definition and behave accordingly?
    a. differential association
    b. cultural transmission
    c. labeling
    d. strain

22. Which of the following is argued by strain theory?
    a. people act to reduce the strain between what others think of them and what they think of themselves
    b. in a situation of social change, a structural strain develops between the culturally prescribed goals of the social system and the socially approved means of attaining the goals
    c. when social obligations strain the resources set aside for their attainment people work to either increase their resources or lessen their obligations
    d. change brings many strains which results in people prioritizing their responsibilities

23. A person who attends college in order to obtain a good job and buy a house is exhibiting which response to strain?
    a. conformity
    b. ritualism
    c. innovation
    d. retreatism

24. Which of the following response to strain is NOT considered deviant?
    a. rebellion
    b. ritualism
    c. innovation
    d. all of the above are considered deviant

25. Why will crime level off or decrease in the United States within the next decade?
    a. actually, crime has been increasing for the past two centuries and we have no evidence that this trend will reverse, so there will not be a decrease at all
    b. the American population is aging and the crime-prone age category is shrinking
    c. local governments are increasing the number of police officers due to FBI funding grants
    d. there will be less white collar crime in the future

True - False

T	F	1. In primary socialization children learn basic knowledge and values of society.
T	F	2. Margaret Mead studied Samoan girls and found that the openness of Samoan society with regard to sexual matters increased the girls' turbulence and conflict.
T	F	3. Very old age is a relatively new stage in the life course.
T	F	4. In all societies the family is responsible for socializing children from birth through independent adulthood.
T	F	5. Agents of socialization are the individuals, groups, organizations, and institutions that provide substantial amounts of socialization during the life course.
T	F	6. A perception of being a distinct personality with a unique identity is the "me."
T	F	7. In role taking we assume the role of another person and then judge ourselves from the viewpoint of that other person.
T	F	8. the main feature of Mead's game stage is that children spend a great deal of time pretending to be someone else.
T	F	9. Symbolic interactionists argue that, "If we define situations as real, they are real in their consequences."
T	F	10. In Kohlberg's preconventional stage of moral development people incorporate societal rules into their own value systems.
T	F	11. Feeling guilt at the mere thought of stealing is an external control mechanism.
T	F	12. Not all crimes are deviant acts.
T	F	13. Cultural transmission theory fails to explain why people who live in high crime areas do not become criminals.
T	F	14. Instead of asking "Why do people commit crimes and deviant acts?" Social bond theory asks, "Why don't people commit crimes and deviant acts?"
T	F	15. Criminals tend to "burn out" of crime as they get old.

Self Test Answers

Multiple Choice

1. c (62)	6. b (67)	11. b (72)	16. a (77)	21. c (84)
2. c (62)	7. d (68)	12. a (74)	17. d (79)	22. b (85)
3. d (63)	8. a (69)	13. d (75)	18. a (80)	23. a (85)
4. b (64)	9. d (71)	14. d (76)	19. d (80)	24. d (85)
5. a (65)	10. c (72)	15. b (77)	20. b (83)	25. b (88)

True - False

1. T (62)	4. T (66)	7. T (71)	10. F (75)	13. T (84)
2. F (64)	5. T (66)	8. F (72)	11. F (77)	14. F (86)
3. T (66)	6. F (69)	9. T (72)	12. T (79)	15. T (88)

Chapter 4

Interaction, Groups, and Organizations

THE GREAT SOCIAL TRANSFORMATION AND INTERACTION, GROUPS AND ORGANIZATIONS

SOCIAL INTERACTION
> *Types of Interaction*
> *Components of Interaction*
> *Role*
> *Sociological Analysis of Interaction*

GROUPS
> *Types of Groups*
> *Group Dynamics*

ORGANIZATIONS
> *Types of Organizations*
> *Bureaucracies*
> *The Corporation*

INTERACTION, GROUPS, AND ORGANIZATIONS IN THE TWENTY-FIRST CENTURY

CRITICAL QUESTIONS
> *Role stress*
> *Group pressure and conformity*
> *Bureaucracies*

SELF TEST QUESTIONS/ANSWERS

CHAPTER SUMMARY and KEY TERMS

The Great Social Transformation and Interaction, Groups, and Organizations

In communal societies, social interaction revolves around personal relationships, and people typically interact with the same group of people for their entire lifetimes. In associational societies, interactions involve many different groups and organizations and are more diverse over the lifetimes of the people.

Social Interaction

One of the core components of the definition of sociology was "social interaction." Sociologists study the many ways people interact interpersonally, in large and small groups, in bureaucracies and corporations. Many interesting insights and facts come from the sociological analysis of social interaction.

Five types of social interaction	**Social interaction** refers to the acts people perform toward each other and the responses they give in return. Social interaction involves communication which may take the form of spoken words, subtle gestures, or visual images. Sociologists recognize five types of social interaction. Often these types are mixed in the same social episode. The five types are: • **Exchange** is the process in which people transfer goods, services, and other items with each other. • **Cooperation** is the process in which people work together to achieve shared goals. • **Competition** is the process in which two or more parties attempt to obtain the same goal. In American culture, competition is seen as the best way to determine social outcomes. • **Conflict** is the process in which people attempt to physically or socially vanquish each other. War is the most obvious form of conflict. • **Coercion** is the process in which people compel other people to do something against their will. It is based on force. Most societies see coercion as disruptive and reserve its use for the agents of the government.
Status	Social interactions are not always a matter of conscious choice. Our **status**, or position in society, effects our interactions with others. Examples of statuses include president of the United States, teacher, parent, and nurse. People will occupy several statuses simultaneously, especially in industrial societies. For any individual, the collection of statuses the person occupies at any one time is called that person's **status set**. Sociologists distinguish between two types of statuses: An **ascribed status** is one that cannot be changed by individual effort. Race, sex, and old age are examples. Religion and social class are also ascribed statuses because we acquire them from our parents when we are too young to have any choice. In contrast, an **achieved status** is one that can be obtained through individual effort. Educational attainment and occupation are examples. In some cases achieved and ascribed statuses are related. For example, sex can be an obstacle to achieving the status of pro football player. Among all the statuses people hold, a few or even one will be more important than the others. Such a status is called a **master status**. It is so important to people's lives that they often organize their lives and identity around it. A master status can be ascribed, as being born into a certain family, or achieved, such as being a nuclear physicist.
Role	A **role** is defined as the expected behavior associated with a status. College students are expected to attend class, study, pass courses, and occasionally party. Roles are guidelines for behavior. People who stray too far from their roles will be socially sanctioned. Usually roles are compatible. However sometimes one or more of our roles will interfere with our other roles. This situation is called **role conflict**—the incompatibility of different roles played by a single person. An example is a working mother whose child becomes ill. Both require her attention at the same time. Should she fulfill her role as employee or mother? With no easy answers, situations such as this lead to **role stress**—the anxiety produced by being unable to meet all role requirements at the same time.

GST and roles

Sometimes people find themselves trying to meet incompatible expectations within a single role. This situation is called **role strain**. One example is being a high school principle. It is a single role but includes norms about administration, teaching, community service, and counseling students. Often the principle will be needed in multiple areas at the same time.

Role conflict and role strain increase with the GST. Despite the increased responsibility, Ruth Coser has found that this can be liberating. We are allowed to continually create new roles for ourselves. Often when one role becomes boring, we can seek new ones. Each person is part of a social network that links them to other people, groups, and organizations. In industrial society the number of social units in each person's network ranges from 500 to 2,500. Industrial societies are criss-crossed with networks that link everyone to a huge number of other persons, groups, and organizations. Social class affects the ability to network successfully.

Dramaturgical approach

The **dramaturgical approach** was developed by **Erving Goffman**. He believes that the world is a stage on which we are players. In essence, we play out social scenes following a "script" written by society. Showing proper manners at a fine restaurant is an example. Goffman states that our role performances are judged as an actor's performance would be judged. If we perform our roles poorly we will be criticized. Sometimes others will help us perform our roles by ignoring our shortcomings. This is called studied *nonobservance*. Goffman also distinguishes between the *front region*, where we play a role before one audience, and a *back region*, where we play a different role before a different audience. Goffman also argues that people engage in **impression management**: the conscious manipulation of props, scenery, costumes, and behavior in an attempt to present a particular image to other people. For example, you would probably present yourself formally and wear a business suit for an interview with the Federal Bureau of Investigation but appear more relaxed for an interview with a sporting goods store.

Ethno-methodology

Ethnomethodology is the methodology for studying the common understanding of everyday life. It is linked to both dramaturgy and symbolic interaction. The goal of ethnomethodology is to bring the everyday social rules to the surface and then to determine what effect they have on our behavior. **Harold Garfinkel** demonstrated the power of these rules by asking his students to pretend to be borders in their own homes, but without informing their parents of the experiment. The students were supposed to address their parents by "Sir" or "Madam" and ask for explanations for common assumptions. Through this *breaching experiment*, Garfinkel hoped to discover unstated rules of social interaction.

Norm of reciprocity

Exchange theory singles out exchange as the most important type of social interaction. Many cultures recognize the **norm of reciprocity**—the strong norm that says that if you do something for a person, then that person must do something of approximately equal social value in return. If someone continually fails to reciprocate, the exchange relationship will be discontinued. Exchange theory is useful in that it recognizes that self-interest and social rewards motivate people to interact. However, it cannot explain true charity or altruism.

Groups

Groups

A **group** is a collection of people who take each other's behavior into account as they interact, and who develop a sense of togetherness. This differs from a *category*, or a cluster of people who share a social trait such as age, sex, or race. It also differs from a *collection*—two or more people who gather together at a specific place without developing a sense of togetherness. Each group develops its own values, norms, roles, and statuses. In essence, culture and structure emerge from the interactions within groups. A group of friends is an *informal* group while a group with a rigid social structure is a *formal* group. The smallest human group is a *dyad*—a group of two. It consists of only one social relationship. Things become more complicated in a triad, a group of three, as these include not one but two additional social relationships.

The feelings we have about groups can also be one way to distinguish groups. An **in-group** is a group to which people feel they belong while an **out-group** is a group to which people feel they do not belong. This distinction is useful when describing group structure and interaction.

Primary groups are characterized by intimate, warm, cooperative, and face-to-face relationships. Primary group members are concerned about each other's well being. They treat each other as valuable individuals rather than as means to an end. The family is one example.

Secondary groups are characterized by limited participation and by impersonal and formal relationships. Secondary groups are a means to an end. Therefore, members are not very concerned about each other's well-being. Secondary groups can be the settings for the development of primary groups. For example, your classes of 50 or more students are secondary groups. But as the term progresses you may become close friends with two or three of your classmates thereby forming a primary group. Secondary groups are more important in industrial societies than in pre-industrial societies as the family can satisfy most needs in the latter society. We do not belong to each group that we identify as important. Even though we do not belong to it, a group could have values, norms, and beliefs that serve as a standard for our own behavior. This is known as a **reference group**. Examples include labor unions, professional associations, or religious orders.

Leaders

Group dynamics refers to the scientific study of the powerful processes that operate in groups. Within a group, it is the **leader** who can consistently influence the behavior of group members and the outcomes of the group. The leader may be formally or informally designated. One way group leaders can be characterized is by their primary concern for or outcome of the groups. An **instrumental leader** is primarily concerned about attaining group goals while an **expressive leader** is primarily concerned with group feelings.

The outcomes characterization is one way to see leaders, another is by leadership style. Three styles of leadership have been identified:

In the *authoritarian* style, communication flows from the top down. The leader retains authority and responsibility for group actions, assigns members to clearly defined activities, and closely monitors their behavior. The benefit in this system is prompt, orderly, and predictable completion of tasks. The disadvantage is the loss of individual initiative and creativity.

In the *democratic* style, communication flows from members to the leader, and from the leader to members. The leader delegates authority and responsibility, discusses matters with group members, and encourages them to divide tasks among themselves. The benefit is the promotion of commitment to group goals. The drawback is the increased time it takes to complete tasks and the possibility of decreased group cohesiveness if members begin to fight among themselves.

In the *laissez-faire* style, the leader exercises authority sparingly and functions mainly as a source of knowledge, skill, and experience that the group can draw on as needed. While this encourages individual initiative and creativity, it may lead to a group standstill if no member takes the challenge.

Groupthink

A group is *cohesive* when its members are strongly attached to it. Cohesion usually occurs when members interact frequently. If outsiders define the group positively cohesion increases. Change in group membership may disrupt cohesion for a while. As discussed in Chapter 3, society usually rewards conformity. This is especially true in small groups where members know each other personally and may exert great pressure on other members. In a small group, if the pressures to conform are so strong that no dissension or critical questioning is allowed, the state is called **groupthink**. Muzafer Sherif and Solomon Asch conducted separate experiments to test group conformity. They each observed that individuals will often change their opinion to fit that of the group, even when they know that the group is wrong. When interviewed, such conformists report that they did not want to be deviant from the group.

Organizations

Organization

An **organization** may be defined as a group with three characteristics: 1) It is deliberately constructed; that is, someone or some group of people decided to create the organization for some purpose. 2) It is structured, with well-defined roles and positions. Typically, the roles differ in prestige and power. 3) It has rules, and sanctions for violations of those rules.

Organizations affect all parts of life in industrial societies. We are born and die in hospitals, are socialized in schools, play in athletic clubs, and visit elders in rest homes. There are about 10 million organizations in the United States. *Voluntary organizations* provide recreation, enjoyment, and the satisfaction of participating in a common activity with other people. Members in such organizations can enter and leave as they wish. *Coercive organizations* take in and keep members against their will. For example, children must attend school whether they want to or not. They are also not permitted to leave each day until the school dismisses them.

Ideal type

Max Weber's analysis of bureaucracies begins with the concept of **ideal type**: a composite of characteristics based on many specific examples.

Bureaucracy

In almost every case, when organizations grow they become bureaucracies. A **bureaucracy** is a form of organization based on explicit rules with a clear, impersonal, and hierarchical authority structure. Examples include your school, the government, and the local library. Max Weber stated that an ideal type of bureaucracy would have these characteristics:

• A complex division of labor among its members with each person having specialized duties and responsibilities.

• A hierarchy of authority with a few people at the top, many people in the middle, and even more people at the bottom. Managers are held responsible for the performance of those under them in the chain of command.

• Detailed and explicit rules and procedures that govern all aspects of the organization. When these rules and procedures are followed a common and predictable outcome is reached.

• A system that rewards people based on performance rather than on family ties, friendships, or other primary relationships. Competence in skills may be determined by tests, past experiences, or formal training. Rewards, salary advances, and promotions are based on job performance.

• Extensive written records of the organization's activities and members. The paper flow becomes the official history of the organization.

In reality, bureaucracies are not perfect. Sociologists have identified several problems or negative consequences of bureaucracies:

• "Service without a smile" occurs in bureaucracies because they are impersonal. Often all customers are treated in the same disinterested way.

• The saying, "rules are rules" illustrates that blind devotion to rules often occurs in bureaucracies. This sometimes interferes with the organization's achievement of its goals. The tendency for bureaucrats to mechanically follow the rules rather than use their imagination is called *trained incapacity*.

• "Goal displacement" refers to the process by which the organization's original goals are replaced by goals that serve the personal interest of the bureaucrat. For example, some charitable organizations spend more money paying bureaucrats' salaries than they give to the people they are trying to help.

• Parkinson's Law states "Work expands to fill the available time." Thus if bureaucrats do not have enough to do, they will fill the time with busywork which provides little benefit to the organization.

• According to Lawrence Peter, "bureaucrats rise to their level of incompetence." They get promoted until they move beyond their ability. Since demotion is rare, Peter argues, every position in the organization eventually comes to be filled by an incompetent bureaucrat.

• According to Robert Michels, every bureaucracy is controlled by an **oligarchy**: a small clique of people who rule the organization for their own benefit. This is known as the "Iron Law of Oligarchy" because Michels believes that the rule by an oligarchy is inevitable in bureaucracies.

• Most bureaucracies supposedly follow a policy of equal opportunity. But some have the problem of "invisible woman." This occurs when women are subjected to sexism in the workplace. This can take the form of condescending chivalry, when a woman's supervisor protects her from criticism even though she may benefit from it; supportive discouragement, when a woman's co-workers discourage her from competing for a new position because she might fail; or benevolent exploitation, when a woman is assigned the boring detail-work of a job but a male superior takes credit for the final product.

Corporation   The corporation is common in industrial societies. A **corporation** is a group that, through the legal process of incorporation, has been given the status of a separate and real social entity. It has rights separate from the people within it. Corporations may be held responsible for the acts of its officers, but the officers are not held responsible for the acts of the corporation.

Interaction, Groups, and Organizations in the Twenty-First Century

In the twenty-first century, a major distinction between societies will be the speed at which their economies operate. Fast societies will have advanced technology which will require fast groups, fast organizations, and fast interaction as the entire business cycle emphasizes the rapid movement of investment capital and the fast delivery of the product to the customer. Interactions, especially those in the workplace, will be greatly impacted by these technological changes.

Critical Questions

CQ: (page 105)   In modern society, is role stress inevitable? Do you think your life as a college student is more stressful than the lives of college students 20 or 30 years ago? Why or why not?

Define the key term role stress. Turn the question around. Is role stress preventable? How? In order to answer the second question, you should put it into a historical context. What was happening in the United States twenty years ago? Thirty years ago? What is happening today? Which generation do you think experienced the greatest social change? What affect does this have on role stress? Is this different in the short run versus the long run?

CQ: (page 113)   Sociologists assert that teenagers and young adults are often subject to strong group pressures to conform. Have you ever felt such group pressure? How did you react?

What forms does group pressure take? What punishments, if any, do groups give to those who do not conform? Do groups exert more pressure over non-members or over members who have gone astray? What is so compelling about group pressure that makes people conform? Have you known any non-conformers? How did their attitudes, goals, values, and personalities differ from those of conformers? Did these non-conformers form their own group or remain isolated? Why do sociologists focus on teenagers and young adults instead of older adults when discussing group pressure?

CQ: (page 119)   What aspects of bureaucracies do you find especially frustrating? Are these the same aspects that create greater efficiency for society?

As with all critical thinking, you must define key terms to intelligently discuss the subject. Define bureaucracy. Review the seven negative consequences of bureaucracies on pages 116-117. Have you ever encountered any of these problems? If so, how much hardship did you suffer as a result? Is it possible to have an modern society without bureaucracies? Why or why not? Do bureaucracies increase efficiency and fairness? Have you encountered any bureaucracies that fit Weber's notion of an ideal type?

Self Test Questions
Multiple Choice

1. Which of the following is NOT a type of social interaction?
      a. coercion
      b. exchange
      c. conflict
      d. all are types of social interaction

2. Which type of social interaction is largely limited to the police or other officials of the state?
   a. coercion
   b. exchange
   c. conflict
   d. competition

3. Jane is five years old. Her parents are Catholic. Which of the following describes Jane's religion at age five?
   a. achieved status
   b. role set
   c. ascribed status
   d. status set

4. Joe is a single father with two children. He is also a chef. When Joe's responsibilities as a parent and as an employee cause him to feel as if he cannot handle all his role requirements, he is experiencing:
   a. master status
   b. role set
   c. role strain
   d. role stress

5. Which of the following best describes the situation of teachers interacting in the teachers' lounge?
   a. They are engaging in impression management.
   b. They are exhibiting dramaturgy.
   c. They are acting in the front region.
   d. They are acting in the back region.

6. If you dress professionally to attend an interview with a large corporation, you are engaging in:
   a. ethnomethodology
   b. impression management
   c. dramaturgy
   d. studied nonobservance

7. Which technique do sociologists use to study the rules underlying everyday life?
   a. dramaturgy
   b. impression management
   c. back region
   d. ethnomethodology

8. Mary pretended to be a guest in her parents' home in order to discover the unstated rules of interaction. Harold Garfinkel called this:
   a. back region
   b. breeching experiment
   c. exchange theory
   d. dramaturgy

9. Professor Lee is not a member of the American Sociological Association but she uses the organization as a standard for her research. In this case, the organization is a:
   a. primary group
   b. reference group
   c. secondary group
   d. democratic group

10. Which type of leader provides the group with his or her knowledge and skill but forces the members to assume leadership tasks for themselves?
    a. authoritarian
    b. democratic
    c. laissez-faire
    d. none of the above

11. Which is NOT a characteristic of organizations?
    a. They are constructed for a purpose.
    b. They reward people on the basis of primary associations.
    c. They have well-defined roles and positions.
    d. They have rules and sanctions for rule violations.

12. Girl Scouts is an example of a:
    a. coercive organization
    b. cohesive organization
    c. voluntary organization
    d. none of the above

13. Robert Michels' Iron Law of Oligarchy states that:
    a. work expands to fill the available time
    b. bureaucrats rise to their level of incompetence
    c. rule by a few people is inevitable
    d. none of the above

14. Which is NOT a characteristic of bureaucracies?
    a. hierarchical authority structure
    b. clear rules
    c. written records
    d. simple division of labor

15. The tendency for bureaucrats to mechanically follow the rules rather than use their imaginations is called:
    a. Iron Law of Oligarchy
    b. trained incapacity
    c. goal displacement
    d. none of the above

16. What term is used to describe a situation in which a woman's supervisor protects her from criticism, even though she might benefit from it?
    a. supportive discouragement
    b. goal displacement
    c. benevolent exploitation
    d. condescending chivalry

17. A corporation is a distinct type of organization in that:
    a. it has rights that are separate from the people within it
    b. it is not responsible for the actions of its officers
    c. people who work in them are held responsible for the corporation's actions
    d. they have a hierarchical authority structure

18. A status that is more important than the others is referred to as a:
   a. status set
   b. master role
   c. master status
   d. role set

19. Sociologists define teacher as a:
   a. role
   b. status
   c. master status
   d. none of the above

20. Which is NOT a dysfunction of bureaucracies?
   a. they are eventually controlled by a few people
   b. busywork may be created when employees do not have legitimate work to do
   c. blind devotion to following rules may interfere with the achievement of goals
   d. all of the above are dysfunctions of bureaucracies

True - False

T	F	1. War is an example of coercion.
T	F	2. Sometimes a person's ascribed status will affect their achieved status.
T	F	3. Professors sometimes suffer role strain when they are required to teach many classes and publish research articles simultaneously.
T	F	4. The number of units in the social network of a member of an industrial society is less than that of a member of a pre-industrial society.
T	F	5. Pretending not to notice a mistake in a role performance is called studied nonobservance.
T	F	6. Five people waiting at a bus stop constitute a group.
T	F	7. Primary groups often develop within secondary groups.
T	F	8. You must join a group for it to be a reference group.
T	F	9. An in group is a well-liked popular group whether or not you are a member of that group.
T	F	10. Membership turnover tends to disrupt group cohesiveness, at least temporarily.
T	F	11. All organizations are bureaucracies.
T	F	12. An expressive leader is concerned with group feeling; an instrumental leader with group goals.
T	F	13. Group think results when the pressures to conform are so strong that no dissenting or critical questioning is allowed.
T	F	14. Weber's concept "ideal type" means that something is the best it can be.
T	F	15. In the future, the use of technology may cause an increased division between fast and slow societies based on the speed their economies operate.

Self Test Answers

Multiple Choice

1. d (95)	6. b (102)	11. b (114)	16. d (117)
2. a (96)	7. d (102)	12. c (114)	17. a (118)
3. c (98)	8. b (103)	13. c (117)	18. c (98)
4. d (99)	9. b (108)	14. d (115)	19. b (98)
5. d (102)	10. c (109)	15. b (116)	20. d (116)

True - False

1. F (96)	4. F (100)	7. T (106)	10. T (111)	13. T (112)
2. T (98)	5. T (102)	8. F (108)	11. F (114)	14. F (115)
3. T (99)	6. F (105)	9. F (106)	12. F (108)	15. T (119)

NOTES FOR FUTURE STUDY AND REVIEW:

Chapter 5

Population, Ecology, and Urbanization

THE GREAT SOCIAL TRANSFORMATION AND POPULATION, ECOLOGY, AND URBANIZATION

DEMOGRAPHIC ANALYSIS
Fertility
Mortality
Migration
The Demographic Transition and the Growth of Population

POPULATION GROWTH AND THE ENVIRONMENT
The Lesson of Easter Island
The Malthusian Trap
The Contemporary Debate Over Malthus' Predictions
Human Ecology
Attitudes about the Environment

URBANIZATION
The Historical City
Cities Today
Urbanism: The Urban Way of Life

POPULATION, ECOLOGY, AND URBANIZATION IN THE TWENTY-FIRST CENTURY

CRITICAL QUESTIONS
Population explosion
Theories of the internal structure of cities
Urban life

SELF TEST QUESTIONS/ANSWERS

CHAPTER SUMMARY and KEY TERMS

The **Great Social Transformation** looks at the changes that take place as societies move from communal to associational, from agricultural to industrial. One major change has been the increasingly fast rate of population growth. Many parts of the world have experienced a **population explosion** or the rapid, unchecked growth in the number of people inhabiting an area. This chapter will look at the causes of population growth and the patterns of growth on the formation of cities.

Demographic Analysis

Demography   **Demography** is the scientific study of the size, growth, and composition of the human population. The goal of most demographers is to understand how social forces affect the population and how the population affects society. Only three factors affect population change. They are fertility, mortality, and migration.

Fertility   **Fertility** is the number of births that occur over a specific period, usually one year. It is the most studied of the three factors because it has the most long-term impact on the growth or decline of a population. It is mainly discussed in relation to women as only women can bear children. Women are capable of having children from the onset of menstruation to the onset of menopause. This lasts about 30 years. The Hutterites were one of the most fertile social groups in history. They averaged about 12 children per woman. This is far above even the most high fertility regions of the world today. American society once valued large families. But many American women now marry at a later age and work full-time after having children. It is also economically difficult to have many children. As a result, women in the United States have an average of less than two children each. This is below *replacement level*: the number of children required to replace the population as people die. Even though it is illegal in many places, abortion is the most used method of birth control worldwide. The simplest measure of fertility is the **crude birth rate**: the annual number of births in a population per 1,000 members of the population. This is not very precise because it includes members of the population who cannot bear children. The **general fertility ratio** is more sensitive. This is the annual number of births in a population per 1,000 women aged 15-44 years.

Mortality   **Mortality** is the number of deaths that occur during a year. **Life expectancy** is the number of years people will probably live. Life expectancy has increased dramatically in the United States. In 1900, the average person could expect to live 49 years while the figure is 75 years today. This varies by race and sex with whites and women living longer than African Americans and men. **Life span** is the theoretical maximum length of life. There are well-documented cases of a Japanese man living to age 119 and a French women living to 120. Thus, life expectancy could increase even more. The most critical time in a person's life is in the first year, when mortality is high. Mortality decreases after the first year and stays low for a number of years. The major cause of death in the United States between the ages of 1-44 is accidents rather than diseases. The **crude death rate** is the annual number of deaths per 1,000 members of the population. The **natural increase** is the number of births in a given time period minus the numbers of deaths in the population for the same time period. When births exceed deaths, there is natural increase. When the number of deaths exceeds the number of births, there is **natural decrease**.

Migration   **Migration** is the movement of people from one area of residence to another. **Immigration** is movement into a place while **emigration** is movement out of a place. Migration is increasing throughout the world. Places which were once homogeneous are now becoming heterogeneous. People migrate for two general reasons. The first, *push factors*, are the reasons for leaving a place. These reasons are usually economic and political. *Pull factors* are the forces that attract migrants to a place, such as good weather or job opportunities. Most migration is *internal migration*, that is, it occurs within a country. The pattern of internal migration in the United States used to flow south-to-north. However, it now flows east-to-west. Migration is more difficult to measure than fertility or mortality. People move freely and are not required to report their move to a central authority. The **net migration rate** is the annual difference between the number of people who enter a place and the number who leave, per 1,000 people of that place. In 1990, 3 people moved to the United States per 1,000 residents. Despite the media's descriptions of the "flood" of migrants, this number has been about the same for the past 30 years.

Demographic transition

Demographic transition involves the link between the birth rate and the death rate of a population. It occurs in four stages:
- *Stage 1: High Birth Rate and High Death Rate.* This stage describes stable populations found in pre-industrial societies. These societies had little technology to overcome diseases or harsh environments. They had little control over their food supply. Therefore the death rate was high. The birth rate was also high because children were needed as laborers and caretakers for aged parents. In this stage the birth and death rates offset each other and the population does not grow rapidly.
- *Stage 2: High Birth Rate and Declining Death Rate.* This stage characterizes societies that are moving from the communal to the transitional. Advances in technology, medicines, and social conditions cause the death rate to fall. However, people continue to have many children, even though the material gains of large families has declined. Deaths no longer offset births and these populations grow rapidly.
- *Stage 3: Declining Birth Rate and Low Death Rate.* Societies in this stage are moving from transitional to associational. Members have smaller families and the gap between fertility and mortality declines. These societies grow very slowly.
- *Stage 4: Low Birth Rate and Low Death Rate.* In the final stage of the demographic transition both birth and mortality rates are low. Societies in this stage neither grow nor decrease but are stable.

Population Growth and the Environment

The story of Easter Island points out how unrestrained population growth and cultural values that neglect the environment will quickly destroy an **ecosystem** or the interlocking, stable group of plants and animals living in their natural habitat.

Thomas Malthus

Thomas Malthus lived during the Industrial Revolution. He was influenced by the poverty and misery he witnessed. Malthus blamed overpopulation as the source of these problems. He said that when the population is small, there are enough resources for everyone. When population is large, resources are spread thin. He also stated that human population grows exponentially (i.e. 2, 4, 8, 16, 32) while food production grows arithmetically (i.e. 1, 2, 3, 4, 5). As you can see, the population size will be much larger than food production after only five cycles with this system. Malthus concluded that if nothing were done, human population would quickly outpace food production and everyone would starve. He also predicted that nature would produce "positive checks" to control population size. These included famine, war, and plague. Although he was not optimistic about them, Malthus also stated that "preventive checks" including postponement of marriage and abstinence from sex within marriage, could also slow population growth. Malthus' ideas did not hold true for most of the world.

Cornucopian View

The Cornucopian view disagrees with Malthus' view. According to the Cornucopians, humans will use their intelligence and inventiveness to overcome any scarcities caused by overpopulation. They support their success by citing the "Green Revolution" in which new plants and fertilizers were used to increase farm productivity. Between 1960 and 1986 the world's grain harvests doubled even when the amount of land under cultivation actually declined. The Cornucopians believe that the earth could support twice as many people as we now have. Neo-Malthusians have modified Malthus' original work. They emphasize two trends. The first concerns the consequences of relying on technology as a cure for scarcity. They point out that the use of heavy chemical fertilizers may harm the environment. The second points out that we are already experiencing a Malthusian disaster.

Human ecology	The perspective of **human ecology** examines the relationship between society and the environment. It rests on the assumption that groups cooperate and compete with each other for the use of environmental resources. It also assumes that the relationship between the environment and society determines the outcome of each. The ecological approach was used to explain air pollution in Los Angeles. Otis Dudley Duncan proposed a model, called POET, which includes the four components of population, social organization, environment, and technology. The POET model applies to Los Angeles as follows: **P**opulation. Migration had caused the Los Angeles population to grow enormously. **O**rganization. Although Los Angeles had a system of public transportation, for the most part people traveled around in their private cars. **E**nvironment. Los Angeles is ringed by mountains that trap and concentrate the polluted air, thereby intensifying its effects. **T**echnology. The relatively inefficient gasoline engine created byproducts that combined with sunlight to form toxic chemicals and smog. Any one of these factors could have produced smog. But the effect was intensified by the combination of the four. The human ecological perspective is very applicable to analyzing environmental problems caused by human activity.

Many people in the United States now express concern about the environment. Unfortunately, these attitudes are not always put into action. Most people say they support efforts to save the environment but most of them are unwilling to make sacrifices to do so.

Urbanization

Urbanization	Native Americans had formed cities by the year AD 1,000. One such city, Cahokia, had a population of 10,000 and was inhabited for 700 years. **Urbanization** is the increase in the percentage of the population residing in cities. A **city** in turn is a densely settled concentration of people.
GST and cities	Hunting and gathering societies were not efficient enough to provide a food surplus. It required everyone's participation. This changed with the rise of horticultural and agrarian societies. Now it was possible for some surplus to accumulate and for a few people to be freed of the daily responsibility of food production. These people could serve as political and religious leaders, build permanent structures, create art, and develop technology. As a result, people began to form permanent settlements. Some of these grew large and became cities. The first cities evolved in the valleys of great rivers such as the Tigris and Euphrates (3,5000 BC), the Nile (3,300 BC), the Indus (2,500 BC), and the Huangho (1,650 BC). The terrain, climate, and technology enabled farmers to produce enough food to feed themselves, with enough left over to feed the people living in the city. Urbanization spread throughout Europe with the rise of the Roman Empire. By contemporary standards, early cities were small. Rome probably never exceeded 350,000 people. Cities were points of defense and centers of government, religion, and art. The Industrial Revolution allowed cities to grow tremendously. The growth of manufacturing also required a different form of social organization, one based on rationality. This led to the development of modern cities. Today, about 40% of the world's population is urban. However, this distorts the difference between industrial and traditional societies. Traditional societies are about one-third urban while industrial societies are about three-fourths urban.
Urban primacy	In traditional societies, urbanization takes place unevenly. One city will grow very large while other areas remain rural. This pattern is called **urban primacy**. For example, in Thailand, about 80 percent of the population is rural but the capital city of Bangkok has five million people. This is 50 times more than the population of the second largest city. Urban primacy results both from natural increase and from migration. Migrants are attracted to primate cities by both push and pull factors. Push factors include the understanding that, however bad the situation in the city might be, it is better than rural areas. Pull factors operate when potential migrants have a relative in the city who can help them get established. Housing in these cities is scarce. Many migrants live in

spontaneous settlements. These are shantytowns, slums, and other areas that they take over without official permission. Life in these settlements is harsh. But residents do experience some communal life. City officials have found it impossible to permanently disband spontaneous settlements. Recently, some authorities have begun to work with residents of these settlements to initiate community development.

Theories of urban growth

The course of urbanization has been very different in industrial societies. It has been much slower than in traditional societies. Industrial societies do not have primate cities. For example, the largest city in the United States is New York City with a population of 20 million. Los Angeles is the second largest with 15 million. During the 1920s sociologists at the University of Chicago developed an explanation of city growth called the concentric zone model. According to the model, cities grow as a series of rings, or concentric zones. The first zone consists of the central business district or the "downtown." The next zone is the "zone of transition" which mainly contains light manufacturing and wholesaling activities. Bars, pawnshops, cheap hotels, and some inexpensive residences are also found in this area. It usually has the reputation of a "bad neighborhood." The next three rings contain residential housing. The ring next to the zone of transition is the poorest while the outermost ring is the most affluent. This model accurately described city growth in the United States for about the first half of the twentieth century. It was proposed before communities developed which had metropolitan areas outside of the central city. These new communities were the **suburbs** and with them came privately owned cars, freeways, and industry that had moved to the outskirts of the city. Other models were developed as these changes occurred. The sector model proposed that some parts of the city grew along irregularly-shaped sectors moving outward from the central city. Another model recognized the existence of multiple nuclei, or several areas that adopt specialized uses. For example, one section of the city might specialize in finance and another in tourism.

Metropolitan community

Recently, cities have begun merging into one single **metropolitan community**: a large city and the surrounding areas that are integrated on a daily basis with the city. In the past 20 years, some metropolitan areas have grown fairly close to each other to form a *megalopolis*: a giant metropolitan complex that functions, in many ways, as a single community. One example is the New York megalopolis which contains New York City as well as cities in New Jersey and Connecticut. Three-fourths of the United States population now lives in one of the 21 recognized megalopolises. They are called consolidated metropolitan statistical areas. *Global cities* are also emerging. These are cities which contain the organizations that run the worldwide economy. Examples include New York, London, and Tokyo.

Urbanism

The concept **urbanism** refers to the patterns of social life found in cities. The differences in size from rural communities to urban communities influence the quality and patterns of social interaction. Many sociologists have commented on these changing patterns. The quality of social interaction may differ between cities and rural areas. Sociologist Ferdinand Toennies developed the concepts of *Gemeinschaft* and *Gesellschaft* 90 years ago. *Gemeinschaft* describes places where people know each other personally and are deeply concerned about each other. They follow old traditions, they believe in the family, and they worry about the well-being of their community. This usually describes small rural communities. *Gesellschaft* refers to places where social relationships are based on pragmatic, practical interests. People do not know each other personally. Therefore they become formal and impersonal. They do not follow tradition very closely and they are not very concerned about the well-being of their communities. Toennies stated that cities are usually Gesellschaft in orientation. This negative view of urban life was shared by Louis Wirth in the 1930s. Wirth stated that urban life was characterized by three characteristics:

• *Size*. Wirth believed that size was associated with social diversity. According to him, the modern city was a collection of ethnic communities, specialized land uses, and neighborhoods of different social classes. In this environment, communal bonds are replaced by formal institutions such as the law, the police, and government. Large population sizes also force people to interact in terms of roles rather than whole personalities.

- *Density.* Urban areas are highly dense because many people live in a small area. The sheer number of contacts with strangers means that each interaction must be transitory and brief. Stimulation from strangers, shop signs, and the media cause people to screen out the unimportant forces. Peace, quiet, and privacy are also difficult to obtain in the city. As a result, people become anxious, hostile, and sometimes violent.
- *Heterogeneity.* Urban areas are called heterogeneous because they are home to many different religious, ethnic, racial, and social groups. Wirth stated that diversity makes people tolerant of different lifestyles and more open to different ethnic groups.

Population, Ecology, and Urbanization in the Twenty-First Century

In the future, world population will continue to grow and put pressure on the environment. A large part of the growth will take place in poorer, traditional societies. In those societies, urban growth will be especially great, and urbanites will suffer even more from overcrowding, pollution, congestion, and poverty.

Critical Questions

CQ: (page 134) Are you concerned abut the population explosion? How do you think it will affect your life in the next century?

As you think about this issue, think about it as you may experience it directly and as you may note the impact of the population explosion globally. Will you have direct personal experience of the population explosion? Do you plan to travel to countries that are in stage two or three of the demographic transition? Have you thought about going into the Peace Corps? Globally, think about the resources you may consume or produce. Will your ability to obtain resources be affected by greater numbers of people world wide? Population increases can cause disaster, disease, and/or the need for land and resources that is sometimes the catalyst for war. Would disaster and conflict in parts of the world impact you or your family in the twenty-first century?

CQ: (page 147) Figure 5.7 illustrates three theories of the internal structure of cities. They are Concentric Zone, Sector, and Multiple Nuclei. The Critical Question asks: Can you identify characteristics of a nearby city that correspond to one of these three models?

The best way to answer this question is through direct observation. Take a bus downtown or ask a friend to drive you. Now choose a route that takes you out of the central business district. Take notes on what you see. What does the downtown look like? What types of economic activities are happening there? What types of jobs are available? Do you think the people you see live there or commute there for work? As you move out of the central business district, do you notice a change in these answers? Is the quality and availability of housing changing? Are the types and number of businesses changing? How? Do the people look richer or poorer as you move through the city? After traveling several miles in one direction, return to the downtown. Now travel in a different direction. What do these sections of the city look like? Do you observe any difference between this route and your first? If so, describe the changes. When you are satisfied with the quality and quality of your observations, turn to page 146 in your textbook. Does the city you observed apply to any one of these models? If it does not, draw a model depicting the differences.

CQ: (page 152) Do you want to spend your life in a large city? What is it about urban life that most appeals or does not appeal to you?

In Chapter 4, Ruth Coser stated that the complexity of contemporary industrial society can liberate us (p. 99). Can this be especially true in large cities? Will you have more opportunities for career and personal growth in a large city? (What is it about the quality of social interaction that is appealing or not?) Are you basing your opinions on direct experience or what you think urban life is like? How has your own socialization influenced how you answer this question? Find someone in your class that grew up in a large metropolitan area and hear what they liked or did not like about that lifestyle.

Self-Test Questions
Multiple Choice

1. The scientific study of the size, growth, and composition of the human population is called:
    a. ecology
    b. urban sociology
    c. demography
    d. fertility

2. A large population provides:
    a. soldiers for the military
    b. workers for farms and industry
    c. people to fill the many roles required for society to run
    d. all of the above

3. The number of births in a population per 1,000 members of the population is:
    a. fertility rate
    b. crude birth rate
    c. specific birth rate
    d. general fertility rate

4. The number of births in a given period of time minus the number of deaths in the same time period is:
    a. natural increase
    b. mortality rate
    c. morbidity rate
    d. population increase

5. Gene's family migrated from Milwaukee to Omaha to take advantage of Omaha's low unemployment rate. This incentive to move is known as:
    a. migration factor
    b. push factor
    c. immigration
    d. pull factor

6. Moving from Columbus, Ohio to Cincinnati, Ohio is an example of:
    a. pull factors
    b. external migration
    c. push factors
    d. internal migration

7. Which of the following describes societies in the first stage of demographic transition?
    a. high birth rate and declining death rate
    b. low birth rate and low death rate
    c. high birth rate and high death rate
    d. high death rate and low birth rate

8. Which of the following describes the situation in many transitional societies today as they move from pre-industrial to industrial?
    a. high birth rate and high death rate
    b. high birth rate and declining death rate
    c. declining death rate and low birth rate
    d. low birth rate and low death rate

9. Which of the following can be learned from a population pyramid?
    a. the number of females in a society
    b. the number of very young versus the number of very old in a society
    c. potential for future population growth
    d. all of the above can be learned from a population pyramid

10. The Easter Island example shows:
    a. how unrestrained population growth and cultural values that neglect the environment will quickly destroy an ecosystem
    b. how brave seafaring people can migrate from one place to another and take their material culture with them
    c. how a society's population concentrated in the young ages can grow explosively
    d. how giant statues, called the moi, can bring a divided people together in times of trouble

11. Which of the following did Thomas Malthus argue?
    a. that the Green Revolution would provide sufficient food for the world's population
    b. that nature did not provide sufficient food for the world's population
    c. that population growth eventually would outpace growth in food supply
    d. none of the above

12. Which point of view argues that human inventiveness will cope with any scarcities caused by overpopulation?
    a. Malthusian
    b. Cornucopian
    c. Green Revolution
    d. New-Malthusian

13. The study of the relationship between society and the environment is:
    a. environmental sociology
    b. demography
    c. human ecology
    d. none of the above

14. Which is NOT part of Otis Dudley Duncan's ecological model?
    a. environment
    b. exchange
    c. population
    d. technology

15. Positive attitudes about the environment on the part of Americans:
    a. has translated into aggressive actions to clean up the environment
    b. does not always translate into action
    c. has led to a majority of people picking up trash when they come across it
    d. has led to a majority feeling that we are overly concerned about the environment

16. Where did the first cities appear?
    a. near the Tigris and Euphrates rivers
    b. Mesoamerica
    c. in the Niger river valley
    d. on sea coasts

17. Mexico City is eight times larger than Mexico's second largest city. This is an example of:
    a. urbanization
    b. urban primacy
    c. Gemeinschaft
    d. Gesellschaft

18. As compared to growth in traditional societies, urban growth in industrial societies has been:
    a. slower
    b. faster
    c. about the same
    d. none of the above

19. Which is consistent with Burgess' Concentric Zone Model of city growth?
    a. The outer-most ring is the most affluent.
    b. The ring next to the zone of transition is the richest area.
    c. The zone of transition contains high-rent luxury apartments
    d. the inner-most ring has a reputation for being a "bad neighborhood."

20. A large city and its surrounding areas that are integrated with the city on a daily basis is called:
    a. metropolis
    b. metropolitan community
    c. metroplex
    d. megalopolis

21. Which of the following describes the type of city that contains organizations that run the worldwide economy?
    a. primate
    b. metroplex
    c. global
    d. megalopolis

22. According to Ferdinand Toennies, small farming villages most likely exhibit which of the following?
    a. Gesellschaft
    b. organic solidarity
    c. Gemeinschaft
    d. none of the above

23. Which is NOT one of the ways Louis Wirth distinguished cities from rural areas?
    a. social relationships
    b. diversity
    c. density
    d. population size

True - False

T	F	1. Overpopulation has been a problem for most of human history.
T	F	2. A population's fertility level is at replacement if enough children are born to replace the population as people die.
T	F	3. If the United States did not allow any immigrants to enter the country, its population would eventually grow smaller, given the current fertility rates.
T	F	4. Life expectancy in the United States has increased about 25 years since 1900.
T	F	5. For the young and middle aged in the United States, the major cause of death is diseases.
T	F	6. Migration is currently increasing the heterogeneity of many countries in the world.
T	F	7. The current migration pattern within the United States is between northern states and southern states.
T	F	8. Postindustrial societies will be characterized by low birth rates and low death rates according to demographic transition theory..
T	F	9. In comparing the population pyramids of Sub-Saharan Africa and Western Europe we find that Africa's population has a much greater potential for future growth than does Europe's.
T	F	10. Malthus referred to famine, war, and plague as positive checks which would increase the death rate and reduce a population's size.
T	F	11. Food surpluses are associated with the development of the first cities.
T	F	12. Today, three-fourths of the world's population lives in urban areas.
T	F	13. Urban primacy develops in industrial societies.
T	F	14. Developments in transportation technology, such as the interstate highway system, resulted in the development of cities which did not fit the Burgess Concentric Zone Model.
T	F	15. New York, London, and Tokyo are global cities because they contain the organizations that are associated with the United Nations.

Self Test Answers

Multiple Choice

1. c (126)	6. d (131)	11. c (136)	16. a (143)	21. c (147)
2. d (127)	7. c (133)	12. b (137)	17. b (144)	22. c (147)
3. b (129)	8. b (133)	13. c (136)	18. a (145)	23. a (148)
4. a (131)	9. d (128)	14. b (138)	19. a (146)	
5. d (131)	10. a (135)	15. b (140)	20. b (146)	

True - False

1. F (126)	4. T (130)	7. F (131)	10. T (136)	13. F (144)
2. T (129)	5. F (130)	8. T (134)	11. T (142)	14. T (145)
3. T (126)	6. T (131)	9. T (128)	12. F (143)	15. F (149)

Chapter 6

Inequalities of Social Class

THE GREAT SOCIAL TRANSFORMATION AND THE INEQUALITIES OF SOCIAL CLASS

CASTE AND CLASS
    Caste Systems
    Class Systems

SOCIOECONOMIC STATUS AND CLASS IN THE UNITED STATES
    Determinants of Socioeconomic Status
    The Class System of the United States
    Description of the American Classes

THE MYTH AND THE REALITY OF MOBILITY IN THE UNITED STATES
    Amount of Mobility
    Determinants of Mobility
    Ideological Support for Inequality

POVERTY IN THE LAND OF RICHES
    What is Poverty?
    The Truly Disadvantaged
    The Culture of Poverty

SOCIOLOGICAL ANALYSIS OF STRATIFICATION AND CLASS
    The Functionalist Perspective
    The Conflict Perspective
    Distributive Systems Theory
    The Symbolic Interactionist Perspective

SOCIAL CLASS INEQUALITY IN THE TWENTY-FIRST CENTURY

CRITICAL QUESTIONS
    Caste and class systems
    Social class membership
    Would you eliminate poverty?

SELF TEST QUESTIONS/ANSWERS

CHAPTER SUMMARY AND KEY TERMS

The Great Social Transformation and the Inequalities of Social Class

The story of the sinking of the Titanic demonstrates the impact of social class on life and death. It also illustrates social stratification: the arrangement of society into a series of layers or strata on the basis of and unequal distribution of societal resources, prestige, or power, such that the stratum at the top has the most resources. All of the children in the first and second class decks of the Titanic survived while only 55% of children in third class survived. The same pattern held for women. The Titanic only had enough lifeboats for about half of the passengers. The first class deck was in closest proximity to the lifeboats and the third class was farthest away. This was known before the Titanic set sail.

Caste and Class

Social stratification	**Social stratification** has changed greatly with the Great Social Transformation. Traditional hunting and gathering societies have little stratification. Stratification systems become more complex with the accumulation of wealth in horticultural and agrarian societies. With industrialization, the intensity of stratification lessens and permits social mobility.
Caste system	A **caste system** consists of a fixed arrangement of strata from the most to the least privileged, with a person's position determined unalterably at birth. The boundaries between castes are discrete— that is, distinct and sharply drawn. Caste boundaries are regulated mainly by controlling marriages. Marriage across castes is strictly prohibited. India has the most extensive caste system today. Discrimination based on caste is illegal, but it still exists. Caste membership determines what type of work a person will do, where they will live, whom they marry, and even from which well they draw water. The highest caste, or *varna*, is Brahmin and the lowest is Shudra. Below the Shudras are the Harijans, or the "untouchables." They are ranked so low that they are outside the caste system. India's dominant religion, Hinduism, supports the caste system by teaching people to accept life as it is. Industrialization and globalization in India are making caste boundaries increasingly difficult to maintain. In addition, some estimates state that 20 to 25 percent of India's population is now or will soon become middle class.
Class system	In contrast to a caste system, in a **class system** social standing is determined by factors over which people can exert some control, such as their educational attainment, their income, and their work experience. In practice, the amount of control may be small but in principle the possibility of obtaining a better position exists. Boundaries between classes are continuous because they merge into each other without a clear distinction between them. Class systems also have a fairly high amount of class consistency. This refers to the similarity among the characteristics that define class strata. The British upper class, which is one to five percent of its population, exhibits a high degree of class consistency. Its members enjoy wealth, high prestige, and a great deal of political influence. It is a self-perpetuating class because its members are trained in exclusive, elite schools. Britain's lower class contains 50 percent of the population. This percentage is influenced by the growth or slowing of the British industrialist economy.

Socioeconomic Status and Class in the United States

The United States prides itself on being an egalitarian society. However, a look at **socioeconomic status** and class tells us that reality is different. Max Weber stated that social standing consists of three parts: class, which he regarded as determined by economic standing or wealth; party, which was equivalent to political power; and status, or social prestige and honor. Weber noted that these three dimensions were closely related such that a member of the lower class would likely have low status and party.

Socioeconomic status	Contemporary sociologists use the term **socioeconomic status** to refer to a person's ranking along several social dimensions, particularly education, occupational prestige, and income.

♦ *Education*. Education is valuable because it produces income. For example, a woman who has completed four years of college will earn 73 percent more during her lifetime than a woman who has completed only four years of high school. Race and gender affect income distribution, even at equal levels of education.

♦ *Wealth*. Sociologists divide total wealth into assets, such as real estate, jewels, stocks, and income, such as wages, salaries, interest received, and stock dividends. In the United States 0.3 percent of the population owns $1 million or more in assets. Income is also distributed unevenly as the top 25 percent of families get over 50 percent of the income while the bottom 25 percent gets only 6 percent.

♦ *Occupation and Prestige*. The federal government has identified over 20,000 separate occupations. Sociologists recognize the differences between *white-collar* and *blue-collar* jobs as one important distinction. Whereas blue-collar work involves mostly physical labor carried out under close supervision, white-collar work emphasizes mental activity and usually takes place indoors in pleasant surroundings. Sometimes the occupational category of *pink-collar* is also used. This category reflects the segregation of women into certain occupations, such as kindergarten teachers, secretaries, file clerks, waitresses, and library science. These jobs are characterized by their relatively low pay and low prestige.

Prestige and esteem

Occupations with the highest prestige often require the longest training. Some positions, such as the clergy, are highly prestigious but do not pay well. In response, sociologists distinguish between **prestige**—honor associated with an occupation or other position in the social system, and **esteem**—honor that accrues to the individual filling the position.

The following three methods are used to measure class standing:
• The *objective method* ranks individuals into classes on the basis of measures such as education, income, and occupational prestige.
• The *reputational method* places people into various social classes on the basis of reputation in the community. This works best in small communities in which people have detailed information about each other.
• The *self-identification method* allows people to place themselves in a social class. Most people place themselves in the middle class, regardless of their actual class standing.

U.S. class differences

The following will give you examples of class differences in the United States.
• The *upper-upper class* is also known as the elite. Usually membership is ascribed. This group comprises 3 percent of the population and possesses 25 to 30 percent of the private wealth in the United States, owns 60 to 70 percent of the corporate wealth, and receives 20 to 25 percent of all yearly income. Members of the elite are close-knit. Their children go to exclusive boarding schools where they begin to form long-lasting social networks. Many elites participate in finance, education, the arts, and government. They often exert their political power from behind the scenes.
• The *lower-upper class* ranks just below the elite. About 4 percent of the population falls into this class. These are people who have recently achieved success and wealth, such as Les Wexner, founder of The Limited clothing company and Helen Gurley Brown, former advertising executive and editor of Cosmopolitan magazine. Some member may have more wealth than members of the elite. But the lack of an established family name and marginal social ties prevent them from acceptance by the elites.
• The *upper-middle class* consists mainly of professionals with well-paying, respected occupations. Their work usually takes a large part of their time and is a major source of their identity. Members of this class are almost always college educated, but they have not attended the elite boarding schools. Often both spouses work. Their dual income allows them to take expensive vacations and enjoy a pleasant lifestyle. They are usually interested in politics, but do not exert nearly as much influence as members of the upper classes.
• *Lower-middle class* people typically earn a middle-range income and enjoy middle-range lifestyles. This category includes teachers, small-scale entrepreneurs, and middle-level managers. Most jobs occupied by members of this class emphasize conformity to established patterns and

rules. These people are usually less educated than members of the upper-middle class. They have relatively few assets and rely on their incomes to maintain their lifestyle. Members of this class emphasize respectability, proper behavior, and reliability.

• The *working class* consists of service personnel, tradespeople, semiskilled operatives, and other blue-collar workers. Some of these positions pay very well by the hour but are seasonal or periodic. Generally, members of the working class earn about $10,000 per year less than those of the middle-class. They usually do not have assets or a substantial savings. They earn too little to afford college for their children but too much to receive financial aid from the federal government. Working class members often do not participate in politics.

• The *lower-lower class* is made up of people who lack education and skills and who therefore lack steady employment at well-paying jobs. They often live in the most run-down places in the community. They have little interest in politics and almost no control over their own fate. This class may be divided into two subgroups. The working poor are lower-lower class people who have jobs but do not earn an adequate income. This includes day laborers and migrant workers. Members of the second group, the chronically poor, are unemployed or work only occasionally.

The Myth and the Reality of Mobility in the United States

Mobility

In reality, many people in the United States do not experience much mobility within their lifetimes. However, many Americans hold onto the rags-to-riches myth. Sociologists frequently study **intergenerational mobility** of individuals: upward or downward movements in socioeconomic status measured by the standing of children compared with that of their parents. A classic study by Peter Blau and Otis Duncan in the 1970s found that 26 percent of the sons of managers, 43 percent of the sons of clerical workers, and 84 percent of the sons of laborers had occupations that ranked higher than their fathers' occupations. This suggests that a fair-to-moderate amount of upward mobility occurred. One hindrance to upward mobility is that there are limited positions at the top. Another is the position at which you begin climbing the ladder. Even though the odds are against making a long climb, most Americans have risen slightly higher than their parents because of **structural mobility**: the movement of entire categories of people due to changes in society itself. This mainly consisted in the expansion of the labor market after World War II. Today, we may be seeing a reversal of this trend with the loss of many white and blue-collar jobs.

Ideology

The stratification system in American society is justified by an **ideology**, or a pattern of beliefs that legitimizes or justifies a particular societal arrangement. The most famous analysis of class ideology derives from the ideas of Karl Marx. Marx stated that the class in power imposes its ideology on the entire society, thereby leading the culture to fit its own needs. A class's acceptance of an ideology that is contrary to the best interests of that class is called **false consciousness**. Marx argued that false consciousness would exist until the exploited class developed a sense of **class consciousness**: an awareness that it is being oppressed and that membership in the class dooms everyone to the same fate. The stratum will become a true class when class consciousness forms. It will then begin to challenge the ruling class.

Homelessness

Homelessness has been increasing in the United States in the past two decades. Researchers make the following points about homelessness:

• There is a shortage of available housing for the poor.

• The restructuring of the American economy in the 1970s and 1980s has resulted in a major loss of jobs for people already in the labor force and a diminished prospect of well-paying jobs for young people about to enter the work force. Joblessness and low-wage employment often lead to homelessness.

• The deinstitutionalization of the mentally ill has left many people on their own. Many of these people are ill-equipped to take care of themselves.

- Displaced families with children are the largest growing segment of the homeless. Most of these families are headed by young women.
- Substance abusers account for a large percentage of the homeless.
- Increasingly, AIDS victims are becoming part of the homeless population.

Poverty in the Land of Riches

Poverty

Poverty is defined in two ways. First, **relative poverty** is when people are poor only in comparison with others. For example, the least wealthy in the United States may be defined as poor. Second, **absolute poverty** is when people cannot afford some minimum of food, clothing, shelter, and other necessities. In the United States, poverty is measured by an index, called the "poverty index." According to the 1997 poverty index, a family of four with a total income of $16,306 per year or less was considered poor.

Truly disadvantaged

The **truly disadvantaged** consists of people who live predominantly in the inner city and who are trapped in a cycle of joblessness, deviance, crime, welfare dependency, and unstable family life. Sociologist William Julius Wilson argues that poor economic conditions are the main problems facing the truly disadvantaged. Many unskilled jobs that used to sustain a large portion of people living in the urban core have disappeared with changes in the economy. If unemployment becomes a permanent feature of these people's lives, they could become locked into a permanent undercaste which they and their children can never leave.

Culture of poverty

The term **culture of poverty** refers to the set of norms and values that helps the poor adapt to their situation. For example, the poor often spend their money as soon as they get it. They do this because they have no hope for the future and see no benefits in delaying gratification. They also feel that they are at the mercy of others. All of these factors lead them to discount the value of education and to ignore the work ethic. Their children are socialized to conform to the culture of poverty.

Sociological Analysis of Stratification and Class

Functionalist perspective

Functionalist theorists propose that all societies have positions that must be filled. They also state that these vary in attractiveness, pay, and prestige. This results in a social stratification system in which some people have more wealth and prestige than others. From the functionalist perspective, this has two benefits. First, it benefits individuals by ensuring that they are rewarded for their talents and qualifications. Second, it benefits society by ensuring that positions are filled by qualified people. Functionalists propose that even the poor play a function in society. First, they provide a pool of inexpensive laborers willing to do the dirty work like collecting trash and picking fruit. Second, they earn low wages which helps keep prices low. Third, the middle class benefits from the money directed to helping the poor. About one-third of the antipoverty funds are paid to staff governmental bureaucracies that service the poor. Fourth, the poor act as a buffer that protects the middle class from economic changes. Several criticisms have been lodged against functionalism. Critics argue that there is an imperfect link between a position's importance to society and its rewards. For example, major film stars earn up to $40 million for each film while school teachers earn about one thousand times less. Another criticism of functionalism is that people are motivated to enter an occupation by more than just material rewards. The final criticism is that functionalism assumes that society is equally open to everyone. Thus it denies the existence of discrimination.

Conflict perspective

Conflict theorists are strongly influenced by Marx's ideas of class. Marx believed that class was determined by property ownership. The bourgeoisie own the means of production while the proletariat are propertyless laborers. The proletariat have no choice but to work for the bourgeoisie. Marx stated that the proletariat would eventually unite, revolt, and overthrow the ruling class. They would then establish a classless society in which the state owned the means of production. Marx failed to predict the rise of the middle class. The middle class in the United states has increased from 18 percent in 1900 to 55 percent in 1990. The middle class often identifies with the company rather than with the workers. Thus they act as a buffer that mediates conflicts between the proletariat and bourgeoisie. In addition, blue-collar workers do not fit the Marxian model. Rather than feeling alienated and oppressed, many blue-collar workers derive great satisfaction from their jobs and take pride in having helped to construct a house or a machine. Contemporary conflict theorists are developing alternatives to Marx's view of stratification. Some are incorporating Weber's notions of stratification. One such theorist is Pierre Bourdieu. He believes that stratification is due to inequalities in the distribution of four types of capital:

- Economic capital—money or material objects that can be used to produce goods and services
- Social capital—positions and relations in social networks that can be used to create economic capital
- Cultural capital—interpersonal skills, habits, and educational credentials that can be used to advantage in society
- Symbolic capital—the ability to use symbols to legitimize the possession of varying levels of the other three levels of capital

Distributive systems theory

Gerhard Lenski has synthesized functionalism and conflict theory to form **distributive systems theory**. According to Lenski, societal resources consist of necessities, such as food and shelter, and surplus, or luxuries. He argues that people will share their possessions only when it is in their best interests. Thus, in hunting and gathering societies in which survival depends upon everyone's contribution, people are willing to share their food. This reduces inequality and contributes to the group's survival. A very different situation occurs in societies that have surpluses. Lenski argues that people do not benefit from sharing surplus because it is unnecessary for group survival. Individuals can accumulate extensive surpluses. Those with the most power accumulate the most surplus. This is consistent with conflict theory. Inequality can only occur when a society has a surplus. Stratification is more complex in industrial societies. In the early stages of industrialization, the bourgeoisie take most of the society's wealth, creating a large division between themselves and the proletariat. As industrialization progresses, productivity increases so much that the elite can no longer monopolize the wealth. Thus inequality declines. At the same time, a growing middle class forces the government to respond to its demands. A sophisticated ideology about the use of power then develops. Lenski predicts that industrialization and ideology will eventually cause inequality to disappear, but not vanish completely.

Symbolic interaction theory

Symbolic interaction theory studies the reasons Americans tolerate inequality. It assumes that society is created and sustained through interaction and definitions of the situation. Both formal and informal socialization teach Americans to tolerate inequality. School children learn to compete for high grades to distinguish themselves from their peers. They also learn to differentiate people according to their power and wealth. Another process that produces tolerance for inequality is that members of the subordinate classes sometimes adopt the value system of classes above them and begin to view themselves as unworthy. Finally, inequality is tolerated because many stereotypes label the poor as lazy, dumb, and pampered by the welfare system.

Social Class Inequality in the Twenty-First Century

The American middle class seems to be shrinking. If the trend continues long enough, the United States will have only an upper class and a lower class. Many families can afford homes only because both spouses work. Many analysts believe that the loss of industry in the United States has led the shrinking of the middle class. In contrast, some social scientists believe that fears of the declining middle class are unfounded. They indicate that the baby boom generation was so large the when it entered the work force in the 1960s, the number of people with low-paying jobs increased dramatically. This caused the middle class to become smaller, but only temporarily. As the boomers mature, they will have higher-paying positions and the size of the middle class will increase. When they retire, many positions will open for the younger generation.

Critical Questions

CQ: (page 161)   What do you think? Are caste and class systems fair? Why or why not? Are class systems fairer than caste systems? Why or why not?

To answer this question, you must first define the key terms class system and caste system. You should also examine your own definition of "fair". Is fairness when every member of the population has exactly the same amount and quality of goods? Is a system that rewards individuals for the value of their work fair? Does personal ability play a factor in fairness? Are all people created equal? Now you are able to intelligently answer the question. How do class and caste systems fit your definition of fairness? How would each of these systems have to change in order to become fair? Can you envision a social system that is fair to all of its members? What does it look like?

CQ: (page 172)   What social class do you belong to? Do you think that people are really the same regardless of their social class position? Why or why not? What answer is a sociologist likely to give to this question?

Review the characteristics of social classes in the United States on pages 163-167. Do you fit any of these categories? Hint: remember that social class involves not only economics but also lifestyle. Is this different from five years ago? Do you expect your class to change after you graduate from college? Will this be different from the class to which your parents belong? If so, what is responsible for the difference. To answer the second question, think about what it means for people to be "the same." Does this mean that all people have similar attitudes, values, and norms? Or does it mean that all people seek solutions to similar problems throughout life such as obtaining food and shelter and engaging in meaningful relationships? Do people of different classes solve these problems in the same ways? If not, how do they differ? After reading six chapters of your textbook, what do you think sociologists have to say about the effects of class on attitudes, values, norms, and solutions to problems? Do sociologists propose that class makes a difference?

CQ: (page 180)   For the sake of argument, suppose you had the power to make the United States a country without poverty. Would you do it? Why or why not? What are your reasons?

First, you must be specific about the type of poverty you would abolish. Define the key terms relative poverty and absolute poverty. Do we have both types in the United States? Do either of these types perform any beneficial functions for society? If so, what functions do they play and for whom? What are the societal costs of relative and absolute poverty? Do the benefits outweigh the costs? Which type/s would you eliminate? Can you envision a society without absolute poverty? Without relative poverty? What do they look like?

Self-Test Questions
Multiple Choice

1. Which type of society permits some social mobility therefore lessening the intensity of the social class system?
     a. hunting and gathering
     b. horticultural
     c. agrarian
     d. industrial

2. The most extensive caste system today is found in:
     a. Iran
     b. India
     c. Pakistan
     d. Great Britain

3. Class systems typically exhibit:
    a. a fairly high amount of class consistency
    b. little class consistency
    c. moderate class consistency
    d. erratic patterns of class consistency

4. Most people have a similar ranking along the three dimensions of socioeconomic status. Thus, most people are:
    a. aware of class inconsistencies
    b. status consistent
    c. class conscious
    d. class clueless

5. Which is NOT one of Weber's components of class?
    a. occupation
    b. education
    c. lifestyle
    d. prestige

6. Which type of occupation is NOT considered blue-collar?
    a. machine operator
    b. machine repair
    c. laborer
    d. technical

7. Professor Jackson determined his students' social class by asking them to list their parents' levels of education, income, and occupation. Which method did he use?
    a. reputational
    b. objective
    c. self-identification
    d. subjective

8. The main difference between the upper class and the lower-upper class is:
    a. the upper class play polo and the lower-upper class do not
    b. the upper class will marry only the upper class
    c. the lower-upper class have recently achieved wealth and success
    d. the upper class uniformly have more wealth than the lower-upper class

9. A major difference between the upper-middle class and the lower-middle class is:
    a. the upper-middle class emphasize career achievement, interpersonal skills, and creativity while the lower class emphasize respectability and reliability.
    b. the lower-middle class are more interested in sports
    c. the upper-middle class marry only among themselves
    d. the lower-middle class are downwardly mobile

10. The working class:
    a. do not earn enough to accumulate substantial savings
    b. are extremely vulnerable to disruptions in income through temporary layoffs or unemployment
    c. earn too little to afford college for their children but too much to afford financial aid
    d. all of the above

11. Julia is a physician. Her parents were farmers. This is an example of:
   a. intergenerational mobility
   b. downward mobility
   c. structural mobility
   d. economic restructuring

12. What term did Thorstein Veblen use to refer to spending money on useless things in order to gain esteem and status?
   a. conspicuous consumption
   b. class consciousness
   c. false consciousness
   d. structural mobility

13. The post World War II economic expansion in the United states led to an increase in white-collar jobs. Many people from blue-collar backgrounds became upwardly mobile by acquiring these jobs. Sociologists refer to this as:
   a. class mobility
   b. structural mobility
   c. intragenerational mobility
   d. downward mobility

14. Which term refers to a class's acceptance of an ideology that is contrary to the best interests of that class?
   a. class consciousness
   b. structural inequality
   c. false consciousness
   d. none of the above

15. According to Marx, the ruling class exploits the subordinate class because the ruling class:
   a. aims to retain power
   b. does not give the subordinate class just rewards for its labor
   c. creates structural unemployment
   d. keeps it from significant political participation

16. Which is NOT true of the homeless?
   a. the fastest growing segment of the homeless is families with young children.
   b. many of the homeless are substance abusers.
   c. the restructuring of the economy made it more difficult for the poor to find jobs for which they were qualified. Some of these people became homeless.
   d. there is an abundant supply of public housing for the poor

17. Which age group has the largest number of poor?
   a. under 18 years
   b. 18 to 24 years
   c. 25 to 60 years
   d. over 60 years

18. Sociologist William Wilson's term to describe the urban poor who are trapped in a cycle of unemployment, deviance, crime, and welfare dependency is called:
    a. absolute poverty
    b. truly disadvantaged
    c. underclass
    d. lower-lower class

19. The set of norms and values that helps the poor adapt to their situation is called:
    a. oppositional subculture
    b. mobility ethic
    c. culture of poverty
    d. fatalism

20. Which theory would argue that doctors make more money than janitors because it takes much more talent and training to become a doctor than to become a janitor?
    a. conflict
    b. functionalist
    c. distributive systems
    d. interactionist

21. Which type of capital consists of interpersonal skills, habits, and educational credentials that can be used to gain advantage in society?
    a. economic capital
    b. social capital
    c. cultural capital
    d. symbolic capital

22. Which theory argues that people are only willing to share when it is in their best interests?
    a. conflict
    b. functionalist
    c. distributive systems
    d. interactionist

23. Which perspective argues that toleration for inequality is the self-fulfilling consequence of class discrimination, that is, people who occupy subordinate class positions sometimes adopt the value system of those above them, and come to view themselves as unworthy?
    a. conflict
    b. functionalist
    c. distributive systems
    d. interactionist

True - False

T	F	1. Horticultural societies have the least intense stratification systems.
T	F	2. Castes are based on achieved statuses.
T	F	3. Boundaries between castes are maintained by controlling who marries whom.
T	F	4. The boundaries between classes are continuous.
T	F	5. The class system in the U.S. is more consistent than that in Great Britain.
T	F	6. Your paycheck is a component of your wealth.
T	F	7. The term pink-collar refers to women who work in male-dominated fields.

T	F	8. Esteem is the honor associated with an occupation or other position in a social system.
T	F	9. As a group, the elite, or upper-upper class, are a close-knit group.
T	F	10. Structural mobility is the movement of entire categories of people due to changes in society itself.
T	F	11. The deinstitutionalization of the mentally ill contributed to an increase in homelessness.
T	F	12. Poverty determined in comparison to others is called relative poverty.
T	F	13. Functionalist theorists argue that poverty has some benefits for society in that it supplies a pool of inexpensive labor for dirty jobs and their low wages hold down prices.

Self Test Answers

Multiple Choice

1. d (158)	6. d (163)	11. a (172)	16. d (170)	21. c (182)
2. b (158)	7. b (164)	12. a (166)	17. a (176)	22. c (183)
3. a (160)	8. c (165)	13. b (174)	18. b (178)	23. d (184)
4. b (162)	9. a (169)	14. c (174)	19. c (178)	
5. c (162)	10. d (169)	15. b (175)	20. b (181)	

True - False

1. F (158)	4. T (160)	7. F (163)	10. T (174)	13. T (181)
2. F (158)	5. F (160)	8. F (163)	11. T (170)	
3. T (158)	6. T (162)	9. T (165)	12. T (176)	

NOTES FOR FUTURE STUDY AND REVIEW:

Chapter 7

Inequalities of Race and Ethnicity

**THE GREAT SOCIAL TRANSFORMATION AND RACIAL
AND ETHNIC INEQUALITY**

RACE AND ETHNICITY
Race
Ethnicity
Minority

PREJUDICE AND DISCRIMINATION
Stereotypes
Institutional Racism

PATTERNS OF RACIAL AND ETHNIC INTRACTION
Assimilation
Pluralism
Expulsion and Annihilation

RACIAL AND ETHNIC GROUPS IN THE UNITED STATES
White Americans
Native Americans
African Americans
Hispanic Americans
Asian Americans

SOCIOLOGICAL ANALYSIS OF RACIAL AND ETHNIC INEQUALITY
The Functionalist Perspective
The Conflict Perspective
The Symbolic Interactionist Perspective

RACIAL AND ETHNIC RELATIONS IN THE TWENTY-FIRST CENTURY

CRITICAL QUESTIONS
Cultural pluralism
Lynching and law and order
Define the typical American

SELF TEST QUESTIONS/ANSWERS

CHAPTER SUMMARY AND KEY TERMS

Race and Ethnicity

The opening of the chapter tells the story of the "Tuskegee Study" of syphilis conducted by the United States Public Health Service. In 1932, 399 adult males infected with the disease and 201 uninfected males were chosen for the study. All were poor uneducated African Americans. Though a cure was available, it was not given to the infected men. The investigators were white and a few of them suggested that syphilis was a punishment for the supposed sexual promiscuity among African Americans. Many of the African Americans died needlessly of syphilis. The authors use this story to illustrate that sometimes racial and ethnic differences are used to justify the mistreatment of one group by another.

GST and race and ethnicity	Race and ethnicity are related to the **Great Social Transformation**. In traditional societies, race and ethnicity are basic communal relationships which bind people together. In associational societies, however, it is not racial or ethnic identity but rather economic ties, a uniform set of laws, similar values and culture, public education, and shared currency and language that link people. In this system, race and ethnicity become badges which distinguish groups from each other. In the competition for wealth and political power, some of these groups come to dominate others.
Race	Several schemes have been used to classify people into races. The most well-known uses three categories: • Caucasoid, people with fair skin and hair ranging from light to dark • Negroid, people with dark skin and curly hair • Mongoloid, people with yellow skin and distinctive folds in the eyelids This scheme is not useful because it is inaccurate. For example, some Caucasoids have darker skin than some Negroids. In addition, humans have migrated over the earth and intermingled to the extent that no pure race exists. A **race** is a group of people who have been singled out on the basis of real or alleged physical characteristics. Thus race is socially constructed in the sense that biological traits are given social meaning. In the United States we determine race by skin color. It is possible that a society could determine race by hair texture or the presence or absence of freckles.
Ethnicity	**Ethnicity** refers to people who have common cultural characteristics, such as the same language, place of origin, dress, food, and values. People who share these cultural features are said to be members of the same **ethnic group**. Members of an ethnic group also share a unique **ethnic identity**; that is, they have internalized ethnic roles as part of their self-concept. Because they share a common identity, members of an ethnic group have a strong feeling of "oneness," unity, and shared fate. Marriage across ethnic lines is not uncommon but it is also not typical. Both hostility with other ethnic groups and preference within the ethnic group lead to inter-group marriage. Race and ethnicity may overlap. For example, Vietnamese Americans, Chinese Americans, and African Americans are considered races and ethnicities.
Minority	A **minority** is a group that has less power than the dominant group. The sociological definition of minority has nothing to do with size. Minority groups are usually poorer than the majority. They also have less prestige and suffer more discrimination.

Prejudice and Discrimination

Prejudice	Sociologically, **prejudice** is an attitude that predisposes an individual to prejudge entire categories of people unfairly. The attitude is difficult to change. It is emotionally loaded and rigid. It often involves selective perception, that is, only those facts and beliefs that fit the prejudice are seen as valid. Also contradictory arguments and evidence are ignored, not believed, dismissed as illogical, or sometimes not perceived at all. As a result, logic and evidence are rarely strong enough to change a well-established prejudice.

Discrimination	**Discrimination** is defined as the unfair and harmful treatment of people based on their group membership. An example is an employer refusing to hire well-qualified Asian or African Americans because of their ethnic and racial membership. Some people are prejudice but do not discriminate.
Racism	**Racism** is the belief that race determines human ability and that as a result, certain races deserve to be treated as inferior while other races deserve to be treated as superior.
Stereotypes	Racism is supported by other features of society and culture. One of these features is **stereotypes**: rigid and inaccurate images that summarize a belief. Stereotypes are based on beliefs rather than facts. Therefore they are illogical and serve the group that constructs them. Stereotypes persist for several reasons. First, they raise the status of the group that uses them. Second, stereotypes simplify thinking and reduce guilt. Finally, stereotypes continue through ignorance. Most people do not have much contact with members of other racial or ethnic groups. They do not have enough first-hand information to verify the inaccuracy of the stereotype.
Institutional racism	**Institutional racism** occurs when racist practices become part of the social practices and institutions of a society. Housing segregation is an example. In 1990, 70 to 80 percent of all African Americans living in major metropolitan areas would have to move in order to achieve a non-segregated pattern of housing. Similar patterns are true for Asian and Hispanic Americans. "Redlining" is another example. This is when banks refuse to grant mortgage loans to African Americans who live in low-income areas of a city. Standardized tests such as the Scholastic Aptitude Test (SAT) may also discriminate against minorities. Some critics argue that these tests assume knowledge of middle class white culture. Those unfamiliar with this culture may perform poorly on the exam. As these examples demonstrate, institutional racism is often so much a part of our everyday lives that we do not even realize it is occurring.

Patterns of Racial and Ethnic Interaction

Assimilation	**Assimilation** is the blending of the culture and structure of one racial or ethnic group with the culture and structure of another group. **Cultural assimilation** involves a blending of languages, dress, foods, norms, customs, and values. **Structural assimilation** involves a blending of work groups and social networks. When assimilation takes place for a long period of time, the distinction between the two groups disappears. There are several possible outcomes to assimilation. The first outcome occurs when the minority group changes while the majority group remains the same. In the United States, this result is called *Anglo conformity* or **Americanization**. Another outcome occurs when both the minority and majority groups change and a new, blended grouping then emerges that combines some features of both groups. This is called **melting pot** assimilation. In the United States, most melting pot assimilation has occurred among white ethics. Other minority groups have assimilated by Anglo conformity.
Pluralism	**Pluralism** is the opposite of assimilation. It occurs when separate racial and ethnic groups maintain their distinctiveness even though they might have approximately equal social standing. The concept of pluralism implies that ethnic diversity is a desirable social goal and that group distinctiveness is voluntary rather than forced on any group by another group. Pluralism is common throughout the world. With its 106 distinct ethnic and racial groups, the United States is pluralistic. Horace Kallen argues that pluralistic societies are stable for two reasons. First, the groups share a common culture even though they retain some of the distinctiveness of their home culture. They are subject to the same laws and follow some of the same customs of the larger society. Second, all groups are ruled by the same government, and this government provides avenues for resolving disputes. Thus, social cohesion will be preserved if groups participate democratically in government.
Ethnic revival	Race and ethnicity are reemerging as important issues in American society. This new interest has given rise to **ethnic revival**: a situation in which racial and ethnic groups clamor for political autonomy and sometimes demand independence. In the United States, ethnic revival has taken the

form of people's renewed interest in their ethnic ancestry. Some individuals seek a greater sense of community belonging while others want to replace feelings of inferiority with feelings of ethnic pride.

Symbolic ethnicity   Related to ethnic revival is symbolic ethnicity. This is the attempt to preserve and participate in disappearing ethnic roles and culture. Irish Americans present one example. They celebrate St. Patrick's Day with parties, parades, and green beer. They take pride in Irish culture and visit Ireland whenever possible. As a result, Irish Americans are learning about Irish culture and voluntarily reaffirming their ethnicity.

Expulsion   Sometimes societies do not accommodate ethnic groups through assimilation. In some cases, ethnic prejudice has resulted in the forceful **expulsion** of the minority. For this tactic to succeed, one group must have enough political and military power to force the other group to leave. Historical examples of expulsion include the United States government's forcing of 16,000 Cherokee Indians to march from their Carolina homeland to Georgia and the forced evacuation of Asian Indians in Uganda in 1972.

Annihilation   An even more extreme and violent response to a racial or ethnic minority group is **annihilation**, or the process by which one group exterminates the other group. Examples include the killing of six million Jews by the Nazis in World War II and the killing of two million Cambodians by the Khmer Rouge government of Cambodia.

Racial and Ethnic Groups in the United States

White Americans   **White Americans** consist of **WASPS** (White Anglo-Saxon Protestants) and white ethnics WASPs are the most powerful group in the United States. They are of English, Canadian, Scottish, Australian, and Northern European descent. WASPs composed the majority of free immigrants to the United States. White ethnic refers to white European groups that are not WASPs. This includes Italians, French, Poles, Czechs, and Russians. With the exception of Russians, who are mostly Jewish, these groups are mainly Catholic. White Catholics suffered great discrimination in the nineteenth century. For a while, sociologists predicted that white ethnic groups would assimilate and disappear because they are racially similar to WASPs. This has not occurred, however, as many white ethnic groups have maintained ethnically identifiable churches, neighborhoods, social clubs, and businesses. The Irish are probably the most assimilated of the white ethnic groups.

Native Americans   It is estimated that 40 million *Native Americans* lived in North America when European settlers first arrived. By the middle of the nineteenth century, warfare, genocide, and poverty along with diseases brought by Europeans had reduced the Native American population to 250,000. Many Americans are beginning to reclaim their Native American origins. Between 1970 and 1990 the number of people claiming Native American origins rose from 800,000 to 1.5 million. Unemployment, poverty, and alcoholism are serious problems faced by Native Americans. Policies of the federal government determined the fate of this group. This occurred in several stages. The first stage was *separation*. The British claimed all land east of the Appalachian Mountains and forced Native Americans to move west. *Expulsion* and *extermination* comprised the second stage. Under approval by Congress, the federal government forced all Indians out of the East Coast in 1830. Originally, this was to be accomplished via treaties with Indian tribes. But it became a violent forced migration (extermination) in which thousands of Native Americans perished. By the 1880s the relocation-extermination policy gave way to *forced assimilation*. This was inspired by religious groups. It involved the redistribution of land with the hope that Native Americans would become part of the white economic system. This plan failed. Forced assimilation also included the destruction of Indian social structure and culture. Policy changed again in the 1930s to one of *tribal restoration*. Under this policy, Native Americans were encouraged to rebuild their cultural roots, if they wished.

African Americans

African Americans are among the oldest racial-ethnic groups in the United States. The first group was brought to Virginia as slaves in 1619. At the peak of the slave trade, between 1740 and 1760, 5,000 slaves were being imported to the United Sates each year. Slaves came from many different tribes and regions of Africa. The groups had little in common with each other, with the exception of their status as slaves. The institution of slavery destroyed most original African tribal cultures. These were replaced by a slave culture that emerged from their new environment. The Civil War ended slavery, but not the subordination of African Americans. After the Reconstruction period, white supremacist groups openly whipped and lynched African Americans and made it dangerous or impossible for them to exercise their right to vote. Also during that time, the institution of "Jim Crow" emerged. Jim Crow was the set of discriminatory practices that lasted until the 1970s. It included separate restrooms, drinking fountains, and schools for whites and blacks. Two major events occurred in the 1950s. First, the Supreme court ruled that segregated public schools were illegal. Second, in 1955 in Montgomery, Alabama, Rosa Parks refused to give up her seat in the black section of a bus to a white man who could not find a seat in the white section. The arrest of Parks triggered a year-long bus boycott by African Americans. It ended only when buses in Montgomery became desegregated. Sometimes groups held in a subordinate position adopt the values of the dominant culture and come to view themselves as unworthy. This reinforces the dominance of the majority. This has been a struggle for the African American community in the United States. The "black pride" movement emerged in the 1960s to combat this. Things have gotten better for African Americans in the United States, but a great deal of inequality remains. To illustrate, one-third of African-American households earn a middle-class income. However, two-thirds do not. In addition, babies of low birth weight are born to black mothers at twice the white rate.

Hispanic Americans

Hispanic Americans include Mexicans, Puerto Ricans, Cubans, and other groups of Spanish heritage. Mexicans are the largest group of Hispanics in the United States (nine million) followed by two million Puerto Ricans and 900,000 Cubans.

• *Mexican Americans* are the second largest racial or ethnic minority in the United States. By early in the next century, they will be the largest due to immigration and a high fertility rate. Mexican Americans are one of the oldest minority groups in the country. They are overwhelmingly Roman Catholic and have a strong family orientation. Today over 80 percent of Mexican Americans reside in urban areas, usually in ethnic neighborhoods called *barrios*. This has allowed Mexican Americans to retain much of their culture. Mexican Americans face considerable prejudice and discrimination. They are often stereotyped as uneducated, lazy, and cowardly. They have a high illiteracy rate and earn only about 70 percent of what whites earn.

• Puerto Rico became part of the United States as the result of the Spanish-American War of 1989. It is an American commonwealth, meaning that *Puerto Ricans* are United States citizens, can travel freely in the United States, and can serve in the American military. They cannot vote in America and they do not pay federal taxes. Most Puerto Rican immigrants have settled in the Northeast, with half in New York City. Puerto Rican immigration is the result of limited economic opportunities in Puerto Rico, a lack of legal and political restriction, and relatively inexpensive air transportation between San Juan and cities on the East Coast. Puerto Ricans in the United States face the same obstacles as Mexicans: lack of education and job opportunity, poor housing, and discrimination. Many Puerto Ricans have very dark skin. They are discriminated against both for their skin color and for their ethnicity. Puerto Ricans are one of the poorest minority groups in the United States. They have a median family income of 22 percent lower than African Americans and 42 percent lower than whites.

• Large-scale Cuban immigration occurred when Fidel Castro's communist government took power in 1959. Most *Cuban Americans* have settled in Miami. Like Puerto Ricans, many Cubans have very dark skin and suffer double discrimination. In 1990 125,000 Cubans were permitted to leave Cuba. They departed from the Mariel port and are called "Mariel" immigrants. About 95 percent of these people were political refugees. Cubans have done well in the United States. They have the highest family income of any Hispanic group, almost equal to whites. They are also well educated. Cubans have been successful because many early immigrants were middle-class or higher and had experience in business and government. The Cuban community of Miami is also active in politics. Miami Cubans have an uneasy relationship with African Americans. Some blacks feel that Cubans are taking their jobs. In 1988 this led to riots.

Asian Americans

Asian Americans are one of the fastest-growing minorities in the United States. However, they currently represent only two to three percent of the population. Like Hispanics, Asian Americans are comprised of several separate groups.

• *Chinese Americans* were the earliest Asians to arrive in the United States. They began immigrating to California during the Gold Rush of 1984. They dreamed of making a fortune and then returning home. Chinese were employed on the transcontinental railroad. They took these very dangerous jobs because it paid about six times what they could make in China. After the gold rush was over and the railroad completed, the Chinese were viewed as competitors for scarce jobs. The Chinese Exclusion Act of 1882 was the first series of laws aimed at excluding immigrants on the basis of race alone. The Chinese suffered discrimination, protest, and violence. The worst anti-Chinese riot occurred in Los Angeles where Chinese men, women, and children were lynched and hung from street poles. As a result of this hostility, the Chinese-American community turned inward and became a highly urbanized, segregated, and isolated population. Despite the many obstacles, Chinese Americans have been highly successful. This is due to their cultural emphasis on education and a strong work ethic. The Chinese also created many self-help organizations which provided members with economic resources, resolved disputes, and dispensed justice. Early Chinese immigrants came from southern China. Now many are coming from Taiwan and Hong Kong. This has increased the diversity of the Chinese community but it has also contributed to outbreaks of violence among Chinese youth gangs.

• The demand for cheap labor began to increase when the Chinese exclusion went into effect. The newly arriving Japanese filled this brief demand. But, like the Chinese, *Japanese Americans* experienced an anti-Japanese campaign when their labor was no longer needed. In 1908 the United States made the "Gentlemen's Agreement" with Japan to end Japanese immigration. The Japanese Americans who already lived in the United States became farmers in California. But this angered people to such an extent that California passed laws making it illegal for Japanese immigrants to own farmland. To get around this, many Japanese put land titles in their American-born children's' names or they formed corporations with whites. Despite the obstacles, Japanese Americans succeeded in farming for several reasons. First, they were willing to work long hard hours on second-rate land producing labor-intensive crops such as strawberries. Second, Japanese Americans established wholesale and some retail outlets for their crops. These outlets protected them from discrimination in the workplace. Finally, they grew so much produce that white retailers had no choice but to deal with them. At the beginning of World War II, two-thirds of Japanese Americans were American citizens by birth. Most of them had never even been to Japan and most could not speak Japanese. Despite this, all Japanese Americans on the West Coast (120,000 men, women, and children) were rounded up and sent to incarceration centers. Though they had committed no crimes, they lost their homes, businesses, and all of their belongings. It took the federal government almost 50 years to compensate the survivors of the incarceration. They were each paid $20,000. Today, Japanese Americans are doing very well. Their income and education levels exceed that of white levels ant they have dispersed throughout the economy.

• Many Asian groups comprise the newly arriving immigrants. This includes Vietnamese, who began immigrating after the Vietnam War, Koreans, Filipinos, and Asian Indians.

Sociological Analysis of Racial and Ethnic Inequality

Functionalist perspective

Functionalism assumes that societal characteristics that continue over time have positive consequences that help society maintain its current form. They do not argue that inequality is morally good, but that it ensures that unpleasant work gets done. Functionalist theorists believe that jobs with low pay, poor working conditions, and little prestige are assigned to racial and ethnic minorities because they lack the power to compete for desirable positions. They also occupy these jobs because they typically have few job skills and little education and they are not wise to the ways of American culture. This does not benefit the minority group. However, it does benefit the larger society. However, functionalists state that minority group members, or their children, will get better jobs once their skills improve. Newer immigrants will then assume the bottom position. The experience of white ethnic groups supports this but the history of Native, African, and Hispanic Americans does not.

Conflict perspective

Conflict theorists believe that conflict is a continual process that underlies almost all social interaction. They state that racial and ethnic inequality is the result of this endless competition for valuable resources. The winner of such resources becomes the dominant group while the losers become the subordinate groups. It is possible that a group will occupy the top position for only a short time. Often conflict occurs among subordinate groups. This was illustrated during the Los Angeles riots when Korean stores were attacked by angry crowds. Korean immigrants had established grocery stores in African American neighborhoods. African Americans complained that Korean shopkeepers overcharged them, offered poor service, and treated them with contempt. Korean grocers said that they were simply earning a living in the American tradition of free enterprise, and that without their shops, African Americans would have no convenient places to shop. Conflict theorists propose that fighting among racial and ethnic groups benefits the dominant group be diverting the energy of the minority groups away from combating the dominant group.

Symbolic interactionist perspective

Symbolic Interactionists point out that in order for a racial or ethnic group to exist, its members must develop a "consciousness of kind," or feelings of being like each other and different from outsiders. This consciousness of kind results from the interaction between racial and ethnic groups and the rest of society. For example, Native Americans were a very diverse group with different tribal languages, customs, and values. But the United States government and most of its citizens refused to recognize this diversity. Instead, they treated all Native Americans as if they had the same culture. They referred to them as "Indians" rather than Cherokee, Shawnee, or Navaho. As a result, Native Americans have developed a consciousness of kind over the past three centuries. The same occurred to African Americans whose ancestors came from hundreds of different tribes in Africa, each with a unique language and culture. In contemporary America, this may happen to Hispanics, who, despite a diverse heritage, are often lumped into one category.

Racial and Ethnic Relations in the Twenty-First Century

Principle of cumulation

In the 1930s and 1940s, Gunnar Myrdal applied the principle of cumulation to ethnic relations. The **principle of cumulation** is a viscous cycle in which discrimination by the majority keeps the minority in an inferior status and, as a result, the minority's inferior status is then cited as "proof" that the minority does not deserve better treatment. Myrdal also thought that the principle could work in reverse. That is, a reduction in discrimination would allow a racial or minority group to obtain better housing, education, and jobs. This would lead to a decrease in discrimination by the majority. Rather than spiraling downward, this would result in a minority group spiraling upward. It is possible that in the future, African Americans could be split into two groups: one whose members have steady incomes and a middle-class or higher lifestyle, and those who are chronically poor.

Critical Questions

CQ: (page 201)   Are you in favor of cultural pluralism as a general approach to maintaining peaceful racial and ethnic interactions? What are the advantages and disadvantages of maintaining racial and ethnic diversity? If you are not in favor of pluralism, what nonviolent alternatives do you see?

To answer this question you must first define the key term pluralism. (You should also define the terms melting pot and assimilation as they are useful for comparison). If you favor pluralism, to what extent do you think racial and ethnic groups should maintain their identity? Should they apply their unique culture at home but assimilate in the outside world? Should they work in businesses owned by members of their group? With respect to the United States, should they learn English? It is important that you examine your thoughts on pluralism as it represents a continuum of possibilities rather than one distinct adaptation. After you have answered these question, make a list of the advantages and disadvantages of pluralism. (Hint: How easily could a racial or ethnic group operate in this system?

How would members of the dominant culture respond to them? Does the racial or ethnic group's ascribed characteristics have any effect on their experiences with the dominant culture?). If you are not in favor of pluralism, list your reasons. Can you think of any nonviolent alternatives? Do you think members of racial and ethnic groups would benefit from your system? Would members of the dominant culture benefit? If so, what are they? Do you see any disadvantages in your proposed system?

CQ: (page 209) Ida B. Wells-Barnett argued that lynching threatened more than just black people; it threatened law and order. Do you agree or disagree with her?

Before you answer this question, review the story of Ida Wells-Barnett. Now, define order. What factors lead to order? Can you envision a situation in which the powerless in a particular society become powerful? What would that society look like if the newly-empowered treated the previously-powerful in the same way that they were treated? Is it possible to have an orderly society in which a group of people is persecuted because of ascribed characteristics? Can people trust each other is such a society? Why or why not? Is the potential for violence higher in this type of society than in one without such discrimination?

CQ: (page 215)   Suppose someone asked you to define the typical American. Could you do it without reference to racial and ethnic categories? Why or why not?

Would you describe physical features? What age group would you describe? Would you answer rely more on values, beliefs, and attitudes than on ascribed statuses? Are there any characteristics that are distinctly American? It is often said that Americans visiting overseas are immediately identifiable, even if their descendents come from the country they are visiting. How can this be? What is it about Americans that is so easily identifiable? (If you have any classmates from other countries, you may want to ask them this question. They may have great insight on identifying American characteristics). Would you answer differently if you were a member of a different racial or ethnic group?

CQ: (p. 221)   Melting Pot/Pluralism In this set of concepts, how does the meaning of the concept relate to the meaning of the other concept linked to it?

Review the definitions of both words looking closely at the common idea they share. Often the terms are contain opposite ideas; other times there are only subtle differences. Throughout the chapter, the variety of racial and ethnic groups becomes apparent. Both melting pot and pluralism relate to the blending of the culture and structure of one racial or ethnic group with the culture and structure of another group.   And not just the dynamics of that blending, but whether or not it is a desired and sought after outcome to have different racial and ethnic groups blend together or stay separate.

Self Test Questions
Multiple Choice

1. Which is NOT a problem of defining race in terms of biological characteristics?
    a. different societies identify races differently
    b. most schemes of categorizing races are inaccurate
    c. humans have migrated for thousands of years resulting in a mixing of races
    d. all of the above are problems

2. With the Great Social Transformation:
    a. racial and ethnic group ties become more important as the building blocks of society
    b. race and ethnicity become badges which distinguish one group from another as people compete for wealth and political power
    c. race and ethnicity are no longer important in social ties
    d. ethnicity is no longer socially important but race is important

3. Which of the following is true about race?
   a. it is a social construction in the sense that biological traits may be endowed with social meaning
   b. it is a clearly distinguishable set of physical traits so that all people may be classified as either Caucasoid, Negroid, or Mongoloid
   c. it determines our mental and physical abilities
   d. it is a social construction based on a cultural characteristics

4. Who led a campaign against the lynching of blacks in the United States?
   a. Rosa Parks
   b. Martin Luther King, Jr.
   c. Ida B. Wells-Barnett
   d. Harriet Beecher Stowe

5. Which term describes an attitude that predisposes an individual to evaluate an entire category of people unfairly?
   a. prejudice
   b. discrimination
   c. stereotype
   d. institutional hate

6. Which is NOT true of stereotypes?
   a. most people do not have enough contact with members of minority groups to be able to see that the stereotype is inaccurate
   b. stereotypes reduce the guilt of those who use them
   c. they separate the group that uses them from the group to which they are being applied
   d. all of the above are true of stereotypes

7. Which is an example of institutional racism?
   a. housing segregation
   b. believing that affirmative action provides minorities with an unfair advantage
   c. not hiring someone because of their race
   d. stereotyping people on the basis of their ethnicity

8. The blending of the culture and structure of one racial or ethnic group with the culture and structure of another group is called:
   a. acculturation
   b. assimilation
   c. absorption
   d. amalgamation

9. When a minority group adopts majority dress, foods, customs, values, norms, and language, it is:
   a. structurally assimilated
   b. partially assimilated
   c. culturally assimilated
   d. normatively assimilated

10. A situation in which racial and ethnic groups live together and share a common core culture but maintain their group's distinctiveness is called:
    a. melting pot
    b. symbolic ethnicity
    c. pluralism
    d. Americanization

11. Irish-Americans celebrate St. Patrick's Day with parades, parties, and green beer. This is an example of:
    a. pluralism
    b. symbolic ethnicity
    c. ethnic revival
    d. Anglo conformity

12. In the 1970s the Khmer Rouge of Cambodia killed two million fellow Cambodians for supposedly representing capitalist culture. This was an example of:
    a. expulsion
    b. political reprisal
    c. annihilation
    d. ethnic cleansing

13. Based on self-identification, the largest ancestry group in the United States is:
    a. Mexican
    b. English
    c. African
    d. German

14. White ethnic groups are mostly:
    a. Protestant
    b. Catholic
    c. Jewish
    d. Baptist

15. What is the term for the legal and traditional discriminatory practices such as separate water fountains for blacks and whites?
    a. symbolic racism
    b. prejudice
    c. expulsion
    d. Jim Crow

16. What is the term for urban Mexican neighborhoods?
    a. tejanos
    b. barrios
    c. Little Mexico
    d. Hispanola

17. Which is NOT a factor contributing to Puerto Rican immigration to the United States?
    a. economic restructuring in the United States
    b. rapid population growth in Puerto Rico
    c. limited economic opportunities in Puerto Rico
    d. lack of legal and political restrictions on migration to the United States

18. Which did NOT contribute to the success of Chinese immigrants in the United States?
    a. they had a strong work ethic similar to that in the United States
    b. they created many self-help organizations
    c. they placed a high value on education
    d. they became Americanized

19. During World War II members of this group, most of whom were American citizens, were rounded up by the federal government and forced to live in incarceration centers.
    a. Chinese
    b. Japanese
    c. Filipinos
    d. Koreans

20. Which theory states that jobs with low pay and poor working conditions are assigned to racial and ethnic minorities because they lack the resources and power to compete for more desirable positions?
    a. functionalism
    b. conflict theory
    c. symbolic interaction
    d. distributive systems

21. Which theory argues that racial and ethnic minority groups obtain menial, low-paying jobs because they have few job skills and are not sophisticated in the ways of American culture?
    a. functionalism
    b. conflict theory
    c. symbolic interaction
    d. distributive systems

22. Which theory argues that fighting among different racial and ethnic groups benefits the dominant group by dividing the hostilities away from the dominant group?
    a. functionalism
    b. conflict theory
    c. symbolic interaction
    d. distributive systems

23. Which theory argues that in order for an ethnic or racial group to exist, its members must develop a "consciousness of kind" which itself results from the interaction between the racial or ethnic group and the rest of society?
    a. functionalism
    b. conflict theory
    c. symbolic interaction
    d. distributive systems

True - False

T   F   1. An ethnic group is one that has been singled out on the basis of physical characteristics.
T   F   2. A group can be considered both a race and an ethnic group.
T   F   3. A minority group is always smaller in number than the majority group.
T   F   4. Discrimination is the unfair and harmful treatment of people based on their group membership.

T	F	5. With more than one million students taking the SAT each year, even a small bias will translate into a substantial amount of institutional racism..
T	F	6. Ethnic preservation is the attempt to preserve and participate in disappearing ethnic roles and culture.
T	F	7. Native Americans suffered separation, expulsion, and extermination.
T	F	8. Mexicans are the largest group of Hispanics in the United States.
T	F	9. Cuban-Americans have the highest average income of all Hispanics ethnic groups in the United States.
T	F	10. On average, Japanese-Americans have higher education and income levels than white-Americans.
T	F	11. Poverty and employment differ little by race and ethnicity in American society.
T	F	12. Native Americans of different tribal ancestry have adopted a consciousness of kind as the result of Americans' refusal to recognize diversity among tribes.

Self Test Answers

Multiple Choice

1. d (192)	6. d (196)	11. b (200)	16. b (207)	21. a (216)
2. b (192)	7. a (196)	12. c (200)	17. a (210)	22. b (217)
3. a (193)	8. b (197)	13. d (201)	18. d (213)	23. c (217)
4. c (208)	9. c (198)	14. b (202)	19. b (214)	
5. a (194)	10. c (199)	15. d (205)	20. a (215)	

True - False

1. F (193)	4. T (194)	7. T (204)	10. T (214)
2. T (193)	5. T (197)	8. T (207)	11. F (216)
3. F (194)	6. F (200)	9. T (211)	12. T (217)

NOTES FOR FUTURE STUDY AND REVIEW

Chapter 8

Inequalities of Gender

THE GREAT SOCIAL TRANSFORMATION AND GENDER INEQUALITY

GENDER-ROLE SOCIALIZATION
Socialization and Gender
Agents of Socialization
Age and Gender-Role Socialization

PATRIARCHY AND EVERYDAY LIFE
Language and Patriarchy
Social Interaction and Patriarchy

GENDER INEQUALITY AND WORK
Working Women
Work Segregation
Income Inequality

FEMINISM
Gender Equality and the Law
Comparable Worth
Abortion
Resistance to Compulsory Heterosexism
Inclusive Feminism

SOCIOLOGICAL ANALYSIS OF GENDER INEQUALITY
The Functionalist Perspective
The Conflict Perspective
The Symbolic Interactionist Perspective

GENDER INEQUALITY IN THE TWENTY-FIRST CENTURY

CRITICAL QUESTIONS
Advertising and gender socialization
Gender role constraints
Career plans and gender
Old boys network/glass ceiling

SELF TEST QUESTIONS/ANSWERS

CHAPTER SUMMARY AND KEY TERMS

The Tailhook Association is an organization dedicated to promoting naval aviation. In September 1991 two thousand naval officers gathered at the Hilton Hotel in Las Vegas to attend the national convention. One evening 26 women, about half of them naval officers, were assaulted by male aviators. The men lined the hallway of the hospitality suites and fondled, groped, and shouted insults at women who came down their "gauntlet." One woman was Lieutenant Paula Coughlin, a helicopter pilot and aide to Admiral John Snyder. The morning after the incident, Lieutenant Coughlin complained to Admiral Snyder, who did nothing. She then took her complaint to a higher authority. In the meantime, the public found out. It was discovered that two-star admiral Frank Kelso was on the floor that night but did nothing to stop the assaults. Admiral Kelso subsequently retired. Following a long-standing tradition, Congress promoted him in order to increase his retirement benefits. This occurred despite the efforts of seven female members of Congress. Lieutenant Coughlin also retired. But unlike Kelso, she was not promoted. In fact, she was charged $19,000 to cover her training since she did not complete her term. The Tailhook Incident was unique because it was so blatant and involved the military. But **sexual harassment**, the unwanted attention or pressure of a sexual nature from another person of greater social or physical power, is common throughout American society.

Sexual harassment
Sexual harassment is a major social issue that reflects the deeper, broader issue of gender inequality. Throughout the world women are treated as second-class citizens. They have less political influence, lower social status, and earn less money than men. Women are also not fully protected under the law. Almost every society in the world may be described as a **patriarchy**: a social arrangement in which men dominate women. This arrangement is supported by **sexism**: an ideology that maintains that women are inherently inferior to men and therefore do not deserve as much power, prestige, and wealth as men.

The Great Social Transformation and Gender Inequality

GST and gender inequality
We have been socialized into a male-dominated society. Therefore some people assume that men are naturally superior to women. This assumption did not always exist in its present form. Men and women are much more equal in traditional societies than in industrial societies. For example, in hunting and gathering societies, men and women are involved in many of the same activities. No one has much wealth or power and men and women view their relationships in terms of integration and balance. In horticultural and agrarian societies the balance of power shifts to men. This relationship changes even more in the transition to industrial societies. Here, a stratification system develops which places the bourgeoisie at the top and the proletariat, including women, at the bottom. Different traits came to be prized for women and men. Women were rewarded for working inside the home and for being dependent. Men were rewarded for working outside the home and for being independent.

Gender Role Socialization

Men and women obviously have different physical characteristics. They also behave differently beginning at an early age. Female infants respond more strongly to faces than to moving objects. Male infants respond more strongly to objects. Other differences emerge as children grow. Compared with boys, girls are more sensitive to sound, odor, and touch. Girls have greater finger dexterity and are more likely to sing in tune. Men are more sensitive to light, more adept at manipulating objects in space, and better at visualizing spatial relations in their minds. Women and men do not differ in overall intelligence, as measured by standardized tests.

Gender
Sociologists agree that men and women differ in some biological characteristics. However, they do not conclude that the differences are always socially important. Every society goes beyond biology to establish the more complex social concept of **gender**: the cultural and attitudinal qualities that are associated with being male or female. Individuals construct gender roles through their actions in society. A **gender role** is the behavior society expects for males or females. Gender roles are different from one society to the next. For example, before the European conquest, Native American culture contained a role called **berdache**: an individual who took the

part of the opposite gender: Mohave men would cut their upper thighs to simulate menstruation and take drugs to induce cramps to simulate childbirth. A female berdache would accept a masculine role by participating in a ceremony which then allowed her to hunt, farm, and make magic. A study of three tribes in New Guinea also demonstrates the flexibility of gender roles. In one tribe both men and women were passive, gentle, and warm. In the second both the men and women were aggressive and violent. In the third, women were aggressive and uninvolved in childrearing while men were artistic, wore jewelry, and raised children. Gender roles may also change over time.

Gender markers

We learn gender roles through socialization. This begins at birth. Infant girls are cuddled more than infant boys, but the boys are handled more. People often remark on the beauty of a girl and the strength of a boy. In doing so, they are anticipating the gender role that the children will play as adults. As a result of gender socialization, children identify themselves as a girl or boy by the tenth month of life. The ability to identify gender is important because people treat boys and girls differently. To help identify gender, American culture uses many **gender markers**: symbols and signs that identify a person's gender. For example, in hospital nurseries baby girls have pink name markers on their cribs while baby boys have blue markers. Gender markers become more apparent as we grow older. Girls are taught to wear dresses and high-heeled shoes. Boys are taught to behave "roughly."

Agents of gender socialization

Agents of gender socialization are those who teach gender roles and identities. Parents socialize their children to become either men or women almost from the moment of birth. Additionally, relatives, teachers, and mass media all are agents of gender socialization through their influence on the environment surrounding boys and girls as they grow and develop.

• *Living Space* provided for children has implication for gender socialization. A girl's room is decorated with floral wallpaper and ruffled bedspread and filled with dolls and homemaking toys while a boy's room is decorated with sports posters and car shaped bed and filled with trucks and toy guns.

• *Play.* Girls receive toys that encourage them to be passive, receptive, and to stay in the home while boys receive toys that encourage them to manipulate their environments. This encourages girls and boys to play different roles. For example, through playing cops and robbers with toy guns, boys learn shooting, fighting, and aggressive behavior. Through playing house with dolls, girls learn to work out family relationships, shop, and perform other domestic chores.

• *Dress.* In addition, boys' and girls' clothing also reinforces gender identity. Boys' clothes are usually dark (to hide dirt) while girls' clothes are often pastels that are difficult to clean.

• *School* also reinforces gender roles and identities. Traditional children's literature portrays girls as passive and boys as active. Males are usually shown in a wide range of occupations while females are shown in traditional feminine occupations and working in the home. Teachers also call on boys more often than girls and force boys to work through the problem while telling girls the answer. Girls are rewarded for non-academic achievement such as being "nice and neat." This helps to explain why girls receive higher classroom grades than boys but score lower on standardized tests. Recently educators have become more sensitive to the impact of gender socialization.

• *Advertising* also has a strong socializing effect on gender socialization. Men are portrayed as powerful with many diverse interests. Women are depicted as dates, mothers, and occasionally as business people. Women are usually shown as being very concerned about their appearances. A recent trend in advertising depicts men and women in cross-stereotyped roles. This includes showing men with children and women with briefcases. However, advertisements aimed at gender-specific audiences continue to depict women and men in a traditional manner.

Age and Gender Role Socialization

The United States is very youth-dominated. Many of our ideas about gender roles include assumptions about age. Definitions of masculinity and femininity are usually based on young men and women. In American culture, young people embody the values of beauty and physical robustness. The aged are stereotyped as fragile and helpless. Both genders are subjected to these stereotypes. But in a patriarchal society this affects women more than men because women are judged more than men by their physical appearance. When men put on weight as they grow older they are often described as mature and stout while women are described as old and overweight.

Patriarchy and Everyday Life

Gender socialization is so much a part of our lives that we hardly even think about it. But gender is expressed in all aspects of life, ranging from how likely you are to be elected president to your routine thoughts and activities.

Language and patriarchy
Language is a subtle but powerful mechanism that sometimes assaults women's self-esteem and helps to perpetuate male dominance. Many of the slang words for women, such as "bimbo," "chick," or "skirt," have negative connotations. The implication of these terms is that women are only sex objects, and that they lack skills or intelligence for success in business. Forms of address also imply inequality. For example, Mrs. or Miss indicate whether a woman is married or single while Mr. does not indicate the status of the man. For this reason, many people now prefer the neutral term Ms. Also women are often addressed by their first names rather than by Dr. X or Ms. X. This practice may seem harmless, but it *infantilizes* women: it implies that they should not be taken as seriously as men.. Gender also affects the words we use. A woman who swears is perceived as vulgar, but a man using the same words is perceived as rugged and earthy. If a man says no, people assume he means it. But when a woman says no, people assume she really means maybe or yes. This often underlies date rape: when the woman rejects the man's advances but he perceives her rejection as an acceptance. In addition, women often take on their husbands' names when they get married. This further demonstrates patriarchy.

Social interaction and patriarchy
Gender dominance is also expressed in the ways women and men interact with each other. Much of this is physical. When a couple is walking side by side, the man dominates the woman by placing his arm on her shoulder and pushing or pulling her in one direction or another. Also, men tend to take the arm rest when seated on a plane beside a woman. In conversations, men also interrupt women much more than women interrupt men. Men change the topic of conversation and ignore women's attempts to change it.

Gender Inequality and Work

In contrast to the traditional image of women as homemakers, women have always worked outside the family. Which women work, however, has changed dramatically during this century. It used to be that lower-class women worked while middle- and upper-class women remained in the home. Today, women of all social classes participate in the labor force. Even in 1950--when the ideal of the traditional housewife was extremely popular--30 percent of adult women worked full-time. Today, 59 percent work and by 2000 more than 60 percent will work. Having children does not prevent women from working as two-thirds of all mothers still manage to work full-time.

Second shift
Although women have long participated in the labor force, they remain segregated in a narrow range of jobs. About half of all working women work in only two occupational categories: clerical (such as typist or secretary) and service (such as waitress or nurse).In terms of specific jobs, women make up more than 98 percent of secretaries and 90 percent of professional nurses, bookkeepers, and housekeepers. Even within occupations men dominate the better positions. For example, women remain typists while men become administrative assistants. Many women work as much outside the home as men. In spite of this, women continue to be responsible for the household and the children. Sociologist Arlie Hochschild referred to this dual responsibility as the **second shift**, meaning that when the woman comes home from her job, she immediately begins working at her second job: cooking dinner, cleaning house, taking care of the children, and other household tasks. On average, women in the United States are responsible for 70 percent of the housework while their husbands and children are responsible for 15 percent each. While women spend many hours at household tasks, their labor is not counted as productive work. As a result,

statistics on industrial output, productivity, and gross national product do not reflect the labor women put into running their homes and rearing their children.

The gender gap can be expressed in terms of money. For example, women in the United States earn about 71 cents for every dollar a man earns. Overall, 75 percent of working women in the United States earn less than $25,000 per year. There are several causes of gender inequality in the workplace:

- *Sexism.* American culture has historically upheld the sexist belief that women are best suited for jobs that emphasize service, nurturing, or housekeeping while men are best suited for jobs that involve high-level decision making, authority, and production. Many people also believe that men have the responsibility for supporting their family while women work only for extra income. As a result, some people assume that women will quit their jobs when they become pregnant.
- *Lack of qualifications.* Men typically have more education and job experience than women. For example, 26 percent of men 25 years or older have completed at least four years of college. This compares to only 20 percent for women.
- *Glass ceiling.* Even in the absence of deliberate discrimination women may encounter a **glass ceiling**: subtle and unconscious discrimination that prevents women from reaching higher and better-paying positions for which they are qualified. For example, women (and members of ethnic minorities) are absent from the top levels of management. Women and minorities make up 30 percent of the middle managers in the United States but less than 1 percent of chief executive officers or those that report to the chief executive. Glass ceilings may exist because many corporate executives were socialized to believe that a woman's place is in the home. Also, some men feel threatened by competition with women. They may deal with this by excluding women from competing altogether.
- *Networking.* This practice is informal but very important. A great deal of business in the United States is conducted outside the office at recreational sites such as golf clubs, where women are discouraged from participating or are even barred. Executive lunches attended by the "old boys" network also exclude women.

Feminism

Feminism	**Feminism** is a counter-ideology that has arisen to challenge sexism and patriarchy and seeks independence and equality for women. Betty Friedan is usually credited as being an important force in much contemporary feminist thought. In her book, The Feminine Mystique, she stated that as long as women achieve their identity through sexual relationships with men they will remain subordinate. Feminism is often identified as seeking to break up the traditional family. It is more properly understood as seeking independence and equality for women.
Gender equality	Feminist ideology supports "equal rights under the law." This is called **gender equality**. In the past, the law often worked against women and prevented their full participation in society. For example, when the Great Depression struck in the late 1920s and early 1930s, the 1932 Federal Economy Act stated that if layoffs were necessary, married women were the first to go. Federal wage codes also gave women less pay than men for the same jobs. Gender equality under the law was recognized when President John Kennedy signed the Equal Pay Act of 1963. Feminists continued to argue for equal for greater legal protection and advocated the equal rights amendment in the 1970s and 1980s. The amendment failed to pass when only 35 approved it (38 states were required).
Comparable worth	Equal pay for equal work might not do women and minorities much good as they are relegated to low-wage positions. Male and female clerks might earn the same wages, but clerks do not earn much in the first place. Recognizing this fact, many feminists endorse the concept of **comparable worth**: equal pay for comparable jobs. According to this idea, every job in every organization should be rated as to its value for the organization. People performing a job with similar value should be paid a similar wage.

Abortion   Feminist ideology attempts to counter the existing cultural belief that women are "naturally" inclined towards being mothers and care providers. These beliefs often keep women economically dependent. Feminists see limitations on abortion as part of a system of beliefs and practices in which men dictate the types of family and gender roles women should perform. Feminists usually advocate few restrictions on abortion because they believe that a woman has the right to choose what happens to her body.

Compulsory heterosexism   Sexual orientation refers to an individual's preference for a particular form of sexual expression. **Heterosexuality** is the desire for a partner of the opposite sex; **homosexuality** is a preference for persons of the same sex; and **bisexuality** is desire for persons of either sex. Homosexual men are called *gays* and homosexual women are called *lesbians*. All patriarchal societies endorse heterosexuality. In the United States, homosexuality is so strongly condemned that heterosexuality is virtually compulsory, that is, forced upon people, whether they prefer it or not. For example, in 1986 the Supreme Court ruled that states may criminalize homosexual acts even when they occur between two consenting adults in a private home. Some feminists view mandatory heterosexuality or compulsory heterosexism as a form of political coercion that keeps women locked into the biological role of childbearers.

Inclusive feminism   Feminists are coming to realize that inequality in one area of life is related to inequality in other areas. As a result, feminists have begun to address inequalities of race, class, and gender together. For example, a woman may experience inequality not only in relation to her gender, but also as the result of her socioeconomic status and racial or ethnic group membership. This new perspective focuses on the causes of inequality, how the causes are related to each other, and how they affect the individual and society. **Inclusive feminism** states that all forms of inequality are related, and therefore all must be opposed.

Even women who do not identify themselves as feminists have benefited from feminism. Feminists have exerted great pressure to increase the representation of women in higher-status jobs. They have succeeded. In 1971 only 7 percent of law students at Ohio State University were women. In 1991 it had risen to 46 percent. Nationally, women have gone from 17 percent to 29 percent of chemists and 14 percent to 44 percent of economists.

Sociological Analysis of Gender Inequality

Functionalist perspective   From a functionalist perspective, gender inequality has a positive function for society as a whole. Gender inequality provides a way to divide labor. It channels women into domestic roles and men into the paid labor force, commerce, and government. According to this theory, it is efficient for women to conduct the *expressive tasks*: smoothing interpersonal problems among family members, diffusing hostilities, and creating solidarity. It is also efficient for men to assume the *instrumental tasks*: solving problems, providing resources, and dealing with affairs external to the family unit. As a result of dividing the labor in this way, women become dependent upon men for protection and resources. Masculine activities become more highly valued by society and gender inequality becomes deeply ingrained in society. Functionalist theory has a few problems. First, it is often interpreted as an apology for the status quo. Just because women are able to bear children does not mean that they must be responsible for domestic duties. Second, an American woman born today can expect to live almost 80 years and bear (on average) fewer than two children. This means that she will live almost half of her life after her children have grown. Thus it is not an efficient use of labor to tie her down to domestic duties. Third, functionalists assume that it is efficient to assign tasks on the basis of gender. Some men are naturally more nurturant than some women while some women are exceptionally well qualified for leadership in business and industry.

Conflict perspective   From the conflict perspective, gender inequality is a form of social stratification. The difference between women and minorities is that women are found at all levels of the class hierarchy while minorities are generally found at the bottom. This does not mean that men and women occupy equal statuses. Generally an upper-class woman will have lower prestige than an upper-class man. Like functionalists, conflict theorists state that the ability of women to bear children contributes to gender inequality. Conflict theory claims that men value women because they can bear children and without them, the society would cease to exist. It also proposes that the power of men to shape society to serve their needs means that women will inevitably be a subordinate group. Women continue to accept sexism because they have been socialized into a culture that defines women as subordinate. Women have come to believe in sexism and to accept a secondary place in society. Conflict theorists state that women suffer *false consciousness* because they accept and support an ideology that works against them. One problem with conflict theory is that it does not recognize that throughout history women have fought to end sexism.

Symbolic interactionist perspective   Much of the symbolic interactionist perspective of gender inequality was presented in the discussion of gender role socialization. Symbolic interactionists emphasize the role of meaning and the self in gender socialization. Children must first learn the meaning of "girl" and "boy" and then place themselves in the appropriate category. The definitions are incorporated into the self and become the basis for choosing relationships and activities that reinforce gender identity. As adults, women and men take societal distinctions of gender for granted. As parents, they socialize their children with similar expectations, thus reproducing gender inequality.

Gender Inequality in the Twenty-First Century

Gender is a social construct based on biological differences between males and females. As a result of the biological differences, gender will not totally disappear. However society may place less emphasis on unimportant gender differences and focus more on people's characteristics. Women have entered the labor markets in large numbers in the past few decades. This has resulted in an increased flexibility of gender roles. In the past, sexual intercourse was necessarily linked with pregnancy. Contraceptives have almost severed this link in many parts of the world. Technology has also decreased the importance of physical strength. Most women are strong enough to perform most jobs as well as men..

Men are also beginning to realize that a gender role that requires them to be aggressive, dominant, unemotional, and economically successful can be self-destructive. For example, men are three times more likely than women to commit suicide, three times more likely to suffer from severe depression, and six times more likely to be alcoholic. In the future, young men might pay less attention to filling their roles in a traditional manner. This would lead to the blurring of gender roles.

3. The aging of the baby boom generation will have a profound impact on the future of gender roles. As the baby boomers retire, they will be replaced by a smaller generation. As a result, an even larger number of women will be drawn into the work force. A broader range of occupations may open up to women, further blurring the distinction between "women's work" and "men's work."

Critical Questions

CQ: (page 228) Play is an important aspect of gender socialization. What gender roles are these children learning through their play? (This question refers to the picture on page 227).

First, define the key terms gender socialization and gender roles. What toys are these children playing with? What types of skills are associated with these toys? Which toys take the child's imagination outside the home? Which take the child inside the home? Visualize this picture with the boy and girl reversed but the toys they are playing with remained the same, in other words the girl is playing with the truck and the boy is hugging the doll. What would your reaction be? Why? This practice of mentally switching males/females can be a powerful tool in "seeing" what is going on.

CQ: (page 229) Have you ever felt constrained by your gender role? Do you feel that society creates too much pressure on young people to be "real men" or "real women?" Why can't we just be ourselves?

If you have ever felt constrained by your gender role, describe the situation? Were you expected to do something that you did not want to do or did you want to do something that was frowned upon due to your gender? Were there any other factors which affected the situation (the gender of others involved, your age, your class)? Describe these intervening factors. How do you think the situation would have been different if you were of the opposite sex? How did you handle the situation? How did the others react? How did your response make you feel? How did the reactions of others make you feel? How much affect did your audience have on your response? Did it make you more willing or did you capitulate? Do you encounter these situations frequently? Do you feel much pressure to conform to a gender role?

CQ: (page 237)   What career plans do have? Is your career path open equally to men and women? If not, why not?

If you have not already done this, it would be useful to look up some statistics concerning the representation of men and women in your prospective field. What percentage of the jobs in your area are held by women? Is this a traditionally male or female occupation? What are the requirements for the occupation? Are these just as easily achieved by women and men? If your college or university has an alumni network, you may want to conduct an informational interview with an alum in your field to get the "inside story" as to gender differences in the work place. What is the starting salary for each group? Your career services office may have a quarterly publication called the NACE Salary Survey which gathers data on entry level salaries and reports it by major and occupational area and also breaks down the data of the salary offers made to men and women. Is there a pattern for the career area in which you are interested?

CQ: (page 236)   Old boys' network/Glass ceiling.   How does the meaning of each concept relate to the meaning of the other concept linked to it?

When people were asked how they obtained their jobs, seventy percent replied that they received their jobs through networking and contacts. If networking is the key to obtaining a job, what are the gender differences for men and women hoping to enter upper management positions? Review the concepts of old boys' network and glass ceiling. Are there women in upper management positions so that there can develop an old girls' network? As you do your own career search, ask those who are in upper level career positions how they obtained their jobs. Also ask questions about opportunities for advancement.

Self Test Questions
Multiple Choice

1. The men involved in the Tailhook scandal in which 26 women were assaulted were not punished for their crimes. In fact, one Admiral was promoted. This demonstrates the ideology that women are inferior to men and therefore do not deserve as much power, prestige, and wealth. Such an ideology is called:
   a. patriarchy
   b. sexism
   c. glass ceiling
   d. gender discrimination

2. Although sexual harassment is a major social issue, it is a reflection of the deeper broader issue of:
   a. lack of discipline in the military
   b. unreported crime in the U.S.
   c. genetics determining social characteristics
   d. gender inequality

3. A social arrangement in which men dominate women is:
    a. sexism
    b. sexual discrimination
    c. patriarchy
    d. matriarchy

4. In which of the following society/societies does the balance of power between women and men shift to men?
    a. industrial
    b. hunting and gathering
    c. horticultural and agrarian
    d. postindustrial

5. The role in Native American culture in which men simulate menstruation and childbirth is called:
    a. gender marker
    b. matriarchy
    c. berdache
    d. inclusive feminism

6. Which is the term for the cultural and attitudinal qualities associated with being male or female?
    a. sex
    b. gender
    c. masculine/feminine
    d. gender role

7. The example of the New Guinea tribes shows that:
    a. gender roles are flexible
    b. "boys will be boys and girls will be girls"
    c. gender is rigid
    d. sex is learned through socialization

8. Dressing infant girls in pink and infant boys in blue to identify their sex is an example of:
    a. berdache
    b. gender role
    c. gender identity
    d. gender marker

9. In which of the following ways do parents socialize their children into gender roles?
    a. they encourage girls to sit quietly and display proper manners
    b. they give to boys toys which encourage them to manipulate their environment
    c. they decorate girls' rooms with homemaking toys such as doll houses and tea sets
    d. all of the above

10. Which of the following does NOT play a role in gender socialization?
    a. parents
    b. schools
    c. mass media
    d. all of the above play roles in socialization

Chapter 8 Inequalities of Gender

11. Definitions of femininity and masculinity are based on:
    a. mature women and men
    b. middle-aged women and men
    c. young women and men
    d. young women and middle-aged men

12. Which of the following is true about gender?
    a. gender roles are socially constructed
    b. gender roles are similar from society to society
    c. gender roles are constant within a society through time
    d. all of the above

13. Practices that infantilize women:
    a. keep women from having children
    b. imply that women should not be taken as seriously as men
    c. keep women in the home
    d. prevent women from inheriting property

14. Sue has a full-time job. At the end of her work day, she cooks dinner, helps her two children with their homework, and prepares lunches for the next day. Sociologist Arlie Hochschild refers to this as:
    a. the second shift
    b. sexism
    c. the gender gap
    d. inclusive feminism

15. Which is NOT a cause of gender inequality in the workplace, according to sociologists?
    a. sexism steers women away from high-level jobs
    b. men typically have more years of education than women
    c. there are not enough good jobs available
    d. women are often excluded from the old boys network

16. Many women rise to the middle-management level in corporations but very few become executives. One reason is the subtle and unconscious discrimination by men in high-level positions. This is an example of:
    a. old boys network
    b. glass ceiling
    c. berdache
    d. gender exclusion

17. Sarah realizes that the key to promotion in her corporation is making contacts with her superiors. But the men in her company socialize at the racquetball court, golf course, and in the locker room. Sarah is being excluded from:
    a. the second shift
    b. the old boys network
    c. the glass ceiling
    d. inclusive feminism

18. Gender inequality in the workplace has been attributed to all of the following except one. What is the one?
    a. sexism
    b. lack of effort on the job
    c. lack of qualifications
    d. networking

19. What is the goal of feminism?
    a. achieving a matriarchal society
    b. the break-up of the traditional family
    c. independence and equality for women
    d. the establishment of an "old girls network"

20. Professor Morgan's research focuses on feminist issues, but also on inequalities of race and social class. She is practicing:
    a. inclusive feminism
    b. radical feminism
    c. comparable worth
    d. berdache

21. Which theory proposes that gender inequality is a mechanism for dividing labor and rewards among members of a society?
    a. symbolic interactionism
    b. conflict
    c. functionalism
    d. feminism

22. Which is NOT a criticism of the functionalist theory of gender inequality?
    a. it fails to recognize the inefficiency of assigning tasks on the basis of gender alone
    b. it converts the biological fact that women can bear children into the perspective that they must be best-suited to household work
    c. it fails to recognize that women are not suffering false consciousness but have been fighting for equality for centuries
    d. it fails to recognize that, on average, women live about 40 years after their children are grown and thus it does not make sense to keep them tied to the household

23. Which sociological perspective argues that gender inequality is a form of social stratification?
    a. symbolic interactionism
    b. conflict
    c. functionalism
    d. feminism

24. Which sociological perspective argues that as a consequence of dividing labor and roles along gender lines, women become dependent on men for protection and resources?
    a. symbolic interactionism
    b. conflict
    c. functionalism
    d. feminism

True - False

T   F   1. Sexual harassment is the unwanted attention or pressure of a sexual nature from another person of greater social or physical power.

T   F   2. Men and women are more equal in hunting and gathering societies than in agrarian societies.

T   F   3. The structure of gender roles is universal, that is, the same in all cultures.

T   F   4. Girls are more highly rewarded than boys for getting along with others and handwriting neatness.

T   F   5. Advertisements aimed at women are less likely to contain strong gender stereotypes than ads aimed at a general audience.

T   F   6. Pejorative slang words such as "bimbo," "chick," or "skirt" show that language itself can be an assault on the self-esteem of women.

T   F   7. In none of the more than 4,000 occupations tabulated by the federal census does the average woman earn as much as the average man.

T   F   8. Working outside the family is a relatively recent development for women.

T   F   9. Over half of all working women have clerical or service jobs.

T   F   10. Topping off is the subtle and often unconscious discrimination within organizations that prevents women from reaching higher and better-paying positions for which they are qualified.

T   F   11. Comparable worth is another way of describing equal pay for equal work.

T   F   12. Pan-feminism is the view that sexism is related to all forms of oppression, and that feminist ideology therefore must fight against race and class oppression.

T   F   13. Symbolic Interactionism focuses on gender role socialization to explain gender inequality.

T   F   14. A major influence on the future of gender roles will be the aging of the baby boom generation

Self Test Answers

Multiple Choice

1. b (223)	6. b (225)	11. c (228)	16. b (236)	21. c (242)
2. d (223)	7. a (225)	12. a (225)	17. b (237)	22. c (243)
3. c (223)	8. d (226)	13. b (230)	18. b (236)	23. b (243)
4. c (224)	9. d (224)	14. a (234)	19. c (237)	24. c (243)
5. c (225)	10. d (228)	15. c (236)	20. a (241)	

True - False

1. T (223)	4. T (228)	7. T (235)	10. F (236)	13. T (242)
2. T (224)	5. F (228)	8. F (232)	11. F (238)	14. T (244)
3. F (225)	6. T (230)	9. T (233)	12. F (239)	

Chapter 9

The Economy

CHAPTER SUMMARY AND KEY TERMS

The chapter opens with the rags to riches story of Stephen Jobs who pioneered the development of the Apple personal computer. While Jobs was the driving force behind the Apple Computer Company, he was not immune from a power struggle with a man he had personally hired which resulted in Jobs being forced out of Apple altogether. Jobs went on to found the hugely successful Pixar, a software development company. Jobs is an example of a successful **entrepreneur.** Entrepreneurs are people who take great risks in order to achieve success in the marketplace and represent one form of work..

The Great Social Transformation and The Economy

GST and the economy
Work is part of the **economy**: the social institution that determines what will be produced, how production will be accomplished, and who will receive what is produced. All societies must address these problems; therefore, all societies have an economy. Work was a communal activity throughout much of human history. The nature of work began to change dramatically in the nineteenth century with industrialization. Factories replaced the family as the primary unit of production, and bureaucratic rules replaced traditional authority. Work became an associational activity and has remained as such since that time. Just as work was transformed by industrialization, human relations were transformed by bureaucratization. Most people in the United Sates work for bureaucratic corporations. Even small businesses have taken on many characteristics of bureaucracies.

Economy and Society

At the present time, two economic systems are very important. The first, **capitalism**, is an economic system in which the means of production are privately owned and market forces determine production and distribution. The other system, **socialism**, is an economic system in which the means of production are collectively owned and the state directs production and distribution.

Capitalism
Capitalism is an economic system in which the means of production are privately owned and market forces determine production and distribution. Philosopher Adam Smith developed a set of economic principles over 200 years ago. This later became the foundation for capitalism. Capitalist systems have these defining characteristics:
• *Free-market competition.* According to Adam Smith, impersonal economic forces will guarantee the greatest good for the greatest number of people within a society--provided that the marketplace is free from artificial obstacles. This is called **free market competition.** To ensure free-market competition, the government must follow a laissez-faire policy, or one of non-interference. As a result, the laws of supply and demand will ensure that incompetent companies fail and competent companies will succeed. This will produce a marketplace with the highest quality goods and services available at the lowest prices. Adam Smith's ideas do not apply to public goods and services as these offer no incentives to private firms. Instead, these must be offered by the government.
• *Private ownership.* Technically, *ownership* refers to a bundle of rights associated with the use and disposal of an object or an idea. For example, if you own a textbook, you have the right to sell it, keep it, or destroy it. **Private ownership of property** refers to ownership of a business, factory, or other means of production (it does not refer to the right to own a car or a private home). Private ownership is allowed in a capitalist system. Ownership may be direct, as when a person owns a business, or it may be indirect, as with anyone who owns stocks.
• *Pursuit of profit.* Adam Smith argued that the **pursuit of profit** eventually produces the greatest good for the greatest number of people. When this system is followed, the entrepreneur earns money, the consumer saves money, and the society becomes more efficient and vigorous. Critics of capitalism state that it is a heartless system in which entire industries may be wiped out overnight and families may be destroyed through unemployment. They also point out that the system ignores the poor, even in times of prosperity. They cite that South-Central Los Angeles

had only 11 grocery stores to serve more than half a million people because servicing the poor yields little profits.

Socialism

In contrast to capitalists, socialists believe that everyone should share equally in goods and services produced by society. Socialists argue that the government should decide which goods are produced, how they are distributed, and at what prices they are sold. The clearest distinction between capitalism and **socialism** concerns ownership of the means of production. In a socialist system, the government owns all of the society's important businesses and industries including railroads, airlines, television stations, banks, and factories. Some of the economy may be privately owned but the government is the dominant economic power. Socialists believe that the government should own the means of production in the name of the people (public ownership) while capitalists believe individuals should own the means of production in their own name. Socialists argue that private ownership increases inequality and thus harms everyone. In order to exert such great control, the governments of socialist systems establish huge and complex bureaucracies. Citizens often experience red tape, or excessive bureaucratization, as a result. Cuba is an example of a contemporary socialist system.

Mixed economy

Capitalist and socialist systems are very different in theory. But the two systems may be converging toward a middle ground, or **mixed economy**. There are several reasons for this convergence. First, all industrial societies are affected by similar forces such as new technology, the division of labor, major population shifts, urbanization, and bureaucratization. Industrialization creates similar problems which must be met with similar solutions. The United States is probably the most capitalistic system in the world. However, it began to move toward socialism during the Great Depression of the 1930s. A new version of capitalism emerged from this period which included **social insurance**: the idea that the government is responsible for guaranteeing a minimum standard of living for everyone. During this era, the federal government also established Social Security to provide retirement benefits. In addition, governments of all types frequently support businesses by granting tax exemptions, issuing favorable regulations, and sometimes by providing direct loans to rescue companies from collapse.

The Corporation and Society

Interlocking directorate

Corporations appear to be highly democratic because stock shares are divided among many people, all of whom have the right to vote for directors of the company. However, few small stockholders attend annual meetings. The major shareholders--many of whom are officers of the company--usually approve of the policies offered by top management. The board also routinely approves new board members, most of whom are selected by top management. As a result, board members typically support top managers. The same directors often sit on boards of more than one company, and most top managers know each other personally. This is called an **interlocking directorate**. For example, the directors of General Motors Corporation sit on the boards of many other companies. As a result, General Motors has direct and indirect links with about 700 other corporations. Interlocking directorates yield a great deal of power.

Conglomerate

Some corporations grow extremely large by acquiring other companies. This often results in **conglomerates**: giant corporations composed of other corporations that produce a variety of products and conduct business in several markets. The major incentive for forming conglomerates is that they help stabilize profits. If one market is depressed, a conglomerate can make money in another market. Another reason to form conglomerates is to gain access to the technology, skills, and experience of the acquired company. They are also formed to prevent unfriendly takeovers.

Multinationals

Companies that conduct business in several countries but have their central headquarters in one country are called **multinationals**. The Caterpillar Tractor Corporation is an example. It operates plants in Scotland, Austria, and Brazil but its headquarters is located in Peoria, Illinois. Multinationals present problems in both power and control. They are difficult to control because they conduct business in different countries with different laws. Some critics claim that multinationals operate outside the law. The largest multinationals control economies as large as some countries. As a result, they greatly influence the economies and political systems of countries in which they operate. Multinationals benefit their host nations by providing jobs, income, training, and technology and by paying local taxes. On a broader scale, they establish a climate conducive to economic growth. On the negative side, they increase inequality among nations and make poor nations more dependent on wealthy nations.

Unemployment and Job Loss Anxiety

Unemployed

Unemployment, or not having a job when you want one, does not exist in traditional societies because the concept of "having a job" does not exist. In industrial societies, employment takes on great significance. It is regarded as a measure of social worth. At the societal level, unemployment wastes human resources. It also costs the government money to support the unemployed. In some cases, unemployment leads to depression, feelings of shame and worthlessness, and/or crime. The economy in most industrial societies changes over time. The possibility of unemployment always exists. The federal government takes a monthly survey to track unemployment. It defines the **unemployed** as consisting of people who are without jobs but who are seeking work. Children, retired people, and others who are not actively seeking work are excluded. The survey undercounts the homeless, migrants, and people without permanent addresses. These are the people most likely to be unemployed. The unemployment rate is one of the most closely watched indicators of economic performance. No society can possibly achieve a zero percent unemployment rate. A number of people will be unemployed at any given time due to changing jobs, illness, moving residences, or other personal reasons. The seasons also affect the unemployment rate. High school and college students enter the job market in the summer and are considered officially unemployed until they find jobs. During the Great Depression of the 1930s, unemployment reached an all-time high of 25 percent. The lowest unemployment rate in the United States occurred shortly after this, during World War II, when it fell to 2 percent. Since that time, it has fluctuated between 5 and 7 percent. Though it is low, a 5 percent unemployment rate has serious implications for some ethnic groups. The black unemployment rate is always about twice the white rate. The situation is even worse when class is taken into account. In 1997 the unemployment rate for young African Americans reached 37 percent.

Job loss anxiety

Many people in industrial societies suffer **job loss anxiety**: anxiety caused by the insecurity of their jobs. Individuals realize that their company might be bought by another company and then "downsized" to increase cost efficiency. More than one in ten Americans now feels that they are fairly likely to loose their job within the next 12 months, whereas in 1972 only 5 percent felt that way. Job loss anxiety reduces people's confidence in their future, affects the amount of money they are willing to spend, and contributes to voter dissatisfaction. In the United States, both political parties blame each other for job loss in order to take advantage of people's anxieties.

Sociological Analysis of the Economic Order

Functionalist perspective

1. Functionalist theorists maintain that social stability is achieved by fulfilling the following functions:

• *Distribution of goods and services.* Functionalists propose that capitalism is well designed to encourage the production and distribution of goods due to its emphasis on free market and profit. If a market exists for a new service or product, some entrepreneur will probably discover it and try to earn a profit. Socialist economies do not respond to such potential as quickly because they do not provide the high rewards that encourage people to take risks.

• *Production of wealth and power.* Functionalists argue that a close link between the political institutions and the economy increases efficiency in directing and managing society's resources. For example, in capitalist societies economic success allows people to accumulate wealth which they can then convert to power. Power allows them to influence the government and to explore new areas of interest. In socialist societies, the economies produce wealth. However, it does not become concentrated in the hands of a few. This means that entrepreneurs receive only a small profit for their work and ideas.

- *Innovation.* Functionalists state that capitalist systems adapt well to changes because they are always innovating new products and processes. This forces companies to constantly compete for customers. This forces the companies to produce the best products at the lowest prices. In socialist economies, customers may be asked to pay more for some products in order to protect inefficient companies.

Conflict perspective
Conflict theorists emphasize the instability that is built into the economic order. Some argue that capitalism is doomed to fail because it contradicts itself. Conflict theorists point to the great inequalities produced by capitalism as well as the ideology that justifies "winners and losers." They also indicate that inequalities generated by capitalism are self-perpetuating. For example, children of rich parents attend elite schools and interact with other rich people. This ensures that they will attract the best-paying and most prestigious jobs.

Symbolic interactionist perspective
Symbolic interactionists examine the interactions between the individual, the group, and the economy. They stress the impact of **career socialization**: the process of acquiring knowledge and ways of thinking about work and careers. Work and career socialization occur throughout the life cycle. Much of this learning is conducted by the agents of socialization: individuals and other sources that are especially influential in the learning process. Both informal and formal agents are responsible for work and career socialization:
- *Informal agents of socialization.* Parents are usually the earliest informal agents. They influence their children's orientation toward work and set them on certain career paths. Children often enter the same occupation as their parents. This is called **occupational inheritance**. Parents may take their children to work at an early age, thus teaching them about a particular occupation. Peers are also informal agents of career socialization. They can be role models or give advice. The mass media is another informal agent. It reinforces cultural values about work and dramatizes rewards attached to certain occupations.
- *Formal agents of socialization.* This consists of schools, employers, and work training programs. Colleges and universities employ career counselors to help students identify potential career tracks.

The Economy in the Twenty-First Century

Deindustrialization
Today, the United States has the single largest economy in the world. But the American economy is also experiencing fundamental changes. One of these is **deindustrialization**: a process of economic change in which an economy is losing jobs in the industrial sector and adding jobs in the service sector. Service jobs now outnumber manufacturing jobs in the United States. About five million jobs created in the postindustrial economy will be in executive, managerial, administrative, or professional occupations. These jobs are well-paid and provide high worker satisfaction. However, the majority of new jobs (11 million) will be in the low-paying sector of the service economy: clerical, retail sales, food preparation, and cleaning services. These jobs require less education, do not pay well, and do not provide high worker satisfaction. A second major trend is the increase of women in jobs that were once male-dominated.

CRITICAL QUESTIONS

CQ: (page 255) This question refers to the "Society Today" Table on page 255 of your text. IBM and Hewlett-Packard made the top 25 corporations. Both of these corporations are involved in the computer industry. As we move into the postindustrial era would you expect their ranking in sales among the top 25 to increase, decrease, or stay about the same? What other corporations on this list might be expected to thrive in the postindustrial economy?

First, review the definition of postindustrial economy. With this in mind, how do you think computer corporations will fare in the future? Will the market become saturated, resulting in a decrease in sales? What do we know about the rate of innovation in modern society? What impact will this have on the computer industry? Refer back to the table. What other types of corporations are listed? Can you make a prediction about these corporations' ranking in the future? If a corporation's ranking dropped from 2 to 25, would that necessarily mean that the company was doing poorly? Is it possible for the annual revenues of the top 100 corporations to increase simultaneously? What do you think will happen to the stocks of industrial corporations in the postindustrial economy? Does postindustrial mean that all manufacturing stops? Can you envision a future in which there are fewer jobs in manufacturing but in which output actually increases due to increases in productivity? Would you buy stock in industrial corporations? We know that new markets are opening continuously throughout the world. These markets include individuals with increasing amounts of money to spend. How will this affect the future of top corporations such as these?

CQ: (page 264)   Are you personally concerned about unemployment and job loss? How can you best protect yourself from these unpleasant features of the economy? How important is a good education?

On what evidence do you base your concerns about unemployment and job loss? Are you planning to enter a field that is currently experiencing downsizing or one in which jobs are increasing? Are you willing to move across the country to take a new job? Do you have skills that are transferable to other jobs? If so, what are these skills? What types of skills are highly valued in a postindustrial economy? Do you have friends who are unemployed? What steps are they taking to alleviate their situation? How much education are you planning to obtain? How will this affect your potential of unemployment?

CQ: (page 268)   What are the influences of your choice of career? Do you plan on visiting a career counselor at your college before you graduate? Why or why not?

Did one or both of your parents take you to their place of employment when you were young? Did they discuss potential careers with you? How did these factors affect your career choice? Are you planning to enter the same career as one of your parents? Why or why not? Have you informally interviewed someone from your prospective occupation? If so, did this change your views of the career? Did it cause you to completely change careers? Did income earning potential or job security affect your decision? What might a career counselor be able to tell you that you do not already know? Have you received instruction on how to interview properly?

CQ: Industrialization/deindustrialization. How does the meaning of each concept relate to the other?

The Great Social Transformation talks about the change in societies from hunting and gathering to industrial. Review the concept deindustrialization which is, for many societies, the stage after industrialization. What part of the economy will grow with deindustrialization? What part of the U.S. economy once associated with industrialization will shrink? How will that effect people in those industries? The previous chapter on gender discussed occupations and gender. If there are fewer manufacturing occupations and more service sector occupations, what will be the implications for men and women? How might your choice of occupation be influenced by deindustrialization?

Self-Test Questions
Multiple choice

1. What is the name for people who take risks in order to gain a profit in the marketplace?
    a. business people
    b. entrepreneurs
    c. venture capitalists
    d. free-marketeers

2. What is the term for the social institution that determines what will be produced, how production will be accomplished, and who will receive what is produced?
    a. marker
    b. exchange field
    c. economy
    d. none of the above

3. Which of the following did NOT occur as the result of industrialization?
   a. the family became the main economic unit
   b. bureaucratic rules replaced traditional authority
   c. factories replaced the family as the primary unit of production
   d. work became more impersonal

4. What is the chief economic unit in communal societies?
   a. husband/wife couple
   b. small business
   c. central bureaucratic committee
   d. family or kinship group

5. In industrial societies, the economy is organized to facilitate:
   a. large-scale productivity
   b. big business
   c. mass consumerism
   d. all of the above

6. Which is NOT a characteristic of capitalism?
   a. private ownership of the means of production
   b. extensive red tape caused by excessive governmental intervention
   c. laissez-faire government economic policy
   d. pursuit of profit

7. What is the term for the bundle of rights associated with the use and disposal of an object?
   a. private ownership
   b. copyright
   c. patent
   d. civil rights

8. Which economic system believes that the government should own the means of production in the name of the people?
   a. capitalism
   b. socialism
   c. mixed
   d. communism

9. Which is NOT a criticism of capitalism?
   a. the free market ignores the poor because they do not yield a high profit
   b. capitalism is unfair because its governments ensure all people a minimum standard of living
   c. capitalists will pollute the environment in pursuit of profit
   d. individuals and communities may be devastated by changes in business patterns

10. Which of the following is NOT a characteristic of socialism?
   a. the government decides which goods are produced and how they are distributed
   b. the government owns and operates strategic businesses and industries
   c. the government encourages the pursuit of profit
   d. the government is responsible for guaranteeing a minimum standard of living for everyone

11. When the United Sates adopted the welfare program, it became what type of economy?
    a. capitalist
    b. socialist
    c. mixed
    d. communist

12. Socialism and capitalism have been:
    a. growing more unlike each other
    b. converging toward some middle ground
    c. incorporating elements of communism
    d. by-passed by the postindustrial economy

13. Which is true of corporations?
    a. they may not be as democratically run as they seem to be
    b. they separate ownership and management
    c. they may be part of a conglomerate
    d. all of the above

14. General Motors has direct and indirect links with 700 other corporations because members of its board of directors sit on other corporations' board. This is called:
    a. conglomerates
    b. multinationals
    c. interlocking directorates
    d. all of the above

15. Corporations that are composed of other corporations that produce a variety of products and conduct business in several markets are called:
    a. conglomerates
    b. interlocking directorates
    c. multinationals
    d. deindustrialized

16. Honda is headquartered in Japan but it has many plants in the United States. Honda is a/an:
    a. conglomerate
    b. interlocking directorate
    c. entrepreneur
    d. multinational

17. Which is NOT true of unemployment?
    a. it causes stress in individuals
    b. it wastes human resources
    c. it costs the government money
    d. all of the above are true

18. Many employed persons fear that they will loose their jobs due to a change in the economy or downsizing. This fear is called:
    a. job despair
    b. job loss anxiety
    c. career de-socialization
    d. unemployment anxiety

19. Which is NOT true according to functionalism?
    a. capitalism encourages innovation
    b. capitalism encourages entrepreneurialism
    c. capitalism allows people to convert wealth into power
    d. capitalism is self-contradictory and will destroy itself

20. The process of acquiring knowledge and ways of thinking about work and careers is:
    a. entrepreneurship
    b. occupational inheritance
    c. social insurance
    d. career socialization

21. Ted's father was an engineer. When Ted was young, his father would take him to work and teach him about engineering. Ted subsequently became an engineer. What is the term for this process?
    a. entrepreneurship
    b. occupational inheritance
    c. social insurance
    d. none of the above

22. Which sociological perspective argues that capitalism produces great inequalities among people?
    a. functionalism
    b. conflict
    c. symbolic interaction
    d. rational choice

23. Which perspective argues that work and career socialization take place throughout the life cycle?
    a. functionalism
    b. conflict
    c. symbolic interaction
    d. rational choice

24. Which sociological perspective argues that the mass media play a role in career socialization by providing a steady stream of work-related models?
    a. functionalism
    b. conflict
    c. symbolic interaction
    d. rational choice

True - False

T	F	1. Adam Smith's idea behind free-market competition is that it will produce the highest quality goods at the best prices.
T	F	2. The economic policy "laissez-faire" means not interfering with the free play of economic forces.
T	F	3. In socialist systems, people are not allowed to own their homes.
T	F	4. In a socialist economy the government owns society's strategic businesses and industries.
T	F	5. Socialists believe that everyone should get what they work for.
T	F	6. Income inequality is greater in socialist systems than in capitalist systems.

T	F	7. Capitalism seems to be more efficient than it actually is often seeking profits in the short term thus destroying prospects for profit in the long term..
T	F	8. To a certain extent, multinational corporations benefit their host country by creating jobs, generating income, and training local work forces..
T	F	9. The concept of unemployment does not exist in traditional societies.
T	F	10. The definition of unemployed is people who are without jobs.
T	F	11. Zero unemployment is attainable.
T	F	12. Conflict theorists propose that most people in the United States do not have a problem with the inequalities created by capitalism because the have an ideology that supports and justifies winners and losers.
T	F	13. The process of economic change in which an economy is losing jobs in the industrial sector and adding jobs in the service sector is called industrial contraction.
T	F	14. In the future, service jobs will be divided into two tiers, one offering well-paying jobs a high satisfaction and the other offering low-paying jobs with little satisfaction.

Self-Test Answers

Multiple Choice

1. b (247)	6. b (249)	11. c (253)	16. d (257)	21. b (267)
2. c (247)	7. a (250)	12. b (253)	17. d (258)	22. b (266)
3. a (248)	8. b (252)	13. d (255)	18. b (262)	23. c (267)
4. d (248)	9. b (251)	14. c (255)	19. d (265)	24. c (267)
5. d (248)	10. c (252)	15. a (255)	20. d (267)	

True - False

1. T (249)	4. T (252)	7. T (252)	10. F (259)	13. F (268)
2. T (249)	5. F (252)	8. T (258)	11. F (260)	14. T (269)
3. F (253)	6. F (252)	9. T (258)	12. T (266)	

NOTES FOR FUTURE STUDY AND REVIEW:

Chapter 10

The Political Order

THE GREAT SOCIAL TRANSFORMATION AND THE POLITICAL ORDER

POWER AND THE POLITICAL ORDER
   Traditional Authority
   Legal-Rational Authority
   Charismatic Authority

THE STATE AND THE EXERCISE OF POWER
   Types of States
   Nations and States
   States and Human Rights

POLITICAL PROCESSES IN THE UNITED STATES
   Political Parties
   Special-Interest Groups
   Voting

POWER ELITE AND PLURALIST MODELS
   The Power Elite Model
   The Pluralist Model

SOCIOLOGICAL ANALYSIS OF THE POLITICAL ORDER
   The Functionalist Perspective
   The Conflict Perspective
   The Symbolic Interactionist Perspective

THE POLITICAL ORDER IN THE TWENTY-FIRST CENTURY

CRITICAL QUESTIONS
   Charismatic leaders
   Human rights
   Political socialization

SELF TEST QUESTIONS/ANSWERS

CHAPTER SUMMARY AND KEY TERMS

The Great Social Transformation and the Political Order

Political

The **political** refers to the distribution of power across the institutions, organizations, and individuals of a society. The political order was relatively simple in hunting and gathering societies. Tribes were organized into kinship networks and tribal elders held the power. In horticultural and agrarian societies, aristocracies developed and governments became more formal and complex. With industrialization in England and northern Europe, the aristocracy lost power, the middle-class formed, and liberal democracy emerged.

Power and the Political Order

Power

The political order rests on a base of **power**: the ability to achieve ends despite resistance. Power is a very valuable resource in every society. Those who have it can control those who do not. Different types of power exist. Max Weber distinguished between using power legitimately and using it illegitimately. A legitimate use of power occurs when society approves of the way in which it is applied. An example is putting a bank robber in prison. Weber called this type of power **authority**. Illegitimate uses of power are those that lack society's approval. A teacher who fails a student because she or he dislikes the student's parents is an example. Weber called this illegitimate use of power **coercion**.

Authority

Weber divided legitimate power into three types: traditional authority, legal-rational authority, and charismatic authority.
  • Authority that is legitimated by the historical beliefs and practices of the society is called **traditional authority**. It is often seen as almost sacred due to its roots in tradition. Monarchs and emperors rule by traditional authority. This type of power is rarely questioned and is therefore slow to change.
  • **Legal-rational authority** derives its legitimacy from the rules and laws that define the rights, duties, and obligations of rulers and followers. In most cases, these rules are written in official documents. Political leaders in associational societies rule by legal-rational authority. The power in a legal-rational system rests in the position rather than in the individual who fills it. For example, the President of the United States is allowed to veto bills only while in office. Once a new president has been elected, the former president must relinquish the power.
  • Weber defined **charismatic authority** as the power that is legitimated by an individual's exceptional personal attributes, such as a magnetic personality, an extraordinary driving energy, or a powerful aura of wisdom and grace. Individuals who possess these qualities can inspire devotion and command obedience. Weber stated that charismatic leaders are convinced that they were divinely chosen to perform a great task that is usually outside the existing political order and they are also able to convince others to share this perception. Examples include Joan of Arc, Abraham Lincoln, Joseph Stalin, and Martin Luther King Jr. Charismatic authority cannot easily be transferred from one person to another.

Ideal type

These three types of authority do not exist in pure form. All three types may be present in a society at the same time. In addition, each category of authority is an **ideal type**: an abstract description, constructed from a number of cases, that reveals the essential features of a concept.

The State and the Exercise of Power

State and government

The **state** is the highest political authority within a given territory. **Government** is the set of people who currently are engaged in directing the state. All governments exercise power, though not in the same way. There are three main categories based on the extent to which people are included or excluded from the processes of government, if the government tolerates opposition, and if the government is interested in the daily lives of the people.

Authoritarian state

• The **authoritarian state** has three major characteristics. First, the people are excluded from the process of government; second, little or no opposition to the government is permitted; and third, the government has little interest in the daily lives of the people--provided the people do not threaten the government or its politics. At one point in history the most common type of authoritarian government was the **monarchy**: a system in which political power is passed from person to person on the basis of hereditary claims. Saudi Arabia and Kuwait are still ruled by monarchies. Another form of authoritarian government is more common: the *junta*, or rule by a small group of military officers. Juntas frequently hold power in underdeveloped nations because they are often so unstable that only the military can create order. About half of the African countries that have gained independence since 1960 are ruled by juntas. Authoritarian regimes are often of short duration or unstable. Power in this system is obtained by overthrowing the government. Also, periods of instability often follow the death of an authoritarian ruler.

Totalitarian state

• In contrast to an authoritarian state, a **totalitarian state** is one in which the government has unlimited power, tolerates no opposition, and exercises close control over its citizens. Some totalitarian regimes are *autocracies* (ruled by a small group), but most are dictatorships (rule by one person). Examples of dictators include Joseph Stalin, Adolph Hitler, and Saddam Hussein. Totalitarian governments are a relatively new development. It emerged in the 1900s and was made possible by technological advances including microphones, secret television cameras, and telephone taps. Totalitarian regimes often inflict great human suffering. For example, during the late 1970s the Chinese government punished almost one million college students for supporting Chairman Mao Zedong, the founder of the Chinese communist state. Only one political party is allowed in totalitarian states. It controls all aspects of life from who holds public office to what music is played in the radio.

Democratic state

Democratic states are at the opposite end of the continuum from authoritarian and totalitarian states. A **democratic state** allows the people to have an input into government divisions, and permits the people to elect and dismiss leaders. Carried to its extreme, a democracy would permit every citizen to participate in every division made by the government. Because this is impractical in large societies, the *representative democracy* has evolved. In this system, elected officials become the representatives of the people. Many authoritarian and totalitarian systems claim to be democracies because they hold elections. However, they are not true democracies because only one party is allowed to run.

Nation
Nation-state

It is important to distinguish between a nation and a state. A **nation** is a group that lives within a given territory and that shares a common history, culture, and identity. The concepts of nation and state are not always completely separate. They may be combined to produce the **nation-state**: the supreme political authority within a territory that incorporates and represents a nation. For example, Japan is a homogeneous country with a common culture; therefore it is a nation-state. Many countries have borders that do not correspond to the geographic location of the nations in the region. This is the case in many parts of Africa which were formerly colonized by England, France, German, and Belgium. In some cases, a single tribe was divided into two or more states. This has resulted nations that do not have their own states and has led to great turmoil.

Human rights

Human rights--those broadly defined rights to which all people are entitled by virtue of their humanity--play an important role in preserving individual freedoms. A Universal Declaration of Human Rights was signed by many governments in 1948. It states, "Everyone shall live in free and equal dignity and rights." This has not stopped several of the signing governments from ignoring human rights. Amnesty International was developed in 1961 through the work of British attorney Peter Benenson. Benenson became enraged when he read of two Portuguese students being imprisoned for seven years after toasting to freedom in public. Amnesty International is now a worldwide organization with 4,200 local groups. Amnesty International raises the point that states and governments routinely violate the rights of their own citizens and that no effective international organization exists that can prevent these violations.

| **Politics of Exclusion** | The politics of exclusion involves the identification of people we define as "we" and the people we define as "they." The people defined as they are the people to whom we feel we owe no moral obligations. The politics of exclusion is made possible by these techniques: |

- *Demonizing.* This occurs when a group defines "they" as evil and "we" as good thus making it natural to destroy the evil.
- *Shifting-the-Blame.* "They asked for it" or "They deserve what they get" are the types of statements that support extreme violence against other groups.
- *Routinizing-the-Violence.* This occurs when killing and destruction become defined as "normal."
- *Dehumanizing.* This involves treating the other group members as less human thereby redefining violence against them as violence against a subhuman species.

Political Processes in the United States

| **Political parties** | Political organizations that are meant to legitimately influence the government are called **political parties**. Large political parties, such as the Republican and Democratic parties, are large bureaucracies. They stand for certain causes and ideologies, they state opinions, and they propose solutions to problems. In the United States third parties rarely win elections. The Democratic Party is the traditional home to labor unions, ethnic minorities, and liberal causes, while the Republican Party is home to management, the upper-class, and conservative causes. Political parties serve many functions and purposes: |

- *Influencing government policy* is an important goal of a political party. Parties can exert influence by controlling appointments, such as the Supreme Court, in addition to winning elections.
- Political parties are also becoming a *basis for forming coalitions*. Under this system, a party can influence its members to vote along party lines most of the time. But on some issues, some members will cross party lines and vote with the other party. The party in power determines who becomes *chair of a committee* in Congress. The chairpersons determines the order in which legislation will be considered.
- Political parties are also *focal points for conflict* between different segments of society. The Republican party represents mainly the white middle- and upper-classes while the Democratic Party represents working- and lower-classes, including most racial and ethnic minorities. The effects of this is seen in the **party platform** of each political party. The party platform is the official statement of the ideology, goals, and plans that the party will implement if its candidates are elected to office. The Republican Party generally stresses individual initiative, free enterprise, less government, technological development, and a strong national defense. The Democratic platform emphasizes welfare programs, the expansion of government, less defense spending, and the elimination of barriers to equal opportunity through affirmative action.

| **Lobbyists Interest groups PACs** | Influencing legislation has become a big business in the United States. **Lobbyists** are people who are employed by a large corporation, a union, or other organizations who aim to influence congressional votes on certain bills. Lobbyists are valuable because they have special insights into the workings of government and they have informal contacts with "people in the right places." There are about 38 lobbyists for every one member of Congress. Lobbyists usually work on behalf of an **interest group**: an organization formed for the express purpose of swaying political decisions. The National Rifle Association is one of the largest interest groups in America. Special interest groups that establish organizations to raise money are called **political action committees**, or **PACs**. PACs are very influential in politics because they contribute millions of dollars to candidates' elections. Even though they are rooted in legal-rational authority, parties, lobbyists, interest groups, and PACs are all part of the informal political process. |

Voting

Though democracy offers people the opportunity to elect government officials, many Americans do not take advantage of it. In only five of the past 16 presidential elections has more than 60 percent of the voting-age population cast a ballot. This contrasts with a voting rate of 95 percent in Belgium, 92 percent in Austria, and 91 percent in Sweden. Race, class, and gender may be used to explain why so few Americans vote. According to federal criteria, almost one person in ten is poor, and the poor are not very politically active. African Americans are less likely to vote than are white Americans. The reasons are mainly due to social class, as middle- and upper-class African Americans vote at about the same rate as middle- and upper-class whites. Women are more likely to vote than men. Women also live longer than men which enables them to vote in more elections.

Power Elite and Pluralist Models

Power elite model
Developed by C. Wright Mills, the **power elite** model proposes that a small group of people control the United States. These people are wealthy, socially well-placed, know each other personally, and frequently marry among themselves. They share a similar worldview and work together to achieve a political agenda that fits their interests. The power elite control the country by exerting control over the economy, government, and the military. Its members are the presidents and board chairmen of major corporations; they hold powerful positions in government; and they are the high-ranking generals and admirals of the military. The power elite consolidates its power by rotating from one institution to the next. The power elite model implies that democracy means very little because elites always have the power to achieve their goals. President Eisenhower warned of the potential dangers of the "military-industrial complex"--a coalition among industrial, military, and political leaders.

Pluralist model
The pluralist model argues that power is diffused throughout society. It points out that in complex societies such as the United States, multiple centers of power exist such as business associations, unions, schools, churches, civic associations, and special interest groups. As a result of this wide distribution, a group can rarely achieve all of its goals. Instead, each group must accommodate and cooperate with others. The pluralist model recognizes that some people in society have more power than others. But it also states that even the most powerful must answer to various constituencies. Power centers that are able to block the actions of other groups are called **veto groups**. Examples include the American Medical Association, the National Chamber of Commerce, and The National Association of Manufacturers. The pluralist model proposes that democracy works fairly well in the United States. However, the diffusion of democracy can hinder problem solving. Too much pluralism translates into poor leadership, a lack of coordination, and a lack of focus.

Sociological Analysis of the Political Order

Functionalist perspective
From the functionalist perspective, the state has achieved a dominant position because it provides society with cohesion and order. The state does this by filling the following functions:
• *Maintaining order.* This is a major function of the state. The state may resort to force, but the continuous use of force is rarely necessary because every society has mechanisms for controlling conflict. In complex societies, the state puts the most important norms into written law.
• *Interacting with other states.* In modern society, states must interact with each other to survive over long periods of time. This results in military treaties, economic alliances, and diplomacy.
• *Directing the system.* States must direct the economic, social, and political systems of their respective societies. For example, the United States government tries to maintain full employment and prosperity. It also regulates important institutions such as banks and insurance companies.

Conflict perspective
Contemporary conflict theorists recognize that conflict exists among many groups in society. For example, racial and ethnic groups compete with the dominant group, liberals compete with conservatives, and women compete with men. The outcome of these struggles often depends on a group's wealth, its ability to raise money, and its power to influence government policy. The weak and the powerless typically lose because they do not even have the resources to organize. Conflict theorists also argue that power can be concentrated in the hands of a few even in a democracy because voting, freedom of speech, and other tools of democracy do not always work.

Change is also difficult to achieve if everyone in the society accepts the dominant group's ideology.

Symbolic interactionist perspective   Symbolic interactionism points out that in addition to being organizations, political parties are also ideas in people's minds and part of their social identities. These ideas and identities are acquired through the process of **political socialization**: the formal and informal learning that creates a political self for each individual. It focuses on the transference of political attitudes, beliefs, and identities from one generation to the next. Symbolic interactionists also indicate that television images are easy to manipulate and give very superficial information.

Political Order in the Twenty-First Century

American voters seem to be losing faith in the political system. Today, politicians are as far removed from the public as movie stars. People view politics as intimidating and uninviting. They become involved only when their personal lives or interests are threatened. One reason for this discontent may be that people do not feel like they have a voice in government and that government is too bureaucratic. It is possible that third party politics will renew people's interest. For example, in the 1992 election, Ross Perot carried no state but received 19 percent of the vote. He gave a populist message by attacking government as being too big, too distant, and too bureaucratic.

Critical Questions

CQ: (page 277)   How can a charismatic political leader further his or her political agenda in a way that other leaders whose authority is based on the traditional or legal-rational cannot?

As always in critical thinking, you must first become familiar with the key terms in the question. Review the section in your text that presents charismatic, traditional and legal-rational authority (pages 275-276). What are the advantages and disadvantages of each? What qualifications must one have in order to obtain each type of authority? What constraints, if any, are placed on each type of authority? Which type does society have the least control over? Why? What impact does this have on an authority figure's ability to motivate people to take action for a particular cause? Can you think of examples of individuals that fit each of these types? What effect did each of these people have on their followers?

CQ: (page 283)   To what extent do you feel that the international community has the right to sanction other states that violate the human rights of their citizens? What should such sanctions consist of?

This question has the potential for a great deal of misunderstanding because answering it requires many assumptions. To alleviate this problem, you must determine your assumptions by defining terms. First, what are human rights? Second, how do you define the international community? Does it include all states in the world, developed countries, countries with standing armies, your country, or a sample of countries? What types of individuals should sit on the international community, government or military leaders, common people, educated elites? Third, how much must a state violate human rights in order to be sanctioned? Should a state be punished for unfairly imprisoning one person, for executing a small group of innocent citizens, for killing a group because of their ethnic identity? What evidence would be required as proof of human rights violation? Can the international community base their decision on rumor or is hard evidence necessary? Finally, what should the punishments be? Should they vary depending upon the extent of the violation? Are all states subject to these rules, even if they do not have representatives on the international committee that makes decisions regarding human rights violations?

CQ: (page293)   What political socialization have you received? Has your family been a significant influence (pro or con) on your political views? What about television?

Define political socialization and review the discussion in your text on page 292. What agents of political socialization do symbolic interactionists identify? Did you receive political socialization from all of these sources? If so, how? Did your family discuss politics over the dinner table while you were growing up? Did you watch and discuss the news together? Now look at the chart on page 284. How do you define your political position? Do you vote along party lines, along issues, or along candidate personalities? How does this compare to the behavior of your parents? What about your siblings? Are your close friends of the same political persuasion as you? Do you discuss politics frequently with your friends?

Self-Test Questions
Multiple Choice

1. What is the term for the ability to achieve one's ends despite resistance?
   a. influence
   b. power
   c. persuasion
   d. all of the above

2. Democracy in general came with the emergence of which type of society?
   a. hunting and gathering
   b. agricultural
   c. horticultural
   d. industrial

3. The political order ultimately rests on which base?
   a. consent of the governed
   b. power
   c. the economy
   d. quality of leadership

4. Which type of authority is rarely questioned, difficult to change, and has a near-sacred quality?
   a. traditional
   b. charismatic
   c. legal-rational
   d. coercion

5. Which type of power did Max Weber define as illegitimate?
   a. traditional
   b. charismatic
   c. legal-rational
   d. coercion

6. The President of the United States has specific powers which are specifically and formally defined and do not accompany him once he leaves office. Which type of power does the president have?
   a. traditional
   b. charismatic
   c. legal-rational
   d. coercion

7. Which is NOT a characteristic of charismatic authority?
   a. it is an illegitimate power
   b. it is based in an individual's personal characteristics
   c. individuals with this power often lead revolutions
   d. it cannot easily be transferred from one person to another

8. Which of the following is a system in which political power is passed from person to person on the basis of hereditary claims?
    a. power elite
    b. monarchy
    c. charismatic
    d. kinship

9. What is the term for an abstract description, constructed from a number of cases, that reveals the essential feature of a concept?
    a. ideal type
    b. working model
    c. theoretical construct
    d. social construction

10. What is the highest political authority within a given territory?
    a. monarch
    b. nation
    c. power elite
    d. state

11. Which is NOT a characteristic of an authoritarian state?
    a. the government is not very interested in people's daily lives
    b. people are excluded from the process of government
    c. the government does not tolerate much opposition
    d. the government exerts complete control over people's lives

12. Japan is a homogeneous country with a common culture and its territory incorporates and represents this culture. Which term best describes Japan?
    a. state
    b. nation-state
    c. nation
    d. none of the above

13. At one time, the Iroquois of the Northeast lived in a specific territory and shared a common history, culture, and identity. They were a:
    a. state
    b. nation
    c. government
    d. political order

14. Which process is NOT involved in defining a group as "they" during times of political upheaval?
    a. treating members of the groups as less than human
    b. blaming the other group for starting the conflict
    c. labeling the other group as evil
    d. all of the above are involved in the definition of "they"

15. Which best describes third parties in the United States?
    a. they have a good record in terms of winning elections
    b. their candidates seldom win elections
    c. they usually do well in state elections but not in national elections
    d. they have done well in times of social turmoil but not in times of social stability

Chapter 10 The Political Order

16 What is the term for the official statement of the ideology, goals, and plans that a party will implement if its candidates are elected to office?
   a. party platform
   b. political ideology
   c. statement of beliefs
   d. party philosophy

17. Which is NOT true of political parties?
   a. they are an important basis for forming coalitions
   b. they sometimes conflict over issues
   c. they employ lobbyists to influence government policies
   d. they attempt to legitimately influence government policy

18. What is the term for professionals who are hired to attempt to influence members of Congress to vote for certain bills?
   a. political action committees
   b. special interest groups
   c. lobbyists
   d. power elite

19. Which model stresses that the United States is controlled by leaders of the military, the government, and business?
   a. pluralist
   b. conflict
   c. power elite
   d. functionalist

20. In the interest of public health, the American Medical Association works to block the actions of tobacco companies. The AMA is called a:
   a. veto group
   b. PAC
   c. power elite
   d. lobbyist

21. Which is NOT a function of the political order according to functionalist theory?
   a. joining alliances with other states
   b. directing the economic, social, and political order
   c. maintaining order, even if force is necessary
   d. teaching people political attitudes, values, and beliefs in order to achieve consensus

22. Which is NOT true of conflict theory?
   a. it recognizes that groups compete for resources
   b. it recognizes that the tools of democracy prevent power from concentrating in the hands of a few
   c. it states that the poor do not have the ability to compete for resources
   d. it proposes that groups with the ability to raise large sums of money tend to have more influence over government policy than groups that cannot raise money

Chapter 10 The Political Order

23. Which sociological perspective argues that political parties are more than just formal organizations; they are also ideas in people's minds and part of their social identities?
   a. functionalism
   b. conflict
   c. symbolic interaction
   d. rational choice

True - False

T	F	1. Power is a valuable resource in every society.
T	F	2. When a person wielding power has a legitimate right to do so it is called authority.
T	F	3. Most communal societies are ruled by legal-rational authority.
T	F	4. A society cannot contain legal-rational, traditional, and charismatic authority at the same time.
T	F	5. Monarchies are often the governing bodies of totalitarian states.
T	F	6. The junta is a form of authoritarian government.
T	F	7. Totalitarian governments are more oppressive than authoritarian governments.
T	F	8. Many totalitarian governments hold elections
T	F	9. Some nations do not have their own states.
T	F	10. There are more members of Congress than there are lobbyists.
T	F	11. Women are more likely to vote than men.
T	F	12. According to the power elite model, democracy in the United States works as it was intended to work.
T	F	13. Too much pluralism in a society leads to poor leadership, a lack of coordination, and a lack of focus.
T	F	14. The pluralist model recognizes that some people in society have considerably more power than others.
T	F	15. It is possible that the development of a third party would increase American's interest in the political system.

SELF-TEST ANSWERS

Multiple Choice

1. b (274)	6. c (275)	11. d (277)	16. a (285)	21. d (290)
2. d (274)	7. a (276)	12. b (279)	17. c (284)	22. b (291)
3. b (274)	8. b (277)	13. b (279)	18. c (285)	23. c (292)
4. a (275)	9. a (277)	14. d (280)	19. c (287)	
5. d (275)	10. d (277)	15. b (283)	20. a (289)	

True - False

1. T (274)	4. F (276)	7. T (278)	10. F (285)	13. T (289)
2. T (274)	5. F (277)	8. T (278)	11. T (287)	14. T (289)
3. F (275)	6. T (278)	9. T (279)	12. F (288)	15. T (294)

Chapter 11

Marriage and the Family

THE GREAT SOCIAL TRANSFORMATION AND MARRIAGE AND THE FAMILY

TYPES OF FAMILIES

MARRIAGE AND KINSHIP
Kinship Patterns
Marriage
Romantic Love
Courtship
Dimensions of Marriage and the Family

ALTERNATIVE FAMILY FORMS IN THE UNITED STATES
Serial Monogamy
The Single-Parent Family
Gay Male and Lesbian Families
Cohabitation
Independent Living

RACIAL AND ETHNIC VARIATIONS IN FAMILY FORMS
The African-American Family
The Mexican-American Family

ISSUES IN MARRIAGE AND THE FAMILY
Marital Dissolution
Explaining Marital Dissolution
Domestic Violence

SOCIOLOGICAL ANALYSIS OF MARRIAGE AND THE FAMILY
The Functionalist Perspective
The Conflict Perspective
The Symbolic Interactionist Perspective

MARRIAGE AND THE FAMILY IN THE TWENTY-FIRST CENTURY

CRITICAL QUESTIONS
Romantic love and endogamy
Typical American family and alternatives
Domestic violence

SELF TEST QUESTIONS/ANSWERS

CHAPTER SUMMARY AND KEY TERMS

Marriage and the Family and the Great Social Transformation

Family The opening story of Albert and Lisa illustrates a traditional family: a mother, father, and children living under the same roof. But defining the family is not always that easy. Sociologists have identified several factors that serve as a basis for defining the family. In short, sociologists define the **family** as a group of individuals who are related in some way, who usually live together, engage in sex, have responsibility for rearing children, and function as an economic unit.

GST and the family Family structure changed a great deal as societies moved from communal to associational. Before industrialization, rural households performed a wide variety of functions and often contained many people such as servants, apprentices, orphaned children, elders, and live-in boarders. Family size decreased as people began to move to cities to take advantage of job opportunities. In urban industrial societies, bureaucracies provide many of the services formerly provided by families. This leaves individuals more freedom to establish intimate relationships with a single person. Changing family functions have also affected child rearing. In preindustrial societies, parenting roles were intermixed with social and economic roles. Children were considered economic assets and members of the work force. Adolescence was not considered a distinct stage of development. Family members participated in common economic activities which blurred the distinctions between age categories and gender categories. As a result of industrialization, the family ceased to be a work unit and in most cases, limited its economic activities to consumption and child care.

Types of Families

Nuclear family The family is the solution to a problem faced by all societies: that the continuation of society depends on replacing the population with children. These children require years of socialization, support, and protection. The family is the social unit which fulfills this responsibility. In industrialized societies, the most common type of family is the **nuclear family**: a unit composed of a husband, a wife, and their children. Most people belong to two families. The **family of orientation** is the nuclear family into which one is born. The **family of procreation** is the nuclear family which one makes with one's spouse and then having children.

Blended family A variation on the nuclear family is the **blended** or **reconstituted family** in which spouses and their children from former marriages live together as a single nuclear family. The blended family is not new. In times when the death rate was high, widows and widowers with children were common. When they remarried they created a blended family.

Binuclear family Today, divorce has resulted in the **binuclear family**, in which each divorced parent establishes a separate household and the children spend time in both.

Extended family The **extended family** is composed of two or more generations of kin who function as an independent social and economic unit. Extended families are the basic social unit of traditional societies.

Marriage and Kinship

Systems of kinship and marriage vary widely across the world. For instance, Nayar girls from India marry before they reach adolescence. Once married, the Nayar wife will probably never see her husband again. When she matures, she lives on her own in a hut near her brothers and takes lovers from the Nambudiri, a rich and powerful tribe that lives nearby. She has children by Nambudiri men, but the biological fathers have nothing to do with their offspring. The mother raises the children while her brothers assume the economic responsibilities. This arrangement is advantageous to both groups. The Nambudiri remain wealthy by passing their wealth to their eldest sons. The eldest son can only marry a Nambudiri woman. This keeps the wealth among the Nambudiri. The Nayar like this arrangement because the children are raised by the mother without interference from the outside.

Kinship	Almost every individual has a system of **kinship**: a network of people who are related by marriage, blood, or social practice (such as adoption). Kinship allows a society to perpetuate itself over time. It does this in two ways. First, children in all societies must be socialized. Property, wealth, and power must be passed through the generations. Kinship fills these needs and provides continuity over generations. Second, kinship allows a society to perpetuate itself over time by creating complex social bonds. A marriage uniting members from different families creates **affinal relationships**: social bonds based on marriage. Affinal relationships may unite hundreds of people. In the United States, kin typically include one's families of procreation and of orientation along with grandparents, aunts, uncles, and cousins. For the most part, all other relatives are treated as non-kin.
Marriage	**Marriage** is a relationship that results when two individuals become involved in a socially-approved relationship that involves intimate, mutual long-term obligations, and when they have fulfilled the customary or legal requirements. Every society has rituals and laws that define a valid marriage. In most societies people marry for practical reasons such as wealth or power. People marry for love only in a small minority of societies (including the United States).
Romantic love	**Romantic love** is an emotional identification between two individuals that is so intense that they are convinced that they cannot be happy without each other. Romantic love was recognized during the nineteenth century but it was not accepted as an important consideration in marriage. Today, romantic love is more valued as a basis for marriage in societies with weak extended family ties. It continues to be less valued in traditional societies where kinship networks reinforce the relationship between spouses. Romantic love provides an incentive to marry in industrial societies. Romantic love also provides support in times of stress. It also helps transfer commitment from the family of orientation to the family of procreation.
Courtship	**Courtship** is the relationship between people who are preparing for marriage to each other. Overwhelmingly, people choose a spouse of their own race, ethnicity, religion, and social class. This is called **endogamy**. When they marry outside their own group, they are engaging in **exogamy**. Several social forces cause people to marry individuals like themselves. They are as follows: • *Propinquity*. Propinquity, or physical closeness, constrains romantic love for the simple reason that people cannot fall in love unless they meet, and they are unlikely to meet if they are far apart. For this reason, people tend to choose a spouse from neighbors, co-workers, and classmates. In these groups, people are likely to meet others like themselves. This promotes endogamy. • *Ethnicity and Race*. Members of racial and ethnic groups usually marry within their own group. Less than 2 percent of whites are married to blacks. Marriage among ethnic groups is more common. For example, 60 percent of Irish Americans and 75 percent of Italian Americans marry someone from another ethnic group. • *Values*. Marital endogamy is reinforced by the values of American culture. For example, television advertisements depict same-race couples. Family and friends also reinforce endogamy by negatively sanctioning those who marry outside the group. Despite these factors, exogamy is increasing in American society.
Male/female patterns	The basic biological unit of a family is the mother and her children. Given this fact, all societies must determine how to fit the man into the family unit. Societies have developed the following resolutions to this problem. • *Limited Marriage Patterns*. Western societies favor **monogamy**, a marriage consisting of one male spouse and one female spouse. Some societies favor marriages containing a number of spouses. This is called **polygamy**. There are three types of polygamy: *polygyny*, one husband and two or more wives; and *polyandry*, one wife and two or more husbands; and *group marriage*, several wives and several husbands. In the nineteenth century, Mormons in the United States practiced polygyny. All forms of polygamy are now illegal in the United States. In most societies, the motivation for having more than one wife is economic and political rather than sexual. About three-fourths of all societies favor a form of marriage other than monogamy. But

Chapter 11 Marriage and the Family

most men in the world only have one wife. This is because the most populous societies are monogamous and where polygyny is practiced, it is practiced by only wealthy men who can support multiple wives..

• *Descent.* Every society has norms regarding **descent**, the system by which kinship is traced over generations. This tells people who their relatives are and who they are responsible for and obligated to. *Patrilineal descent* is kinship and inheritance that is passed through the man's side of the family. In *matrilineal descent*, kinship and inheritance are passed through the woman's side of the family. In *bilineal descent* they are passed through both sides. Unlike most societies, the United States supports bilineal descent.

• *Residence.* Societies must develop norms about where married couples should live. In a *matrilocal* arrangement, the couple lives with or near the wife's mother. In *patrilocal* systems they live with or near the husband's father. In *neolocal* systems, the couple establishes their own, independent housing apart from the relatives. In recent years, a new form of neolocal residence has emerged. Due to job locations, some married couples occupy separate residences in different cities and reunite only on weekends. This is called a *bilocal* household.

• *Power.* A family system in which a man (usually the husband or eldest male) has the most power is called a *patriarchy*. Historically, this has been the dominant pattern. Although a society theoretically could vest most of the family power in women, a system known as *matriarchy*, no known society has ever been truly matriarchal. Family systems in which women hold some power are common. These are called *matricentric* families. Matricentric clans were common among Native Americans before the coming of white settlers. The Creek Indians of Florida were one example.

Alternative Family Forms

The family has been one of the most stable institutions in American history. But its form has changed. In 1970 only one in three American households consisted of a married couple with children under 18 (a "traditional" family). Marriage continues to be strongly related to families, however, as 77 percent of families still include a married couple. Alternative family forms include:

• *Serial monogamy.* American culture and law do permit a person to have more than one spouse, but not at the same time—a pattern called **serial monogamy**. A person can marry, divorce, and remarry without limit. This is now very common, as 46 percent of all marriages in a given year involve a bride or groom (or both) who were married previously. Serial monogamy is popular because marriage is popular.

• *Single parent family.* Single-parent families are another alternative family form. In 1995 there were 9.9 million single-parent families in the United States. This is the second most common family form after the traditional family. Single-parenthood affects women more negatively than men as women experience a 27 percent decrease in standard of living while men experience a 10 percent increase. This is because women typically earn less than men and women do not accumulate as much economic security. Today, about one-fifth of poor families consist of a single mother and her children. Poverty is striking women and children disproportionately, and thus becoming *feminized*.

• *Gay male and lesbian families.* Gays and lesbians are now openly establishing families. At Stanford University gay and lesbian student couples have the same housing, health care, and campus privileges as married students. With few exceptions, however, most religious bodies will not perform marriage ceremonies for a gay or lesbian couple. Legal issues, such as automatic inheritance, concerning gay and lesbian couples is unclear in many states. Some cities such as Seattle and San Francisco have passed legislation that permit gay and lesbian couples to declare publicly and legally that they are "domestic partners." This allows them many of the same rights as married couples.

• *Cohabitation.* When partners share a household and engage in intimate social and sexual relations without being formally married, they are engaging in **cohabitation**. It can be divided into several types. One is "part-time" or "limited" cohabitation in which partners may stay together several nights a week but live in their own residences. These relationships tend to be casual and often last less than six months. "Trial marriage" is a second type. Here the couple lives together and establishes a relationship similar to those in a conventional marriage. The third type is "substitute marriage" in which the partners are not legally married but in all other respects behave as a traditional husband and wife. About two million American couples are cohabiting. It is particularly popular among the young. Almost half of cohabiting couples expect to eventually marry their partner. The law now recognizes that cohabiting partners might have a claim on their partner's assets. This is called palimony. Before the 1960s cohabitation was illegal in most places. It is more widely accepted today but critics state that it weakens family ties. People who cohabitate before marriage are also more likely to get divorced than those who do not.

• *Independent living.* One of the fastest-growing segments of the American population consists of people who live by themselves. Their number has increased from 11 million in 1970 to 25 million today. The majority of these people range from 25 to 54 years of age. This trend is increasing because young people are postponing marriage. The average age at first marriage is 27 for men and 25 for women. Older people are also living alone after the death of a spouse. People also often live alone for a while after divorce. American culture is becoming more accepting of single adulthood as a normal state of living. Because women live longer than men, they constitute 60 percent of those who live alone.

Racial and Ethnic Variations in Family Forms

Race and ethnicity are powerful forces that shape American social institutions , therefore, family forms have differing characteristics in racial and ethnic groups. Two differences are illustrated by African Americans and Mexican American families.

• *African-American families.* Many African Americans live in poverty. As a result, they often have more difficulty than white families in forming a traditional family. Only 46 percent of African Americans live in households consisting of a married couple with both spouses present. This compares with 81 percent for the whites. Many African-American children live in female-headed households. In 1960 Daniel Moynihan argued that the African-American family was a product of slavery and was therefore matricentric. He then stated that this was dysfunctional in modern American society because it produces a continual stream of deviance, poverty, and welfare dependency. He predicted that these problems would worsen over time. His critics charged that Moynihan was "blaming the victim" for problems that were caused by racism. Moynihan's idea that slavery produced matricentric families is incorrect as black families were composed of a husband and wife after slavery. The matricentric family developed later. Also, social scientists believe that matricentric families are not a problem in themselves. Rather, poverty is the problem. Today the African-American population is dividing into the "haves" and the "have nots." About one-third of African Americans have reached middle-class standing, and their family structure resembles that found in the broader society. Lower-class black families are often isolated in neighborhoods filled with crime and drugs. These people have few resources to achieve upward mobility.

• *Mexican-American families.* Mexican Americans (Chicanos) also suffer much discrimination and live in segregated neighborhoods. Since many also live near Mexico, the continual stream of new immigrants results in a relatively slow process of change in Chicano families. Chicano families display three major characteristics which originated during the Spanish colonial period in Mexico and the United States. First, Mexican Americans are very family-oriented. They value the family over the individual. They maintain extended families that include aunts, uncles, cousins, grandparents, and *compadres*—persons outside the family who are chosen to be godparents of the family's children. Patriarchy is a second characteristic. This is closely related to the Hispanic concept of **machismo**, a value system embracing highly masculine behaviors and including a "double standard" in which men are encouraged to engage in sexual relations outside marriage but women are not. Chicana women are considered subordinate to men. Women are responsible for the house and children and are expected to serve the men. The third characteristic of Chicano families is authoritarian child rearing. Chicano fathers are strict with their children and act as the final disciplinary authority. The Chicano family is child-centered. Children develop a strong sense of ethnic belonging and identity by age five or six. Today, with many Mexican-

American women entering the labor force, patriarchy is declining among Mexican-American families.

Issues in the Family

As a basic institution in society, problems in marriage and families become a social concern. Marital dissolution and domestic violence are two major social issues in American families.

Divorce and desertion

Marital dissolution is common in contemporary society. Today, 50 percent of all American marriages end in divorce after seven years. **Divorce** is the dissolution of the legal ties that bind a married couple, but socially it constitutes the recognition that the marriage is over. A *legal separation* is an arrangement whereby spouses agree to take up separate residences. In contrast, an *informal separation* is not recognized by law, but is very common. **Desertion** is the social dissolution of marriage that occurs when one spouse leaves the other or simply walks away from the marriage for a prolonged period. Teenagers are prone to divorce because they often have short courtships and do not know each other very well. They are also often financially insecure. African Americans have a higher divorce rate than whites. This is mainly due to poor economic conditions. Divorce is very low among Asian Americans because it stigmatizes the families. The following factors explain marital dissolution.

• *Society.* In an extended family system, marriage represents the union of kinship lines. Divorce is discouraged or prohibited because it would destroy many of these relationships. In a nuclear family system, however, only the wife, husband, and children are directly affected. This makes marital dissolution much more acceptable.

• *Falling out of Love.* People are expected to marry for love in industrial societies. But romantic love is passionate and unpredictable. When people fall out of love, they may conclude that they no longer have any reason to remain married.

• *Women's Changing Roles.* The changing status of women has also contributed to the increased acceptance of marital dissolution and has reduced the social pressure to marry. Financial security was a primary reason women remained married even if they no longer wanted to be married. This is less a factor today with so many women in the labor force.

• *Domestic violence.* Families are often shattered by domestic violence. It is estimated that about 500,000 cases of spouse abuse occur each year. Women are the victims more often than men. But there are as many wives that kill their husbands as husbands who kill their wives. Often, though, wives kill their husbands in self-defense. The most common form of spouse abuse is battery with fists or weapons. Between 2,000 and 4,000 women are beaten to death by their husbands each year. This is more prevalent than car accidents, rape, or mugging. Lower- and working-class men often punch their wives in the face, leaving visible traces of abuse. Middle- and upper-class men attack the torso and other body parts that are not visible to casual observers. Fear that their husbands will harm their relatives or children is one reason abused women stay with their husbands. Abused wives also often have no other place to go. They may believe that a failed marriage is their fault and that they can change their husband's behavior. Often, too, they have been socialized into playing the part of the victim. The prevalence of wife abuse is becoming more widely known and steps are being taken to alleviate it. Spouse abuse is found throughout the world.

Sociological Analysis of the Family

Functionalist perspective

The functionalist perspective states that the family serves the following functions:

• *Socialization.* Human infants need to be supported for many years. In all societies, the family solves this problem.

• *Replacement of Members and Regulation of Sexual Behavior.* Societies require procreation in order to survive. Therefore all societies must have norms regarding sexual behavior. Family or kin encourage or require individuals to choose their mates from a pool of people with certain characteristics.

- *Economic Functions.* Family assets are passed from parent to children through custom and law. This can result in a great deal of wealth. The family is also embedded in the economic processes of production and consumption. For example, food and shelter are purchased for the family rather than for individuals.
- *Support and Comfort.* For most people, families are a source of support and comfort. Family members count on each other to help out financially in times of need and socially in times of stress.
- *Social Placement.* Children inherit their parents' social class, religion, ethnicity, and place in society.

Conflict perspective

Conflict theorists emphasize the power relationships that exist within the family, the family's role in perpetuating social inequality based on ascribed status, and the dominance of men over women. A study by Friedrich Engels in 1902 stated that agrarian societies were productive enough to generate a surplus. This was controlled by men who became leaders, financiers, and power brokers while women were confined to the areas of childbearers, domestic workers, and providers of sex to men. This resulted in a system of patriarchy that permeated all of industrial society. Engels emphasized that monogamous marriage was essential for inheritance. In contrast, many contemporary conflict theorists state that men's size, strength, and aggressiveness first allowed them to dominate women. Female sexuality became a man's property, and the right to this property became the defining characteristic of a marriage. Critics state that many women find marriage and family life attractive and that conflict theory overemphasizes people's desire for absolute equality.

Symbolic interactionist perspective

Symbolic interactionists state that the family does not exist as an ideal type but that it is constantly being recreated through the members' daily interaction with each other. The family is a source of major roles and identities. These become part of an individual's self concept and help to define the relationships to others. Traditional marriage involves both the taking of the new role and the making of the role into one that is more personalized. Although couples never develop a unified view of their married life, they do develop a common memory and biography over time.

Marriage and the Family in the Twenty-First Century

There is much controversy over this topic today. *Traditionalists* value an idealized family form and believe that families should be male-dominated. These people support government policies designed to prevent alternative family forms. On the other side, the *progressives* view the traditional family as one of many alternatives. These people tend to favor a more equal sharing of household tasks and believe that men should be more involved in childrearing. They seek a view of the family that includes childless couples, homosexual families, cohabitors, and serial monogamists. The future of the American family depends largely upon which of these groups wins the debate.

Critical Questions

CQ: (page 306)   Why does American society emphasize romantic love but practice endogamy?

Before answering this question, define the key terms romantic love and endogamy. Why do Americans tend to marry within their own racial and ethnic groups? (Hint: review the "Courtship" section in your text). What is the most important factor contributing to individuals' choices of dating partners? How does this relate to endogamy? Do you think people consciously choose to date people of their own racial or ethnic groups or does this happen automatically due to the characteristics of those with whom people surround themselves? Is this the same for people of different religions and for members of different classes? Think of your own life. Are most of your dates members of your racial or ethnic group? What about your neighbors, classmates, and co-workers? What are the social sanctions for dating or marrying exogamously? What is the source of these attitudes? Do you predict any changes in patterns of endogamy in the next decade? If so, what are they and what forces are causing the changes?

CQ: (page 310)   Is there a typical American family? Do alternative family forms provide the same functions as the traditional family? Why or why not?

To answer this question, first review the discussion of alternative family forms and the functions of families in your text. Then make a chart with alternative family types down the side and functions across the top. Fill in the chart by answering the question, "How does this family type fill this function?" Also indicate if the family type does not fill the function. Now examine the family forms that successfully fill the functions. What do they have in common? How are they different? Do these families have any advantages over the traditional family? Do they have any disadvantages? Now consider, if applicable, the family types that fail to fill any or all of the functions. What characteristics of that family type put its members at a disadvantage? How do you think a member of this type of family would respond? Would they agree with your assessment? Why or why not? What assumptions are you applying to the question which affect your responses? Do you view one family type as superior over others? If so, what is your evidence? (Remember that personal experience is beneficial in giving you exposure to a situation but it is not evidence).

CQ: (page 316)   In your judgment, is violence in the family a cause for alarm in society? To what extent should society become involved in attempting to limit domestic violence?

First, review the section on domestic violence in your text. Are you surprised by the amount of domestic violence that occurs each year in the United States? If so, did you think it occurred more or less frequently? Americans place a very high value on privacy. How much legal intervention would Americans tolerate in order to decrease domestic violence? Should abusers be given mandatory prison sentences regardless of their spouses' willingness to press charges? Should the police use a less formal mechanism of control such as publishing the abuser's picture in the local newspaper? Would middle and upper class abusers tolerate such public scrutiny or do they have resources and power to prevent such actions? How would the public react to this? Should Americans focus on the abuser and the abused equally? How should child abuse cases be handled? What constitutes sufficient evidence of abuse? Should children be removed from their abusive homes? Should their families receive government-funded counseling? Should abusive parents be allowed to have more children?

Self-Test Questions
Multiple Choice

1. A group of individuals who are related in some way, who usually live together, have responsibility for rearing children, and function as an economic unit are called a:
    a. family
    b. clan
    c. kinship
    d. cohabiting unit

2. What changes in the family occurred as a result of the Great Social Transformation?
    a. its economic activity became limited to consumption
    b. its size decreased
    c. adolescence became a distinctive stage
    d. all of the above occurred as the result of the GST

3. Joe grew up with his parents and his sisters. Which type of family is this?
    a. family of procreation
    b. blended family
    c. reconstituted family
    d. family of orientation

4. Mary and her sons and Ted and his daughters formed a family. Which term describes their family?
   a. extended family
   b. blended family
   c. family of orientation
   d. bilocal family

5. Which type of society is organized by elaborate family networks?
   a. familial
   b. extended
   c. traditional
   d. modern

6. What is the term for social bonds based on a marriage?
   a. kinship
   b. affinal relationships
   c. family
   d. communal relationships

7. Individuals tend to choose prospective spouses from neighbors, co-workers, and classmates due to:
   a. propinquity
   b. affinal
   c. endogamy
   d. exogamy

8. Which is NOT a reason that most people engage in endogamy in the United States?
   a. people tend to marry within their own racial/ethnic group
   b. people tend to fall in love with people who are in close physical proximity to them
   c. the media reinforces endogamy
   d. all of the above are reasons people in the United States engage in endogamy

9. A marriage consisting of one male spouse and one female spouse is:
   a. polyandry
   b. conventional
   c. monogamy
   d. binuclear

10. When a Toda woman (India) marries a Toda man, she becomes the wife of all of his brothers as well. This system is called:
    a. serial monogamy
    b. polyandry
    c. group marriage
    d. polygyny

11. Shannon and Chris got married and moved into an apartment down the street from Shannon's parents. This pattern of residence is called:
    a. matrilocal
    b. neolocal
    c. patrilocal
    d. bilocal

12. In American society, a married couple with children under the age of 18 is considered which type of family?
    a. small
    b. traditional
    c. modern
    d. disappearing

13. Actress Elizabeth Taylor has been married and divorced eight times. She practices which of the following?
    a. serial monogamy
    b. polygamy
    c. polyandry
    d. cohabitation

14. The second most common type of family after the traditional family is the:
    a. divorced couple
    b. single parent
    c. binuclear
    d. gay

15. Which of the following is true of homosexual partners?
    a. lesbian couples tend to be faithful
    b. gay male partners often have sexual relations outside the family setting
    c. courts sometimes grant custody of children to a lesbian in a stable relationship
    d. all of the above are true

16. When a married couple has separate residences but unites on weekends and vacations, they are:
    a. in a trial marriage
    b. in a bilocal pattern of residence
    c. not legally married
    d. in a limited cohabitation arrangement

17. Which is NOT true of African-American families?
    a. they are headed by single parents more often than white families
    b. they tend to be more matricentric than white families
    c. they are more patriarchal than Mexican-American families
    d. many African-American men cannot provide for their families because they have been denied well-paying jobs

18. What is the term for the Hispanic value system that prizes highly masculine behavior, often at the expense of women?
    a. compadrazgo
    b. barrio
    c. machismo
    d. muchacho

19. Which is NOT an explanation for marital dissolutions?
    a. women's roles are changing
    b. divorces are fairly easy to get
    c. people fall out of love
    d. domestic violence

20. Which of the following groups has the lowest divorce rate in America?
    a. whites
    b. African Americans
    c. Hispanic Americans
    d. Asian Americans

21. According to functionalist theory, which is NOT a function of the family?
    a. regulation of sexual behavior
    b. social placement
    c. male dominance
    c. socialization of children

22. Which theory argues that the family perpetuates social inequality based on ascribed characteristics?
    a. functionalism
    b. conflict
    c. symbolic interactionism
    d. rational choice

23. Which sociological perspective fails to realize that women find marriage and family life attractive even though they are usually burdened with most of the housework?
    a. functionalism
    b. conflict
    c. symbolic interactionism
    d. rational choice

24. Which sociological perspective argues that the family exists not as some ideal type, but as people who make decisions daily as they deal with one another?
    a. functionalism
    b. conflict
    c. symbolic interactionism
    d. rational choice

True - False

T	F	1. The family is an economic unit.
T	F	2. Traditional societies have traditional small nuclear families as each person's most important kin relationship..
T	F	3. A family composed of two or more generations of kin who function as an independent social and economic unit is called an extended family.
T	F	4. Kinship is the network of people who are related by marriage, blood, or social practice.
T	F	5. Marriage is a state that occurs when two individuals are involved in a socially-approved relationship that involves intimate, mutual long-term obligations, and have fulfilled the customary ceremonial or legal requirements.
T	F	6. Romantic love is more highly valued as a reason for marriage in societies with weak extended family ties.
T	F	7. Nick is a white-American and his wife, Maria, is a Cuban-American. They are an endogamous couple.
T	F	8. Polygamy has always been illegal in the United States.
T	F	9. Independent living has decreased in the United States since 1970.
T	F	10. Chicano families are very authoritarian but child centered.

T	F	11. Divorce is the dissolution of the legal ties that bind a married couple; socially it constitutes the recognition that the marriage is over.
T	F	12. Each year in the United States, more women are beaten by their husbands than are injured in car accidents.
T	F	13. Low- and working-class wife abusers tend to hit their wives in more visible places than do middle- and upper-class wife abusers.
T	F	14. Functionalists argue that all societies have norms and mores to regulate sexual behavior so that societies will procreate in an orderly way.
T	F	15. The future of the American family largely depends on who wins the cultural debate Progressives or the Traditionalists.

Self-Test Answers

Multiple Choice

1. a (297)	6. b (300)	11. b (306)	16. b (306)	21. c (317)
2. d (298)	7. a (304)	12. b (306)	17. c (311)	22. b (318)
3. d (299)	8. d (304)	13. a (307)	18. c (312)	23. b (319)
4. b (299)	9. c (304)	14. b (307)	19. d (314)	24. c (319)
5. c (300)	10. b (305)	15. d (309)	20. d (313)	

True - False

1. T (297)	4. T (300)	7. F (304)	10. T (312)	13. T (315)
2. F (300)	5. T (301)	8. F (304)	11. T (313)	14. T (317)
3. T (299)	6. T (303)	9. F (309)	12. T (315)	15. T (322)

NOTES FOR FUTURE REVIEW AND STUDY:

Chapter 12

Education

THE GREAT SOCIAL TRANSFORMATION AND EDUCATION

CROSS-CULTURAL COMPARISONS: THE UNITED STATES AND JAPAN
> *Education in the United States*
> *Education in Japan*

EDUCATION AND MINORITY ISSUES
> *The Coleman Report and Unequal Education*
> *Mandatory Busing to End Segregation*
> *The Language of Instruction*
> *Testing and Educational Inequality*
> *The Debate over Cultural Literacy*
> *Tracking and Educational Inequality*
> *Gender Bias*
> *Freedom of Choice*

SOCIOLOGICAL ANALYSIS OF EDUCATION
> *The Functionalist Perspective*
> *The Conflict Perspective*
> *The Symbolic Interactionist Perspective*

EDUCATION IN THE TWENTY-FIRST CENTURY

CRITICAL QUESTIONS
> *Year round school attendance*
> *Bilingual education*
> *Tracking*

SELF TEST QUESTIONS/ANSWERS

Chapter 12 Education

CHAPTER SUMMARY AND KEY TERMS

The Great Social Transformation and Education

The opening story tells of Eugene Lang who grew up in Harlem and later received a scholarship and graduated from college. When giving the sixth grade commencement address to the public elementary school he attended, Lang realized that hard work alone would not get the kids graduated from high school, out of the ghetto, and onto college. Because they were embedded in an environment of poverty, crime, and drugs, the odds were set against them. Lang started the I Have a Dream Foundation which provided college scholarships and guidance to these inner-city kids. The project was an enormous success. Lang concluded that the major problems these kids faced was a lack of support to guide them through school. The sociological moral to this story is that dropping out of school and getting swallowed by a hostile environment has a lot to do with the economic and social resources available to young people and little to do with their innate abilities.

Education   **Education** is the transfer of the knowledge, values, and beliefs of a society from one generation to the next. In communal societies, this occurs mainly through the informal interaction between parents and children. Professional educators came into existence with industrialization. Industrial societies are too complex to adequately educate young people informally. Therefore, industrial societies use a system of **formal education**—the transmission of knowledge, skills, and attitudes from one generation to the next through systematic training. This training usually takes place in organizations that specialize in providing instruction conducted by professional teachers and supervised by professional administrators—that is, **schools**.

Cross-Cultural Comparisons: The United States and Japan

Education in the U.S.   A high cultural value is placed on education in the United States. This is true across all racial and ethnic groups and for women and men alike. Americans see education as necessary for participating in democracy, for righting injustices, and for attaining personal happiness. The United States spends $400 billion each year on education and has the most comprehensive educational system in the world. Americans assume that every citizen has the right to a free primary and secondary education. However, many Americans now feel that our education system is failing. More than 20 percent of 18-year-olds are **functionally illiterate**—unable to read and write well enough to carry out the routines of everyday life. The rate of functional illiteracy may reach 40 percent among disadvantaged minority groups. Much of this is due to dropping out of school which is a major problem in the American educational system especially for some minority groups. The education system in the United States has several unique characteristics:

• *Decentralized Control.* Though the federal government spends a great deal in education, each state is responsible for deciding how to educate its citizens. Within each state, responsibility is also delegated to local communities. There are about 16,000 independent school districts in the United States.

• *Mass Education.* The United States was the first industrial nation to adopt the notion of **mass education**— the idea that everyone is entitled to a certain amount of publicly-provided education and is obligated to obtain it. By 1900 all states required children to attend school. **Mandatory education** had become the norm. Mass education and mandatory education stem from the idea that democracy and education are inseparable and from the work of organized labor and other groups concerned with child welfare. These groups demanded that children attend school rather than work in factories. Another force behind mass education was the factory system which needed workers who were on time, regular in attendance, submissive to authority, and orderly, all of which were learned in school. Lancaster Schools developed nearby and operated like factories. The United States extended the principle of mass education to higher education. Under the Land Grant College Act of 1862 (the Morrill Act), the federal government granted each state 300,000 acres of land for each senator or representative. The states then sold their land to finance the building of "land grant" universities which were initially to be used to teach agriculture and mechanics.

- *Practicality.* American culture emphasizes practicality even in education. As a result, American schools teach subjects related to occupational careers. In a poll of freshmen, half said that they were going to college in order to be well off financially..
- *Credentialism.* Sociologist Randall Collins suggests that in the United States, academic degrees are viewed as credentials that indicate one's qualifications to perform certain jobs. He calls this **credentialism**. Often, a person without the proper degree is not considered for jobs, even though he or she may possess the appropriate skills. Credentialism results in **educational inflation**—the situation in which the credentials required to obtain a job increase while the skills necessary to perform the job remain the same. Many modern jobs are complicated, but the great increase in demand for higher credentials comes more from educational inflation than from increases in job complexity. Many Americans are overeducated for the jobs they hold. This is beneficial in that over-education increases a person's flexibility to change jobs. Education also broadens people's horizons and helps them achieve a more meaningful life.

Education in Japan

Many elements of traditional Japanese culture can be seen in Japan's modern education system. It rests on the traditional values of conformity, selectivity, and standardized planning. Japan's education system looks like a pyramid with many elementary schools supporting a smaller number of academic high schools, which support a tiny number of elite universities. Due to intense competition, only a small percentage of Japanese children who enter preschool will graduate from an elite university. The Japanese believe that all students have the same natural ability and that excellence is achieved through effort. Japanese schools organize children into peer work groups called *han*. Each *han* has a student leader who is responsible for all group members. At age 14 all Japanese students take an exam to determine who goes to an academic high school and who goes to a vocational high school. Those who do not get accepted to an academic high school have almost no chance of getting into college. Many Japanese students attend *juku*—private schools that meet after regular school hours to help them prepare for entrance exams. Students who do not pass the college entrance exams are called *ronin* after the medieval samurai warriors who wandered the countryside without a master. Most ronin study for an additional two years at a private school that specializes in teaching them to pass the exams. During that time their parents often are so embarrassed that they refuse to mention their child's name in public.

Graduation from an elite university is about the only way for Japanese to get jobs in top Japanese corporations. In fact, it practically guarantees a top-level position. Unlike American universities where there is constant evaluation and competition for grades and honors, Japanese universities assume that anyone who passes the entrance exam is qualified to graduate. As a result, Japanese college students often skip classes and fail to turn in assignments and papers.

Japanese society is very patriarchal. Economic opportunities for even well-educated women are more limited than in the United States. Most Japanese women achieve their statuses through their husbands and children. Relatively few Japanese women attend college. Those who do usually attend junior college. Japanese children spend more time in school than American children. At the time of high school graduation, the Japanese student has been in school the equivalent of three to four years more than the American student. Some experts believe that American students make up for this gap in college.

Problems with the Japanese system

For the most part, the Japanese education system is highly regarded. But it does have a few problems. First, the system demands that parents invest a great deal of energy into their children's educations. Mothers are expected to stay home and sacrifice their own identity for that of her children. Second, Japan's system places so much demand on students that the young people must organize their lives around academics. This leaves them little time for sports, dating, and part-time work. Third, the screening examinations make no allowances for the handicapped or the learning-disabled. Finally, students who are left behind are labeled failures and bring shame upon their families.

Education and Minority Issues

With an emphasis on mandatory education and mass education, people in the United States believe that education is the key to individual advancement. As a result of this attitude, issues of fairness and justice are very important. There are a number of issues surrounding education and minority groups.

Coleman Report
- *The Coleman Report.* Americans believe that education is the key to success. Therefore fairness is a very important issue in education. In 1966 sociologist James Coleman published a study of 4,000 American public school and 645,000 students. His study showed that most students attend racially-segregated schools, that predominantly white schools had more educational resources than predominantly black schools, and that African-American students did not perform as well as white students. These findings were not surprising. However, Coleman did find that having an abundance of educational resources did not affect academic performance. The key to superior performance was family background. African-American students performed more poorly because they came from poorer families that did not stress the importance of education. A later study found that students from poor backgrounds benefited greatly from teachers that cared about them, who were well-organized, and who could maintain discipline. Thus, teacher-student interaction and social status affect student performance.

Mandatory busing
- *Mandatory busing.* Historically, the United States has been a very segregated society. So far the only practical way to achieve integration in schools has been to bus students to schools outside of their neighborhoods. Opposition to busing has often been intense. In some communities, it resulted in **white flight**—an upsurge in white families moving to suburban neighborhoods to avoid mandatory busing. White flight had two consequences for schools. First, it increased segregation in many school districts. Leaving many poor minorities behind, this decreases the city's tax base. Schools were spending more on busing and less on classroom instruction. Today, about nine in ten whites believe that students of all races should attend the same schools. However, more than half of whites still oppose mandatory busing. Busing in the United States has failed to produce integration. One-third of African-American children now attend predominantly black schools. Many communities have developed **magnet schools** to integrate their students. These schools offer specialized programs in certain subjects such as math or science.

Language of instruction
- *Language of instruction.* The United States has no official language. But English is usually used in schools. This has become a political issue due to the increasing number of non-English-speaking immigrants. Immigrant children are likely to fall behind if they are placed in special classes while they learn English. But they will also fall behind if they are placed in classes taught in English before they can understand it. One solution is to teach some classes in their native language while they learn English. However, this would place a great burden on schools that are already having financial difficulties. There are also too many language groups in the United States to provide instruction in each. Some critics also argue that multilanguage instruction will encourage immigrants to remain isolated in their ethnic group and that it will fragment American culture into distinct regional and ethnic cultures.

Testing
- *Testing.* Almost two million high school students each year take standardized achievement exams, usually the Scholastic Aptitude Test (SAT) and/or the American Achievement Test (ACT), as part of the process of applying to colleges and universities. The scores vary widely by racial-ethnic background and gender. Asian Americans usually score the highest followed by whites, Native Americans, Mexican Americans, Puerto Rican Americans, and African Americans. Explanations for the differences in scores range from genetics (which most sociologists reject) to cultural factors. No standardized test is free of cultural bias. Some questions assume that the student has a particular set of cultural knowledge. The tests are geared toward middle- or upper-class, English-speaking, well-educated students.

Cultural literacy
- *Cultural literacy.* E.D. Hirsch, Jr. popularized the term **cultural literacy**: the extent to which a person possesses "the basic information needed to thrive in the modern world." Examples in the United States include familiarity with the named John Adams and Susan B. Anthony and the meaning of "e pluribus unum." Hirsch states that cultural literacy is important because it enhances communication and understanding. Without a common culture, unity would erode. Hirsch lays the responsibility for teaching cultural literacy on schools. Cultural literacy has been criticized by **multiculturalists**—individuals who believe that culture should be viewed from the perspective of

different groups. Multiculturalists state that most of the items deemed necessary to learn by cultural literacy advocates are drawn from Western European traditions and reflect the thinking of DWEMs—dead white European males. The viewpoints of racial minorities, women, and members of the lower class are largely ignored. For example, children are taught that Columbus discovered America in 1492 and thus began the development of the New World. Multiculturalists point out that the Americas were already inhabited by native peoples, many with highly complex civilizations.

Tracking

- *Tracking.* Most high schools in the United States **track** students: that is, they assign them to different programs on the basis of their ability or interests. Sometimes these decisions are based on standardized tests that contain cultural assumptions as previously discussed. Schools usually provide three tracks: vocational, general, and college preparatory. Supporters of tracking claim that it uses resources more efficiently because it matches positions in the classroom with individuals' qualifications. Ideally, tracking should occur without concern for race, ethnicity, gender, or class. In reality, however, the poor, women, and minorities are not served by the tracking system.

Gender bias

- *Gender bias.* The American belief that education is the key to success is often applied differently to men and women. Until the 1970s schools prepared women for domestic roles and childbearing by requiring them to take home economics classes. Women were expected to quit their jobs when they married. It was also assumed that women went to college only to find a suitable husband. In early grades, girls and boys show the same ability in math. By high school, girls score lower on standardized tests. Some say that math is labeled "masculine" and therefore girls do not try to excel in it for fear of appearing unattractive to their peers. Also, guidance counselors still often steer girls away from college preparatory classes in math and science. Gender inequality is highly visible at the college level. Even though women make up half of the students, they constitute only one third of the faculty. Women are also underrepresented in physics, math, computer sciences, and biology. However, gender bias may be declining. Gender discrimination is now illegal and schools that receive federal funds must provide equal opportunities for men and women.

Freedom of choice

- *Freedom of choice of schools.* There has recently been a call for parents to have greater choice in selecting schools for their children. One version of this freedom of choice approach would give parents vouchers which they would use to send their child to any school they choose. Currently 62% of Americans favor this approach. One consequence of this system is that money would flow out of the public school system to private schools. It would also do away with the principle of neighborhood schools and of community control of schools. Critics also argue that parents might use the vouchers to send their children to religious schools, which would violate the separation of church and state.

Sociological Analysis of Education

Functionalist perspective

From the functionalist perspective, education helps to maintain an orderly and efficient society in the following ways:

- *Socialization.* In advanced societies the knowledge required to live prosperously is so great that a system of formal education develops to help children prepare for their adult roles. In addition to teaching specific subjects, schools also teach the **hidden curriculum**: the dominant cultural values and norms of the society which are taught unconsciously. For example, teachers teach obedience to authority and competitiveness through daily activities.

- *Integration into Society.* The United States is a heterogeneous society which must confront the problem of integrating various ethnic, racial, religious, and language groups into a national culture. The school system is used to help assimilate new immigrants. Most of this burden falls on urban school systems. For example, more than 28 ethnic groups are represented in the Los Angeles school system. Functionalists believe that assimilation is the most efficient way to handle large numbers of immigrants. They tend to prefer English as the main or only language of instruction and to emphasize cultural literacy.

- *Social Placement Based on Ability.* Functionalists propose that the school system helps sort young people into various social statuses. Schools accomplish this by evaluating students and tracking them into certain areas. As a result, functionalists believe that the "best and the brightest" students attend the most selective colleges and eventually obtain the best jobs. While they recognize the existence of discrimination in the education system, functionalists indicate that even members of minority groups continue to view education as the key to success.

Conflict perspective
The conflict perspective emphasizes how the educational system leads to the continuation of inequality. Conflict theorists state that most people fail to realize that academic merit is defined and measured in terms of middle- and upper-class expectations. Members of the working- and lower-classes are socialized in ways that put them at a disadvantage. Conflict theorists also argue that the prestige hierarchy of colleges and universities contributes to the reproduction of inequality. They see issues of language of instruction, standardized testing, and cultural literacy as issues of power in which the powerful force their views on the less powerful. Conflict theorists also take issue with tracking because it undermines individual achievement and reinforces social inequality. They cite social class bias in the tracks, the unequal effects on income, and the unequal amounts of materials taught as evidence that tracking promotes inequality.

Symbolic interactionist perspective
Symbolic interactionists emphasize that schools are places in which young people learn social roles and develop their self-concepts. This affects all aspects of life. When teachers label a child as a "poor learner" that child may adopt a negative self-image and, as a result, perform more poorly thus fitting the teacher's initial definition. This is called a **self-fulfilling prophecy**. Such labeling may negatively affect the child's behavior outside the classroom as well. Unlike functionalists or conflict theorists, symbolic interactionists emphasize that interaction is important to study. The interaction between students and teachers is often affected by ascribed statuses of race ethnicity, class, and gender. They also emphasize that students placed in lower tracks may develop a negative self-esteem which will affect all aspects of their lives.

Education in the Twenty-First Century

Education reflects the dominant structure and concerns of society. In postindustrial society, the ability to solve problems is very important. While the economic core of industrial societies is the production of material goods, the economic core of postindustrial societies will be problem solving, creativity, individuality, and an ability to work with others from diverse backgrounds.

Critical Questions

CQ: (page 333)   What implications does year-round attendance have for financing education. Thinking back on your own experience, would year-round attendance have improved your academic skills?

Review the discussion of year-round schooling on pages 287-289. Make a list of the advantages and disadvantages of the current system and year-round schooling. Compare the two systems. Which is most costly to the school districts? Which is most beneficial to the education of students? Which system would working parents prefer? Can you think of a system which contains the most advantageous elements of each system? Knowing the advantages and disadvantages, what arguments would you use if you were in charge of a campaign to pass or defeat a ballot initiative for a school operating levy that was necessary in order to have year-round schooling?

CQ: (page 336)   Some people claim that bilingual and multilingual education will weaken national cohesion. Other people say that diversity will strengthen American society. What do you think?

Review the controversy over bilingual and multilingual education. What are the advantages and disadvantages of each? Do you think bilingual and multilingual education would hinder assimilation? If so, how? Would this benefit or harm immigrant groups? Would such a system lead to pluralism? What advantages and disadvantages would bilingual and multilingual education have for the dominant ethnic group?

CQ: (page 346)   Were you assigned to a "track" in your high school? How did you feel about that? Compare how functionalists, conflict theorists and symbolic interactionists view tracking. Which perspective do you agree with the most?

Most likely you took a college prep track, but one should not assume everyone in college took such a track. Would all schools have a college prep track? Which schools would be less likely to have a college prep track? Which schools would be less likely to have a vocational track? What would functionalism and conflict theorists say about types of schools determining what is available to students? In many schools, the vocational track trains a student for a particular trade or occupation, however, those in that track are somewhat stigmatized or looked down upon. Why is training at the high school level stigmatized while training at the college level (engineering or nursing) highly valued? What implications does tracking have in a post-industrial society that values persons with critical thinking skills and creativity?

Self-Test Questions

Multiple Choice

1. Education to a certain age that is required by law is called:
    a. mandatory education
    b. tracking
    c. required education
    d. legal education

2. It is assumed in America that every citizen has the right to what level of education?
    a. grade school
    b. junior high school
    c. high school
    d. college

3. The principle of mass education in the United States goes back to Thomas Jefferson's belief that education and what go hand-in-hand?
    a. religion
    b. democracy
    c. farming
    d. industrialization

4. Which is NOT true of education in the United States?
    a. it is criticized because many young people are functionally illiterate
    b. control of education is highly centralized
    c. the United States was the first industrialized nation to implement mass education
    d. it is based on the value of practicality

5. Universities funded by the Morrill Act that originally emphasized agriculture and mechanics but over time became large comprehensive research universities are called:
    a. liberal arts universities
    b. magnet schools
    c. Ivy League
    d. land grant universities

6. Joe has the skills necessary to performs the duties of a manager but the company will not hire him because he does not have a college degree. This is called:
    a. education inflation
    b. mass education
    c. credentialism
    d. cultural illiteracy

7. Brenda's father was hired at the local factory without a high school diploma. However, now the company requires a high school diploma for the same jobs. This is called:
    a. education inflation
    b. credentialism
    c. practicality
    d. mass education

8. Which is NOT true of Japan's education system?
    a. Japanese students enroll in extra classes to help prepare for entrance exams
    b. it places great demands on parents, especially mothers
    c. Japanese students engage in many extra-curricular activities such as sports
    d. there are few programs for learning disabled students

9. Which was NOT included in the Coleman report?
    a. African-American children perform more poorly than white children
    b. American children attend racially segregated schools
    c. predominantly white schools had more educational resources than predominantly black schools
    d. students in schools with more educational resources perform much better than those from schools with fewer educational resources

10. What was the result of white flight?
    a. increased racial and ethnic segregation
    b. decreased city tax base
    c. increased financial problems in central city schools
    d. all of the above were the results of white flight

11. Schools that offer specialized subjects like science, math, and arts are called:
    a. neighborhood schools
    b. hidden curriculum schools
    c. magnet schools
    d. tracking schools

12. Which is NOT a problem of multilanguage instruction?
    a. it is very expensive
    b. it may lead to increased isolation of ethnic groups
    c. it may fragment American culture into ethnic groups
    d. it will result in immigrant children falling behind American children

13. Which is NOT true of magnet schools?
    a. they attract students from all areas of the city
    b. they are usually located in minority areas
    c. they are cheaper to run than neighborhood schools
    d. they are usually more integrated than neighborhood schools

14. People of individual societies share knowledge that enhances communication and helps them understand each other. In the United States, this includes knowing the meaning of "e pluribus unum," the names John Adams and Susan B. Anthony, and the location of the Caribbean Sea. This type of knowledge is called:
    a. functional literacy
    b. mass education
    c. cultural literacy
    d. the hidden curriculum

15. People who criticize the United States' education system for teaching from a dead white European male perspective are called:
    a. multiculturalists
    b. conflict theorists
    c. cultural advocates
    d. functionally literate

16. In Uma's high school, students are placed in one of three groups; vocational, general, or college preparatory. This process is called:
    a. labeling
    b. tracking
    c. magnet schooling
    d. tailored education

17. When Bruce's mother was in high school she was required to take home economics and typing even though she preferred woodworking. Bruce's mother was subjected to:
    a. labeling
    b. tracking
    c. gender bias
    d. prejudice

18. One latent function of education in the United States is that children learn to be on time, to line up properly, and to be patriotic. This is referred to as:
    a. the hidden curriculum
    b. cultural literacy
    c. cultural capital
    d. assimilation

19. According to functionalist theory, which is NOT a function of education?
    a. tracking the best and brightest students into the most intellectually-demanding positions
    b. integrating people into society
    c. teaching students what they need to know to fill their adult roles
    d. all of the above are considered functions of education

20. Which sociological perspective argues that the hidden curriculum works against working-class students because it instructs them not to challenge authority?
    a. functionalism
    b. conflict
    c. symbolic interactionism
    d. rational choice

21. Which sociological perspective argues that assimilation is the most efficient means for society to handle a large number of immigrants and that there should be, therefore, school instruction in one language only?
    a. functionalism
    b. conflict
    c. symbolic interactionism
    d. rational choice

22. Which sociological perspective sees the issues of language of instruction, standardized testing, and cultural literacy as issues of power in which the more powerful force the less powerful to adapt to their customs?
    a. functionalism
    b. conflict
    c. symbolic interactionism
    d. rational choice

23. Which sociological perspective focuses on the social interaction between teachers and students?
    a. functionalism
    b. conflict
    c. symbolic interactionism
    d. rational choice

24. One consequence of the freedom to choose schools will be that:
    a. money would flow out of the public school system to private schools
    b. most people will desert public schools
    c. property taxes would be increased to pay for increased busing
    d. all of the above will be consequences

25. Mark was labeled a slow learner. As a result, he developed a negative self-image and started performing poorly in school. This is called:
    a. cultural illiteracy
    b. self-fulfilling prophecy
    c. functional illiteracy
    d. gender bias

True - False

T   F   1. In communal societies, education is highly formal and takes place mainly in schools.
T   F   2. People who cannot read or write well enough to carry out routines of everyday life are called functionally illiterate.
T   F   3. The federal government plays a very small role in the United States education system.
T   F   4. The factory system held back the development of mass education in America.
T   F   5. The Japanese believe that all students have about the same innate ability.
T   F   6. College life for Japanese students is much easier than college life for American students because the Japanese assume that anyone who passes the entrance exams is qualified to graduate.
T   F   7. Summer vacation started in the nineteenth century when children were needed to work on the family farm.

T	F	8. Coleman found that racial integration was the key to successful student performance in school.
T	F	9. In American schools, English is the official language of instruction.
T	F	10. Most standardized educational tests, including the ACT and SAT, are free of cultural and class bias.
T	F	11. If given a chance to choose, 68 percent of parents with children in public school would change schools.
T	F	12. Functionalist theorists believe that tracking is based on ascribed statuses.
T	F	13. Regardless of your major, problem solving, creativity, individuality, and the ability to work with others from diverse backgrounds will be universal skills necessary in post-industrial society.
T	F	14. The economic core of an industrial economy is the production of material goods whereas the economic core of a post industrial society is creativity.

Self-Test Answers

Multiple Choice

1. a (327)	6. c (329)	11. c (335)	16. b (339)	21. a (343)
2. c (327)	7. a (329)	12. d (336)	17. c (340)	22. b (344)
3. b (327)	8. c (331)	13. c (335)	18. a (342)	23. c (345)
4. b (327)	9. d (334)	14. c (338)	19. d (342)	24. d (341)
5. d (328)	10. d (334)	15. a (338)	20. b (344)	25. b (345)

True - False

1. F (326)	4. F (328)	7. T (332)	10. F (337)	13. T (348)
2. T (329)	5. T (330)	8. F (334)	11. F (341)	14. T (347)
3. F (327)	6. T (331)	9. F (335)	12. F (343)	

NOTES FOR FUTURE STUDY AND REVIEW:

Chapter 13

Religion

CHAPTER SUMMARY AND KEY TERMS

The Great Social Transformation and Religion

Religion

Religion is defined as a system of beliefs, rituals, and ceremonies that focuses on sacred matters, promotes community among its followers, and provides for a personal spiritual experience for its members.

GST and religion

In communal societies, religion is woven into all aspects of life. In contemporary industrial society, religion has become separated from many social and economic activities. Most of our daily activities do not involve religion. Religion in industrial societies is more private, with silent prayers instead of communal rituals. In The Protestant Ethnic and the Spirit of Capitalism, Max Weber illustrated the close connection between the virtues of hard work, honesty, and prosperity as a sign of God's favor on the Protestant Reformation and the values of initiative, thrift, and competition of a capitalist economic system.

The Elements of Religion

There are several characteristics of religion. All religions contain these common elements, however, throughout history and today globally, religions differ on the amount to which they fit the characteristics. Some religions such as Catholicism are elaborate with a complex set of doctrines and rituals while others such as that of the ancient Romans are less defined. The Romans practiced *pantheism*—the tolerant acceptance of the worship of all gods. These characteristics are as follows:

Characteristics of religion
- *Beliefs.* Emile Durkheim was one of the first sociologists to study religion scientifically. He pointed out that many people believe in the teachings of various religions even though they cannot test their truth. For example, Christians believe that Jesus' mother, Mary, was a virgin. The validity of this argument is based on faith.
- *The sacred and the profane.* According to Durkheim, all religions distinguish between the sacred and profane. The **sacred** are those things that have supernatural significance and qualities. The **profane** are those things that are regarded as part of ordinary life. Anything can be determined to be sacred.
- *Rituals and ceremonies.* All religions have some form of routinized behaviors that express and reinforce faith; that is, all religions have **rituals**. Prayers, chants, and incantations are common rituals. Durkheim argued that rituals are social mechanisms which bring together the sacred and the profane. Rituals permit worshipers, who might be contaminated by the profane, to approach their respective deity temporarily and safely. This helps bind people of a society together.
- *Moral communities.* Religions are organized around communities of people who share the same beliefs and values. The religious community provides continuity from one generation to the next. It also provides social support for its members.
- *Personal experience.* Religion is intertwined with personal experiences. The born-again Christians are probably the most well-known group in the United States that requires personal involvement. Individuals' personal experiences with religion can be a powerful force that gives meaning to their lives.

All religions exist in the broader society and must accommodate other social institutions. Some religions are well accepted while others are not. Religions are divided into types on the basis of this variation.

Church

A **church** is a formal religious organization that is well-established and well-integrated into society. A church has an organized bureaucracy, a large membership, follows well-established rituals, and is accepted by the wider population. Churches are stable. They claim authority over both the profane and the sacred. As a result, they reserve the right to judge and supervise morality.

Ecclesia   Some churches enjoy so much favor that they become the state's official religion. When that occurs, everyone in the nation is automatically a member of the religion by virtue of birth. This type of religion is called an **ecclesia**. For example, some Latin American countries recognize Roman Catholicism as their official religion. Protestantism is the dominant religion in the United States, however, the government does not recognize it as the official religion. Therefore, it is not an ecclesia.

Denomination   In pluralistic societies, such as the United States, religions usually take on a specific form of a **denomination**: a religion that maintains friendly relations with the government and with other religions but does not claim to be the nation's only legitimate faith. There are over 1,500 religious denominations in the United States. Some examples include Baptists, Lutherans, Reform Jews, and Methodists. Members of a particular denomination may believe that their faith holds the only truth, but they recognize the right of other people to hold different views. Many denominations compete to get people to convert to their faith.

Sects   **Sects** are religious groups that actively reject the broader society in which they exist. This rejection is their defining characteristic. Members of sects are very dedicated to their beliefs. Sect services tend to be spontaneous and emotional. Sects are loosely organized and are nonbureaucratic as compared with the church. As a result, sects are vulnerable to economic problems and mismanagement. Usually, sects do not last long. However, Baptists, Presbyterians, Seventh Day Adventists, Quakers, and Jehovah's Witnesses were all once sects and survived to develop into major denominations and churches.

Cults   **Cults** are religious organizations that have little or nothing to do with conventional religious traditions. They believe that society is degenerate and that the members of the organization must withdraw together from normal life and live apart in group quarters or in a commune. Some people join cults to alleviate loneliness and isolation. Some recruits are attracted by the cult's philosophy. Others join as a result of social pressure. But the most common reason for joining is the leader's charisma. For this reason, cults are often associated with one particular person. Examples include David Koresh and Sun Myung Moon, of the Unification church (the "Moonies"). Cults are usually smaller and less structured than sects. Most die out quickly. However, a few last for years. When cults become established, they typically become less hostile to society.

Varieties of Religion

Christianity   Christianity is the world's single largest religion, with 1.96 billion believers divided among three branches. The largest branch is Roman Catholic, followed by Protestant, and then Orthodox Christian. Large groups of Christians are found throughout the world, but most live in Europe, North America, and South America. Christianity began as a tiny cult whose members believed that Jesus of Nazareth was the long-promised Messiah of the Jews. He was then arrested, tried for treason, and crucified. Followers believe that he rose from the dead and ascended to heaven. Christianity split into the Roman Catholic Church and the Orthodox Church in the tenth century. A second split occurred when Martin Luther (1483-1546) broke away from the Roman Catholic Church to found Protestantism.

Islam   Muslims are the followers of the **Islamic** religion. It is the world's second largest religion with more than 1 billion followers. Muslims believe that the Qur'an (Koran) is the word of Allah (God) as written by the prophet Muhammad over a span of 20 years. Muslims believe that Allah is the only god. They pray daily, give alms, fast during religious periods of the year, and hope to make a pilgrimage to the holy city of Mecca at least once in their lifetime. Many Muslims live in the Middle East, Indonesia, Pakistan, India, the republics of the former Soviet Union, Europe, and North America. In contrast to the Catholic Church, Islam does not have a bureaucratic and centralized leadership. Local clerics act as leaders. In strict Islamic countries, such as Saudi Arabia, there is no distinction between religious and civil life. The deepest split within Islam is between the Sunni (orthodox) and Shiite Muslims. This occurred centuries ago, following the death of Muhammad.

Judaism

Numerically, **Judaism** is the smallest of the world religions. With less than 20 million followers, it accounts for less than one percent of the world's population. Most Jews live in North America, but large Jewish populations are also found in South Asia and the former Soviet Union. Israel is the official Jewish state. A distinctive feature of Jewish faith concerns the agreement under which Jews became God's "chosen people." The first five books of the Bible are called the Torah by Jews. According to Jewish beliefs, God revealed the *Torah* to Moses on Mount Sinai more than 3,000 years ago. The *Talmud* are the commentaries on the Jewish law by Torah scholars. The major factions within Judaism are Orthodox, Conservative, and Reform.

Monotheism
Polytheism

Christianity, Islam, and Judaism have some common beliefs. Each worships one god, a practice called **monotheism**. In addition, each uses the portion of the Bible known to Christians as the Old Testament. For this reason these three groups are called the *"People of the Book."* Monotheism is contrasted to **polytheism** or worshipping more than one god.

Hinduism

With 793 million followers, **Hinduism** is the largest of the Eastern religions (Buddhism and Confucianism are the other two). It is one of the world's oldest religions. Almost half of all Hindus live in India. Unlike Christianity and Islam, Hinduism does not rest on the teachings of a single person. The central belief of Hinduism is the *dharma*: the idea that a special moral force exists throughout the universe. This force places demands on the individual and makes day-to-day life sacred. The dharma reinforces India's caste system. Hinduism includes a belief in *karma*: the development of the spirit as expressed in reincarnation. After death, a person's spirit is reborn in another body. The quality of the new life depends on the quality of the old life. Spiritual perfection, or *nirvana*, is the only escape from this cycle. Hindus believe in a universal moral order. Hindus are free to be monotheists or polytheists.

Buddhism

More than 325 million people follow **Buddhism**. It originated with Siddhartha Gautama, who was born the son of a king in 563 BC. In what is now southern Nepal. Gautama's father confined him to his home because a sage had warned him that his son would threaten him and become a universal monarch. Gautama later escaped and wandered around Asia in search of peace. Eventually, he came upon the Tree of Enlightenment. After living under the tree for many years and practicing meditation, he became *Buddha*, the enlightened one. Today various forms of Buddhism are found in southern Asia, Sri Lanka, the Himalayas, Tibet, Mongolia, China, Korea, and Japan. Many Buddhists do not worship a god but try to live a good life inspired by Gautama. They believe that life is full of suffering but that it is transitory. Like Hindus, they believe that the goal of existence is nirvana and that one's life on earth represents spiritual achievements of an earlier life.

Confucianism

Five million people follow Confucianism. It also began with a single person: K'ung Fu-tzu, or Confucius, as he is known in the West. Confucius was born in northern China around 551 BC. He devoted his early teachings to solving the practical problems of everyday life. Most of his wisdom is written in the *Analects*: a collection of precepts that deal with the proper management of society. Confucius wrote of *jen*: a human-hearted sympathy that binds all people together. Jen is most frequently expressed in the five basic relationships of human life: sovereign and subject, parent and child, older brother and younger brother, husband and wife, and friend and friend. He emphasized parent and child as the most important. Confucius also emphasized *Li*: proper etiquette and ritual. In contrast to religions that emphasize a supernatural being, Buddhism and Confucianism are **ethicalist** belief systems. That is, their followers aspire to attain spiritual excellence by practicing rituals and by following the ethical principles set forth in their religion.

Sociological Analysis of Religion

Functionalist perspective

In <u>The Elementary Forms of the Religious Life</u>, Durkheim laid the foundations for the functionalist approach to religion. Durkheim argued that religion played an important role in society. He states that all religions have a social rather than a supernatural origin and therefore they can be explained sociologically. Durkheim stated that all social institutions, including religion, contribute to the stability of society. He cited the following functions of religion:

• *Cohesion.* By participating in religious activities, people form groups. This reduces their sense of isolation that they might otherwise suffer. It also increases social solidarity. Religion also provides a moral code and a plan for living a good life. Religion also provides social and emotional support in times of stress.

• *Social control.* Religion has authority over rites of passage including birth, marriage, and death. Religion also increases social control because serious sanctions are perceived for norm violation. Religious punishments can extend into the afterlife.

• *Provision of purpose.* People experience anxieties about the future, about social relationships, and about economic well-being throughout life. Religion helps reduce anxiety by answering broad questions about the meaning of life, existence, and the afterlife.

Conflict perspective

Karl Marx, a conflict theorist, believed that the ruling class used religion as a weapon to achieve its own goals. He stated that it made the working-class passive because they believed that their lives would be better in the afterlife. Marx stated that this legitimated inequality and illustrated the fact that humans can create social institutions, can become dominated by their creation, and can eventually believe that the domination is legitimate. He called the last part false consciousness in its most profound sense. Many scholars disagree with Marx stating that religion can actually decrease inequality. For example, some Christian leaders promote a doctrine called *liberation theology* which combines religion with political activism to work among the poor and counter oppression by the ruling classes.

Symbolic interactionist perspective

From the symbolic interactionist perspective, religion is important because it affects individuals and their social relationships. The most important aspect of this concerns the impact of religion on the development of social identity. A strong religious identity is important because it serves as a reference point for everyday life. Some people keep religion confined to a specific area of their lives. A radical change in faiths, such as converting from Christianity to Islam, may involve a fundamental shift in identity. Some people actively reject their earlier religious identity. These people, called *apostates*, tend to be young, highly educated, single males who are mobile and politically independent. As apostates grow older, however, they often return to religion. Religious identity and values are partially the result of socialization. School is also an agent of religious socialization. Public schools in the United States recognize Christianity by closing school on Christian holidays but not on Jewish of Islamic holidays.

Social Change and Religion

Women and religion

The social position of women has changed dramatically over the past 50 years. However, religions have been slow to accept women into positions of authority. For example, in 1985 Pope John Paul stated that women and men were equal in the sight of God but that each has characteristics that makes them suited for separate roles in the church.

Secularization

To some extent, religion and science compete to explain the same things. As science developed, it increasingly replaced religion as the major source of explanation. As science explains more and more, religion explains less and less. This process is called **secularization**: the declining influence of religion combined with an increasing influence of science. Secularization changes religion, but it does not destroy it. Religion is still widely practiced in the United States, but it is practiced more privately and it does not visibly enter every aspect of life.

Civil religion   Sociologist Robert Bellah states that traditional religion is being supplanted by **civil religion**: quasi-religious beliefs that link people to society and country. "Civil" refers to the non-religious aspects of life. Thus civil religion combines the sacred with the profane. Civil religion is not a direct replacement for traditional religion. Societies with the highest development of civil religion also have the most highly developed traditional religion. One example of civil religion is the prohibition of alcohol sales on Sunday in Ohio, Virginia, and other states. The idea of patriotism also relates to civil religion. We are socialized to believe in the goodness and sacredness of our country. As a result, we respond with love and obedience for our country which we express through rituals worshipping the symbols of the nation.

Religious revival   The United States is experiencing a rise in membership in churches that stress renewed commitment to doctrine, personal experience, and religious morality. This is called "religious fundamentalism." Protestant fundamentalists believe that the Bible is literally true, that moral standards have sunk to alarming lows, and that people can attain salvation only by accepting Christ as their savior. They view society as threatened by sexual lewdness, drunkenness, gambling, homosexuality, and lapses in faith. They oppose pornography and abortion on demand. Today, about one-third of the United States population think of themselves as fundamentalists.

Religion in the Twenty-First Century

Electronic church   Society is increasingly reliant upon far-reaching communication networks. One aspect of this is seen in the **electronic church**. This refers to the broadcasting of religious services through the mass media, notably television. This is now a two billion dollar enterprise with 1,400 radio and 220 television stations devoted exclusively to religious programming. Electronic preachers, or **televangelists**, stress fundamentalism, and like all fundamentalists, they call for a return to what they perceive as traditional values.

Mega-church   In addition to the electronic church, another way to attract more people to religion is by increasing the facilities, services, and activities associated with a church. The **mega-church** typically draws more than 2,000 worshipers each week and offers its members many more reasons to come to church than to hear a sermon or visit with a preacher. These churches replace the idea of a church as a place of worship with the idea of the church as a center around which people organize their daily lives. Some mega-churches offer schools, nurseries, day care, recreational facilities, meeting rooms, and restaurants.

Critical Questions

CQ: (page 357)   Do you know of any cults in your state? What are their major characteristics? Do you consider cults a danger or a blessing to society?

Define the key word cult and review the section on cults in your text. Do the cults in your state fit all of these characteristics? If not, how are they different? How did the cults become labeled as such? It would be informative to look up newspaper articles on the cults to determine the ways they were received by mainstream society. Do the cults have stated goals that work against dominant society? If so, what are they? Is this detrimental to the larger society? Do the people in your community consider the cults a serious threat to social stability? Are cults harmful to members? If so, how? Could a member simply walk away from the cult compound? Have you seen any reports of family members who have difficulty getting a loved one out of the cult? What functions, if any, do the cults play in your community?

CQ: (page 356)   This question refers to the Table 13.1 on page 356. Given the data in this table, how would you describe American society in terms of religious membership? Is the United States a Catholic country or is it a Protestant country or is it religiously pluralistic?

To answer this question, first make a list of Protestant religions. Also look up the population of the United States. (Hint: the *Statistical Abstract of the United States* is an excellent source of population data). Now, use the data in the table to compute the membership in all of the Protestant denominations. Compare this with the number of Roman Catholics. Is the United States more Protestant or more Roman Catholic? What percentage of the population are Jewish? Now add the membership of all of the other religions. How does this compare with the numbers of Protestants, Roman Catholics, and Jews? What percentage of the United States population belongs to a religion other than these three? Is the United States overwhelmingly Protestant, Catholic, or Jewish, or is it pluralistic with respect to religious groups?

CQ: (page 366)   Karl Marx made one of the most famous statements in sociology: "Religion is the sign of the oppressed creature...It is the opiate of the people." What do you think Marx meant by this? Do you agree with him? Why or why not?

Review the discussion of Marx's ideas about religion on pages 364-365. How did Marx relate the notion of false consciousness to religion? Are upper- and middle-class citizens religious or is religion just a lower- and working-class phenomenon? Does religion benefit people in any way other than promising them a better afterlife? How would a functionalist answer this? Is Marx assuming that the upper-class does not suffer many of the same hardships of life as the working-class? If so, is this a reasonable assumption?

Self-Test Questions
Multiple Choice

1. Which is Not a characteristic of religion?
    a. rituals and ceremonies
    b. the distinction between the sacred and the profane
    c. beliefs
    d. all of the above are characteristics of religion

2. From the Christian point of view, the crucifix and the rosary are which type of objects?
    a. sacred
    b. ritual
    c. profane
    d. ceremonial

3. What is the term for the tolerant acceptance of the worship of all gods?
    a. monotheism
    b. pantheism
    c. animism
    d. atheism

4. What sociologist argued that there was a close connection between the virtue of Protestantism and the value of capitalism?
    a. Emile Durkheim
    b. Max Weber
    c. Robert Bellah
    d. Auguste Comte

5. What is the term for a religion that maintains friendly relations with the government and with other religions and does not claim to be the nation's only legitimate faith?
   a. denomination
   b. sect
   c. ecclesia
   d. church

6. The Roman Catholic Church has found so much support in many Latin American countries that it has become the state's official religion in these countries. In such countries, the Roman Catholic Church is a/an:
   a. sect
   b. denomination
   c. ecclesia
   d. cult

7. According to your text, which is NOT a reason that people join cults?
   a. they are attracted to the cult's philosophy
   b. they are lonely and isolated
   c. they want to escape the outside world
   d. they are attracted to the leader's charisma

8. The largest religious body in the United States is the:
   a. United Methodist Church
   b. Southern Baptist Convention
   c. Lutheran Church
   d. Roman Catholic Church

9. Which is the smallest of the world religions?
   a. Buddhism
   b. Judaism
   c. Hinduism
   d. Confucianism

10. Which religion believes in a covenant between the people and God that is expressed in the *Torah* and *Talmud*?
    a. Buddhism
    b. Judaism
    c. Hinduism
    d. Confucianism

11. Which religion is NOT monotheistic?
    a. Christianity
    b. Hinduism
    c. Islam
    d. Judaism

12. Which of the following religious groups are called "People of the Book?"
    a. Confucians, Buddhists, and Jews
    b. Hindus, Muslims, and Christians
    c. Muslims, Christians, and Jews
    d. Muslims, Buddhists, and Jews

13. Which religion proposes that after death, a person's spirit is reborn into another body and that the quality of the new life is determined by the quality of the old life?
    a. Judaism
    b. Hinduism
    c. Islam
    d. Confucianism

14. Which religion emphasizes jen, or human-hearted sympathy that binds all people together?
    a. Confucianism
    b. Hinduism
    c. Buddhism
    d. Islam

15. Which is NOT a function of religion according to Durkheim?
    a. social control
    b. cohesion
    c. answering broad questions
    d. perpetuating inequality

16. Which sociological perspective argues that religion contributes to people's lives by providing answers to questions about the meaning of life, existence, and the afterlife?
    a. functionalism
    b. conflict
    c. symbolic interactionism
    d. rational choice

17. Which sociological perspective argues that the most significant impact of religion on the individual concerns the development of social identity?
    a. functionalism
    b. conflict
    c. symbolic interactionism
    d. rational choice

18. In the United States, science has been growing more influential in explaining disease, climatic changes, and mental health while the influence of religion has been declining. What term do sociologists use to describe this process?
    a. ritualism
    b. secularization
    c. modernization
    d. scientific transformation

19. Most people in the United States believe in:
    a. heaven
    b. hell
    c. the Devil
    d. all of the above

20. In some places, crimes against the state are also crimes against God. One example is that many states such as Ohio and Virginia prohibit the sale of alcohol on Sundays in order to reserve the day for sacred activities. This is an example of:
    a. Christianity
    b. secularization
    c. civil religion
    d. expansive religion

21. Which group typically believes that the Bible is literally true; that moral standards have sunk to alarming depths; and that people can attain salvation only by accepting Christ as their savior?
    a. Protestant Fundamentalists
    b. Liberal Protestants
    c. Roman Catholics
    d. Reform Jews

22. Fundamentalist ministers who espouse traditional religious values and regularly use television to spread their messages are called:
    a. lay-preachers
    b. traditionalists
    c. televangelists
    d. media-preachers

23. Which is NOT a trend in the United States?
    a. religious revival
    b. the rise of civil religion
    c. secularization
    d. decline of fundamentalism

24. The mega-church strives to attain the idea that:
    a. the church should be a life center or a hub around which people organize their daily routines and social commitments
    b. it is important to have large congregations
    c. the church should reach out through the mass media to reach as many people as possible
    d. none of the above

True - False

T	F	1. In communal societies, religion permeates all aspects of life.
T	F	2. A formal religious organization that is well-established and well-integrated into society but that is not the state's official religion is called an ecclesia.
T	F	3. Islam is the world's largest religion.
T	F	4. Compared with Christianity, the authority structure of Islam is very centralized.
T	F	5. Christianity began as a tiny cult whose members believed that Jesus was the long-promised Messiah of the Jews.
T	F	6. Followers of Islam believe that the Qur'an is the word of Allah as set down by the prophet Muhammad.
T	F	7. The central belief of Hinduism is the idea that a special moral force exists throughout the universe that makes demands on the individual and gives everyday life a sacred quality.
T	F	8. Functionalism argues that religion as well as other social institutions contributes to the harmony and stability of society.

Chapter 13 Religion

T	F	9. Durkheim said that religion was a narcotic that dulled the pain of inequality.
T	F	10. According to symbolic interactionism, religion is important because it affects individuals and their social relationships.
T	F	11. To some extent, religion and science compete to explain the same phenomena.
T	F	12. Civil religion is religion that is officially recognized by the state.
T	F	13. An electronic church is a large religious congregation in which the church becomes a center around which people organize their daily lives and which provides members with many non-traditional services and facilities.

Self Test Answers

Multiple Choice

1. d (353)	6. c (355)	11. b (360)	16. a (364)	21. a (370)
2. a (353)	7. c (357)	12. c (360)	17. c (365)	22. c (372)
3. b (355)	8. d (356)	13. b (360)	18. b (368)	23. d (368)
4. b (352)	9. b (359)	14. a (361)	19. d (368)	24. a (373)
5. a (355)	10. b (359)	15. d (363)	20. c (368)	

True - False

1. T (352)	4. F (358)	7. T (360)	10. T (365)	13. F (372)
2. F (355)	5. T (358)	8. T (362)	11. T (368)	
3. F (358)	6. T (358)	9. F (365)	12. F (368)	

NOTES FOR FUTURE STUDY AND REVIEW:

Chapter 14

Medicine and Health Care

THE GREAT SOCIAL TRANSFORMATION AND MEDICINE AND HEALTH CARE

HEALTH AND SOCIETY
The Historical Development of Medicine in the United States
The Social Organization of Medicine
Health Care Organizations

SOCIOLOGICAL ISSUES IN MEDICINE AND HEALTH CARE
Inequality in Health and Health Care
The Cost of Health Care
Health Insurance
The Medicalization of Society

SOCIOLOGICAL ANALYSIS OF MEDICINE AND HEALTH CARE
The Functionalist Perspective
The Conflict Perspective
The Symbolic Interactionist Perspective

MEDICINE AND HEALTH CARE IN THE TWENTY-FIRST CENTURY

CRITICAL QUESTIONS
Your diet and exercise
Florence Nightingale
HMOs and hospitals

SELF TEST QUESTIONS/ANSWERS

CHAPTER SUMMARY AND KEY TERMS

The Great Social Transformation and Medicine and Health Care

Disease and health

Sociologists define **disease** as a pathology that disrupts the usual functions of the body and **health** as the capacity to satisfy role requirements. If you are able to carry out all of the responsibilities associated with your roles, you are said to be healthy. Sickness places strains on individuals and on the social system. It is therefore a subject of interest to sociologists.

GST and medicine

In communal societies, disease is a communal matter. When a member becomes ill, everyone joins in the effort to make the patient well again. They do this because they know each other personally, share a common history, and anticipate a common future. Industrial societies view sickness as a matter of science. Rather than calling on community members to pray, sick people in industrial societies seek the aid of professionally-trained doctors and place their faith in surgery and drugs. The interaction between these healers and patients is impersonal, focused, and rational in nature.

Health and Society

Before the development of scientific medicine, many doctors believed that good health resulted from the proper balance of fluids, or humors, within the body. Treatments often involved cutting a blood vessel to allow the humors to reach a balance. If the patient died, the doctor assumed that the patient had not bled enough. Medical practices remained crude until the middle of the nineteenth century when germ theory was developed. It laid the foundation for understanding contagious diseases. The development of anesthetics then made it possible to perform surgery. Improved sanitation reduced gangrene, blood poisoning, and other infections that had killed most of the people who managed to survive surgery. Physicians began washing their hands and using sterile dressings. Nursing became an accepted profession. Physicians also began to gain prestige in society.

AMA

The American Medical Association (AMA) was founded in the mid 1800s. Influenced by the AMA, legislatures outlawed "quack" healing practices and granted the AMA control over the training of new doctors. The AMA had gained a near-monopoly over American medicine by the early 1900s. The AMA now recognizes 27 specialties in medicine.

Key positions in medicine

There are several key positions in medicine:
- *Physicians.* Although they comprise only 10 percent of all American health care workers, doctors have the most powerful position in medicine. They have the right to diagnose disease, prescribe drugs, and perform surgery. In many places, only a physician can pronounce a person dead, certify that someone is mentally competent, or give expert testimony on medical matters in court. Their prestige is so high that they are treated with deference, respect, and courtesy wherever they go. Doctors are among the most highly paid workers in America earning more than five times the earnings of the average worker. The percentage of doctors in specialized areas is increasing.
- *Nurses.* In the nineteenth century, Florence Nightingale transformed nursing in Great Britain from a position of low esteem to one that was highly respected. Her influence spread to the United States which established its first nursing school, New York's Bellevue Hospital, in 1873. In 1901 nurse Margaret Sanger led the fight to give people access to contraception. She invented the term *birth control* and helped found Planned Parenthood. Nurses used to train at three-year schools, but now many attend four-year universities, major in nursing, and receive a bachelor's degree at graduation. Graduate training in nursing has become a recent development. Nurses can only work under the supervision of doctors, most of whom are men. Though nurses get to know patients better than doctors, they do not have control over the patient's treatment.
- *Hospitals.* People usually associate hospitals with medicine and forget that they are also bureaucracies with rules, regulations, and paper work. Unlike most bureaucracies, hospitals do not follow the usual principles of hierarchy. Rather than having a single, clear line of authority, most hospitals have two lines. The first consists of physicians who have authority over medical

matters. The second is administrators who have authority over business matters. Often these two exist in an uneasy balance. Today, many *multihospital systems* are forming. These are a combination of two or more hospitals that are owned or managed by a single corporation. The corporation can cut costs by taking advantage of pooled resources. Hospitals have also cut costs by hiring physicians directly. In essence, these physicians become high-paid white-collar workers.

HMO
• *Health Maintenance Organizations.* The **health maintenance organization (HMO)** is an insurance plan combined with a physical facility for delivering care. Members of an HMO pay a set monthly fee which entitles them to comprehensive health care at the HMO facility. The HMO group is one variation. In this arrangement doctors, nurses, and pharmacists are contracted to provide members with comprehensive health care under one roof.

Sociological Issues in Medicine and Health Care

Inequality
As illustrated in other chapters, social class, race and ethnicity, and gender are the three major dimensions of inequality. These dimensions are associated with inequality in medicine.

• *Social Class.* In all societies, the upper classes receive the best health care and live in the best health. These people are educated about symptoms and have the resources to obtain the best professional help in times of illness. They also live and work in healthy environments, exercise, and eat properly. In contrast, the poor are more likely to live in unhealthy environments, smoke, eat poorly, and be obese. Hospitals in poor areas often rely on government assistance and lack the resources of those in affluent areas.

• *Race and Ethnicity.* Substantial health differences exist between African Americans and white Americans. Compared with whites, African Americans have a higher incidence of chronic diseases that prevent them from working; an African-American woman is more than three times more likely to die during childbirth; an African-American baby is twice as likely to die; and an African-American male is seven times more likely to die of homicide. One reason for these differences is the interaction between race and ethnicity and socioeconomic status. Many African and Hispanic Americans are lower class and have little control over their health. They may become fatalistic and careless about their diet, exercise, and other preventive measures such as diet and exercise. Discrimination also plays a role as racial and ethnic minorities are often segregated into crowded, unhealthy urban areas.

• *Gender.* Women suffer from the problems faced by people who lack power and wealth. Medicine is a male-dominated institution and it has traditionally viewed women's diseases as less important than men's diseases. For example, menstrual cramps, morning sickness, and difficulties with lactation receive low research priority. Even breast cancer, which will attack about one out of every eight women, has not been given the same research priority as diseases that primarily affect men. Less is known about women's medicine as male patients have been the primary subjects for research and clinical drug testing. Women are underrepresented in the powerful positions of health care. Only about one in five doctors is a women. This is changing as women now constitute 40 percent of new medical students.

Cost
In addition to inequality, the high cost of medical care is a problem. The United States spends about $1 trillion per year on health and related matters. This could reach $2 trillion by the next century. Several factors account for the increasing costs.

• *Physician Fees.* The net income for physicians accounts for about 20 percent of all health care expenditures in the United States. Fees have increased because doctors now conduct extensive diagnoses and treatment. This is partially the result of technology-intensive medicine. Many times doctors order tests to prove that they have not been negligent in case there should be a malpractice suit. This is called "defensive medicine." Malpractice insurance is expensive, and as with most costs, eventually gets passed along to whoever is paying the physician's fees.

• *Hospitals.* Hospitals charge high fees to fund their large bureaucracies. It costs a hospital about $1,000 each day to support a patient. The costs of wages and salaries of support personnel, the cost of equipment, unpaid bills of indigent patients, maintenance of the physical facility, and administrative overhead are included. Private hospitals have also increased costs in order to earn higher profits. Patients have little choice as they cannot often shop around for the lowest prices.

	• *Technology.* The cost of health care increases as medicine becomes more dependent on sophisticated technologies.
Health insurance	About seven of every ten Americans has private health insurance. It is usually purchased through their employer or labor union as part of a benefits package. The employer pays part of the premium while the employee pays the rest. Few health insurance plans cover all medical expenses. Often the uncovered portion is too expensive for people to pay. Today, three categories of people tend to be uninsured. These are racial-ethnic minorities, the young (aged 18 to 24), and the poor. Both the Republicans and Democrats have advocated health care reform. Both seek to reduce the costs of **Medicare**: a federal health insurance program for the elderly financed by taxes on working people and their employers and by a monthly fee for those enrolled in the program. Medicare was created jointly with **Medicaid**: a health insurance plan targeted to the poor and disabled. Despite Medicaid, about one in four poor Americans has no health insurance.
Medicalization of society	One trend in the United States is the **medicalization of society**: the expansion and taking over of areas of life by medicine that were formerly part of another social institution. Childbirth is an example. For most of human history, childbirth has been regarded as a natural occurrence rather than a medical problem. Babies used to be delivered at home by a family member or a midwife. As medicine became more influential, doctors argued that only they could ensure a healthy delivery. Under pressure by physicians, many states outlawed the practice of midwifery. Today, most women routinely seek the care of a doctor as soon as they become pregnant. They also give birth in the hospital rather than at home. Excessive drinking has also become medicalized. Alcoholism is now considered a disease of addiction. Physical attractiveness is also becoming medicalized. Many people wear braces or undergo plastic surgery to alter their appearances.

Sociological Analysis of Medicine and Health Care

Functionalist perspective	From the functionalist viewpoint, the function of medicine is to keep people healthy so they can serve society. If too many people are ill, society will collapse. This happened to civilizations in Central and South America which were decimated by the diseases brought by explorers. Another function of medicine is to treat and cure sickness. Though different societies take different approaches, all societies have the institution of medicine. Contemporary disease treatments rely on science. Therefore medicine serves the function of encouraging scientific research. Medicine also serves the function of encouraging people to follow the norms, values, and behaviors of conventional society. In doing so, medicine acts as an agent of social control. Medicine acts as a gatekeeper by certifying health care providers who are qualified to perform certain tasks. With the development of life sustaining technology, medicine can now act as a gatekeeper to death by preventing premature death and prolonging the lives of the terminally ill. Some people feel physicians should also be able to assist those wishing to commit suicide. Finally, medicine plays the function of generating wealth and prestige.
Malingering	Functionalists also propose that all societies must deal with **malingering**: pretending to be sick to achieve some personal or social goal. Widespread malingering strains the social system. Malingering also violates the sick role: expectations and rights given to people who are ill.
Sick role	Four expectations are associated with the **sick role**: • Sick people are not responsible for their condition. • Sick people may withdraw from normal activities. • Sickness is undesirable and sick people want to get well. • The sick should seek treatment. One problem with this scheme is the idea that the sick are not responsible for their condition. In reality, many diseases carry a stigma. For example, people with a sexually transmitted diseases are often stigmatized for being sexually promiscuous. Another problem is the expectation that the patient will try to recover. Some people develop life-long illnesses and adapt their lifestyles to the demands of their disease. Also, conflict theorists and symbolic interactionists state that the conception of the sick role excludes physicians and fails to account for the interaction between patients and physicians.

Conflict perspective	Many conflict theorists criticize American medicine for being capitalistic in nature. They point out that even with the most expensive and technologically advanced health care system in the world, the United States compares unfavorably with the less expensive and less elaborate health care systems of other industrial countries. They also stress the inequality of medicine and health care with regard to racial and ethnic minorities, women, and the poor. Conflict theorists state that the institution of medicine does not function as smoothly as functionalists believe. They cite the power struggles between doctors, hospitals, insurance companies, drug companies, and governmental regulatory bodies.
Symbolic interactionist perspective	Symbolic interactionists focus on the individual and on social interaction. They are concerned with the following issues: •. *Socialization of Physicians and Nurses.* Doctors deal with life and death matters and must undergo extensive training before being allowed to practice independently. Their education begins in "pre-med" courses in undergraduate school. This is followed by four years of medical school, an intense, stressful introduction to the knowledge, values, and attitudes associated with the medical profession. Here medical students learn to be dispassionate and unemotional about sickness and to view medicine as a technical and scientific process. Nurses usually major in nursing as undergraduates. They are socialized to maintain a high level of altruism and dedication to patients. After nurses graduate, they sometimes find their compassion devalued by the medical bureaucracy. They also find that physicians insist on controlling everything, leaving them little room for independent decision making. • *Physician-Patient Interaction.* Most of this interaction is one-sided with the physician giving the orders. However, doctors have noted that there are some important racial and ethnic differences in how people respond to pain. Some physicians have stated that Asian Americans respond quietly while Italian Americans are more likely to express their discomfort forcefully and demand relief. As a result, the patient-doctor interaction is filled with potential misunderstandings. In hospitals, patients interact with nurses much more than with doctors. • *Social Support and Recovery from Disease.* Symbolic interactionists are interested in the social context in which healing occurs. Often the social context can speed recovery. Usually, patients who belong to a network of family, friends, and co-workers do better than patients who are isolated. These networks provide support to the patient and information to health care providers.

Medicine and Health Care in the Twenty-First Century

Preventive medicine	Historically the main goal of medicine has been to cure disease. In the future, medicine will also emphasize **preventive medicine**: the maintenance of health and the prevention of disease. This will occur for three reasons. First, small lifestyle changes can have a large impact on the health of a population. For example, convincing people to have "safe sex" could dramatically decrease the spread of HIV. Second, changes in the age structure of the population will encourage health maintenance and prevention in the near future. The aging of the baby boomers will place tremendous stress on the health care system. To combat costs, the government must stress health maintenance and prevention. Third, the view of health will change to encompass the world. The World Health Organization (WHO), an international organization with projects in many countries, already defines health as a state of physical, mental, and social well-being. By this definition, achieving health in a society requires full employment, with wages high enough to buy nutritious foods; greater attention to equal rights for women; the implementation of universal education; and the avoidance of war.

Critical Questions

CQ: (page 380) This question refers to Table 14.1 on page 380 of your text. Have you recently changed your diet and exercise program in order to minimize your risk of developing cancer or heart disease? If not, why not?

Do you take time to listen to the results of health research on the news or to read health articles in the newspaper? Would you say that you are well-informed about preventive medicine? Why or why not? Do you believe that you can control your health through your lifestyle? Why or why not? Have any of your family members suffered from cancer or heart disease? Have you spoken with a doctor about this? If so, did they advise you to change your lifestyle? Did you follow the advice? Do you think that insurance companies should pay for a policy holder's health problems that were the result of his or her poor diet and lack of exercise? Should society be responsible for such people? Why or why not?

CQ: (page 383)   What lasting contributions did Florence Nightingale make to the practice of modern medicine? What did she teach us about the importance of nurses in maintaining health?

Review the account of Nightingale on pages 382-383. Which of Nightingale's procedures are still used in medical facilities? What effect, if any, does this have on preventive medicine? When Nightingale began nursing, the profession was not respected. This was because nurses had the reputation for drunkenness and sexual promiscuity? How is this different today? Is there any connection between cleanliness and the prestige of nursing? Do the style and colors of nurses' uniforms contribute to this?

CQ: (page 384)   What is the difference between an HMO and a hospital? Do they serve different purposes?

Define the key term HMO. List the characteristics of an HMO and a hospital. Do they differ in quality of treatment, diversity of specializations, or cost? What are the advantages and disadvantages of each? Can you list cases in which hospitals should be used? Can you think of any situations in which HMOs are more useful? Do you have experience with either of these? Could you have visited the other to fill your needs? In which situations do you prefer a hospital? An HMO?

Self-Test Questions
Multiple Choice

1. When you are able to satisfy all of your role requirements, you are:
    a. disease free
    b. healthy
    c. malingering
    d. all of the above

2. Compared to communal societies, health care in associational societies is:
    a. more scientific
    b. less personal
    c. more rational
    d. all of the above

3. Which is NOT true of the American Medical Association?
    a. it shares control over the practice of medicine with many other professional organizations
    b. it lobbied legislatures to outlaw quack healing practices
    c. it controls the training of doctors
    d. it has great influence in setting national public health goals

4. Which is NOT true of nurses?
    a. they often burn out due to job stress
    b. they can make independent decisions about a patient's treatment
    c. they are increasingly attending four-year universities
    d. in hospitals, they generally spend more time with patients than the doctors do

5. Which is NOT true of the relationship between doctors and hospital administrators?
    a. they often have an uneasy relationship
    b. administrators defer to physicians on medical matters
    c. physicians rely on administrators to provide them with equipment
    d. all of the above are true

6. What is the term for a combination of two or more hospitals that are owned or managed by a single corporation?
    a. multiplex
    b. multihospital system
    c. hospice
    d. joint care facility

7. Which is NOT a reason that members of the upper classes are usually healthier than members of the lower classes?
    a. the lower class is often fatalistic about their health
    b. the wealthy tend to smoke less and exercise more
    c. members of the upper classes are usually educated about diseases and can recognize symptoms
    d. all of the above are reasons that the upper classes are healthier than the lower classes

8. Compared with whites:
    a. African Americans have a higher incidence of chronic diseases that prevents them from working
    b. African American women are three times more likely to die in child birth
    c. African American babies are twice as likely to die
    d. all of the above

9. Why has medicine traditionally viewed women's diseases as less important than men's diseases?
    a. medicine is male dominated
    b. serious diseases are male diseases
    c. women are not as significant a factor of economic production
    d. women live longer than men

10. Approximately what percentage of doctors are women?
    a. five
    b. ten
    c. twenty
    d. thirty

11. Medical costs:
    a. are devouring an increasing share of the nation's resources
    b. could reach $2 trillion early next century
    c. in part reflect the increased technology of medicine
    d. all of the above

12. Which is NOT true of women's health?
    a. problems faced by women often receive low research priority
    b. less is known about women's medicine
    c. most drug research is based on female subjects
    d. today 40 percent of new medical students are women

13. Which is NOT a factor in the increasing costs of health care?
    a. private hospitals are charging higher fees to increase their profits
    b. there are not enough doctors to meet the demand for health care
    c. doctors often order many high-tech tests to diagnose a problem
    d. physicians are increasing their fees

14. At one time, alcoholics were considered immoral people. Now they are defined as having a disease of addiction. This is an example of:
    a. sick role
    b. malingering
    c. stigmatization of the sick
    d. medicalization of society

15. Critics argue that the medicalization of society:
    a. gives courts more control over individual behavior
    b. undermines morality, self-control, and social responsibility
    c. results in fewer people being treated for serious illness
    d. undermines advances in women's health

16. Which sociological perspective argues that the purpose of medicine is to keep people healthy so they can serve society?
    a. functionalism
    b. conflict
    c. symbolic interactionism
    d. rational choice

17. Which sociological perspective argues that medicine acts as an agent of social control by deciding which people can administer it?
    a. functionalism
    b. conflict
    c. symbolic interactionism
    d. rational choice

18. Which sociological perspective argues that medicine encourages scientific research which results in better treatments?
    a. functionalism
    b. conflict
    c. symbolic interactionism
    d. rational choice

19. Pretending to be sick in order to achieve a social or personal goal is:
    a. sick role
    b. humors
    c. malingering
    d. none of the above

20. Which is NOT an aspect of the sick role?
    a. sick people should want to get well
    b. the sick should seek treatment
    c. sickness is an undesirable condition
    d. sick people should try to fill their role obligations

21. Which sociological perspective proposes that physicians have such great influence that they have a legal monopoly on the prescription of drugs and have prevented nurses from expanding their professional spheres?
   a. functionalism
   b. conflict
   c. symbolic interactionism
   d. rational choice

22. Which sociological perspective argues that medical school provides an intense and stressful introduction to the knowledge, values, and attitudes associated with the medical profession?
   a. functionalism
   b. conflict
   c. symbolic interactionism
   d. rational choice

23. Which sociological perspective argues that the social networks provide patients with emotional and material support and information about treatments, physicians, and hospitals?
   a. functionalism
   b. conflict
   c. symbolic interactionism
   d. rational choice

24. Which of the following is NOT a factor in the health maintenance of American society?
   a. it makes sense to emphasize prevention since small lifestyle changes have large effects on health
   b. the population is getting younger and the young are more health conscious
   c. the view as to what is the nature of health is expanding to include medical, social, and political factors
   d. all of the above are factors

True - False

T	F	1. Because sickness places a strain on the social system and on individuals, every society has the institution of medicine.
T	F	2. Improvements in nursing skill reduced gangrene, blood poisoning, and other infections that killed most surgical patients.
T	F	3. Physicians occupy the most powerful position in medicine.
T	F	4. Nurses increasingly have bachelor's degrees.
T	F	5. Most hospitals have two lines of authority: doctors and administrators.
T	F	6. A Health Maintenance Organization (HMO) is an insurance plan combined with a physical facility for delivering health care.
T	F	7. The overlap between race and class is one reason that African Americans have poorer health, on average, than whites.
T	F	8. Medicaid was designed to provide health insurance for the elderly.
T	F	9. Critics of the concept of the sick role state that in reality people are sometimes stigmatized for their illnesses.
T	F	10. Medical students are socialized in medical school to be unemotional about sickness.
T	F	11. There is not much variation in patient-doctor interaction from one racial or ethnic group to the next.

T	F	12. Focus on preventive medicine will probably decline in postindustrial society.
T	F	13. The World Health Organization defines health as a state of physical, mental, and social well-being.

Self-Test Answers

Multiple Choice

1. b (377)	6. b (383)	11. d (386)	16. a (392)	21. b (396)
2. d (378)	7. d (385)	12. c (386)	17. a (393)	22. c (396)
3. a (379)	8. d (385)	13. b (386)	18. a (392)	23. c (397)
4. b (381)	9. a (385)	14. d (390)	19. c (393)	24. b (398)
5. d (383)	10. c (386)	15. b (391)	20. d (393)	

True - False

1. T (377)	4. T (381)	7. T (385)	10. T (396)	13. T (399)
2. F (379)	5. T (383)	8. F (388)	11. F (397)	
3. T (380)	6. T (384)	9. T (394)	12. F (398)	

NOTES FOR FUTURE STUDY AND REVIEW:

Chapter 15

Collective Social Action

CHAPTER SUMMARY AND KEY TERMS

The Great Social Transformation and Collective Social Action

Collective social action

Collective social action is defined as cooperative attempts to achieve a social goal. The pro-democracy demonstrations by 100,000 Chinese students in Tiananmen Square in 1986 was an example of collective social action. Collective social action is not new and has always played an important role in social change in communal and associational societies. However, in contemporary associational societies it takes place at a much faster pace than in communal societies.

Collective Behavior

Collective behavior

Collective behavior is social interaction that is in response to unstructured, ambiguous, or unstable situations. We encounter many situations that are relatively unstructured. Therefore collective behavior covers a broad range of behaviors including being caught up in a crowd, a riot, a panic, or even simply responding to rumors, stories, or news items that turn out to be false. Sociologists do not believe that collective behavior is irrational and unexplainable. Neil Smelser suggests a *theory of structural strain* that links existing societal conditions with the emergence of collective behavior. He states that collective behavior will emerge when all six of these conditions are met:

• *Structural conduciveness.* This refers to the preexisting conditions that make collective behavior likely.

• *Structural strains.* Conditions that cause people to feel anxious or strained set the stage for collective behavior. For example, a racial riot is not likely to break out if relationships between racial groups are not already strained.

• *Generalized beliefs.* Before collective action can occur, people must develop a set of beliefs about their situation and about which actions are appropriate in given situations.

• *Precipitating factors.* An incident that triggers or precipitates the collective behavior must take place. For example, a riot in South-Central Los Angeles was precipitated by the announcement of a not-guilty verdict for the police officers that beat Rodney King.

• *Mobilization for action.* For collective behavior to occur, people must join together or mobilize to achieve their goals. This usually occurs at the encouragement of a leader.

• *Failure of social control.* Collective behavior is more likely to occur if agencies of social control are too slow or indecisive.

Crowds

A **crowd** is a temporary grouping of individuals who are physically close enough to engage in social interaction. In contrast, a **mob** is a special type of crowd, one that is wildly out of control and intent on doing violence and harm. Most people are routinely members of crowds but rarely of mobs. Sociologists identify five different types of crowds:

• **Casual crowd**. A casual crowd consists of people who are passive and have a low emotional engagement and little social interaction with those nearby. People continually move in and out of a casual crowd with little notice. Casual crowds are not usually considered a social problem.

• **Conventional crowd**. A conventional crowd is a relatively structured grouping in which conventional norms govern social behavior. Conventional crowds are goal-directed and each person has little interaction with other people in the group. An example is people gathered at a bus stop.

• **Solidaristic crowd**. A crowd that provides its members with a sense of unity or social solidarity is called a solidaristic crowd. For example, the "Million Man March" on Washington in 1995 was an expression of solidarity for African-American men.

• **Expressive crowd**. When people gather to change their mood, emotions, and behavior, they are members of an expressive crowd. Rock concerts are one example. Sometimes expressive crowds become unruly. As a result, officials are very concerned whenever a situation arises that might influence and intensify the emotions and behaviors of an expressive crowd.

- **Acting crowd.** When crowd members become angry and engage in smashing windows, overturning cars, setting fires, or attacking members of certain groups, the crowd has moved beyond mere expression. It has become an acting crowd and now constitutes a mob. Herbert Blumer studied acting crowds. He stated that they grow through five stages: 1) people become restless, apprehensive, and susceptible to rumors; 2) something startling occurs and people become preoccupied with it; 3) people start milling about and discussing what is going on; 4) people next focus on some aspect of the event or on certain people involved in the event; 5) finally, crowd members come to a general agreement as to the best action to take.

Riot
A **riot** is a relatively large-scale, violent collective behavior that grows from a shared anger, frustration, and sense of deprivation. Compared with a mob, a riot involves many more people, takes place across a wider area, and may last for days. Riots may be set off by a single incident, but they often reflect underlying strains in the social structure. One of the earliest riots in America occurred in New York City during the Civil War. It began as a protest against the government's policy of drafting men into the army but later turned violent.

Panic
Another form of collective behavior that may have serious consequences is a **panic**: a collective but irrational reaction to a serious threat. This is a very dramatic event that attracts media attention. An example from movies is people madly fleeing a monster. Sociologists believe that true panics rarely occur. Even when faced with a flood, hurricane, or invading army, people seldom become hysterical, irrational, selfish, or antisocial.

Rumor
Riots, panics, and other forms of collective behavior are often fueled by **rumors**: false or unverified reports communicated from one person to another. Rumors travel informally and are difficult to verify. The Los Angeles Watts riot of 1965 was started by a rumor that police officers had stopped a pregnant African-American woman and beaten her. In fact, no such incident had occurred.

Theories of crowd behavior
Sociologists have developed three main theories to explain crowd behavior. All three of these theories could apply to a crowd in a given situation. They are as follows:
- *Contagion Theory.* Early sociologists believed that people in collective situations lost their individuality and became swept up in the behaviors of others, in essence, they adopted a "herd mentality." Gustav LeBon proposed that people in crowds felt that they were free to do whatever they wished and that they were caught up in a collective mind. This resulted in a contagion that swept through the crowd releasing people's destructive tendencies. Robert Park states that a circular reaction occurred. A *circular reaction* is false information at one stage that is rapidly communicated to others in a crowd, who then embellish the misinformation and communicate it to other crowd members. Today, sociologists continue to use the idea of contagion to describe collective behavior. However, they have abandoned LeBon's notion of the "herd mentality."
- *Convergence Theory.* This theory assumes that crowd unity results from the like-mindedness of members, and that this like-mindedness exists before people join the crowd. In other words, the crowd's behavior is determined by the similarity of its members.
- *Emergent Norm Theory.* This theory proposes that different norms develop in crowd situations and that people use these norms to guide their behavior. Thus, crowd behavior is not random.

Social Movements

Social movement
A **social movement** is an organized but non-institutionalized effort to change society through collective action. Compared with crowd behavior, a social movement is relatively well organized and may involve literally millions of people. Sociologists recognize four types of social movements:
- **Reform movement.** The goal of a reform movement is to change society in a limited way. Often, a reform movement focuses on the passage or repeal of a specific law. For example, the original goal of the temperance movement was to outlaw the manufacture and sale of alcoholic drinks.

- **Revolutionary.** The goal of a revolutionary movement is to replace the existing social order with a completely new order. These movements usually arise when reforming the existing order seems inefficient. The best known revolutionary movement in the United States occurred in 1776 when Americans decided to break from the British and establish an independent state.
- **Resistance.** A resistance movement is a counter-movement. Its goal is to stop or reverse changes that are taking place. An example is the labor movement which began in order to counter the power of management and to establish a safe work environment for employees.
- **Expressive.** The goal of an expressive movement is to provide gratification through self-expression. One example is the charismatic movement that is currently taking place among Catholics and Protestants. This movement urges people to open themselves to the direct actions of the Holy Spirit.

Theories to explain social movements

Sociologists have developed three theories to explain social movements. They are relative deprivation, resource-mobilization, and mass society theories.
- *Relative Deprivation.* The theory of relative deprivation assumes that a social movement is likely to develop when people perceive a gap between what they feel their situation should be and what their situation actually is. Feelings of relative deprivation often arise when people compare themselves to others who appear more wealthy, more powerful, or more free. This concept explains why people may feel wronged even though they may be fairly well-off in absolute terms. An interesting prediction follows from the concept of relative deprivation, that people are more likely to engage in collective behavior when their situation is getting better rather than when it is getting worse.
- *Resource-Mobilization Theory.* A problem with relative deprivation theory is that in all industrial societies, some people have less than others. Therefore relative deprivation is always present but does not always result in collective action. *Resource-mobilization theory* argues that resources are the key to successful social movements. Resources include money, members, leaders, offices and communication facilities, ties with other active groups and influential people, and contacts with the media. In addition, people must agree that the movement is legitimate. This theory also suggests that social movements are more likely to occur when prosperity is increasing.
- *Mass Society Theory.* According to mass society theory, industrialization results in highly impersonal political, religious, and social systems. It assumes that these changes bring alienation, anomie, and excessive rationalization. Out of this condition, people may be drawn together and provided with a common cause and sense of community. The democratic movement in Czechoslovakia is an example of a social movement explained by mass society theory.

Social Movements in the United States

Civil Rights Movement

The Civil Rights Movement fought for racial and ethnic equality. The end of the Civil War in 1865 ended slavery. But it did not end the economic and political oppression of African Americans. Many states passed Jim Crow laws that legalized segregation. These laws were often enforced by violence against African Americans. The National Association for the Advancement of Colored People (NAACP) was established in 1910 and took the social protest into the courts. It won several victories, including the pivotal 1954 Supreme Court decision Brown v. Board of Education. The decision, that separate educational facilities for whites and blacks is unequal, banned racial segregation in public schools. This led to a full-fledged civil rights movement including boycotts of segregated busses and restaurants and marches. Martin Luther King, Jr. and his followers in the Southern Christian Leadership Conference (SCLC) began another wave of protests. Dr. King favored a nonviolent approach to social change. This made him very popular among whites. More militant groups began to follow leaders such as Bobby Seale of the Black Panthers and Elijah Muhammad and Malcolm X of the Nation of Islam. This branch advocated that African Americans take their situations in their own hands and turn away from whites. The Black Power movement argued for the development of economic, cultural, educational, and political institutions created and shaped by African Americans and for African Americans. Today, the civil rights movement is an institutionalized part of American society. Most people agree on the goals of the movement but many disagree about how they should be achieved.

Women's Movement

The women's movement began in the 1840s when feminists sought the rights to vote and divorce. At first, the movement was viewed as an attack on the sexual morality of the time and on the integrity of the traditional family. It was greatly undermined in 1872 when the Supreme Court ruled that the "innate weaknesses" of women made them unfit for many occupations. About 20 years later the Supreme Court ruled that women were not even "persons" under the law. The Women's Christian Temperance Union (WCTU) had gained legitimacy by the early 1900s. It actively crusaded against alcohol abuse and prostitution and for better employment conditions, child labor laws, kindergartens, and moral purity. In 1920 women gained the right to vote. The women's movement suffered setbacks during the Great Depression. The 1932 Economic Act mandated that if layoffs were necessary, married women were the first to go. The federal wage code also gave women less pay than men for the same jobs. During World War II, many women entered the labor force. But after the war, they were displaced by returning veterans. The Equal Pay Act was signed in 1963 and the Civil Rights Act in 1964. The 1964 act made it illegal for companies with over 15 employees to discriminate on the basis of race, color, national origin, religion, or sex. During the 1970s the National Organization for Women (NOW) heavily supported the Equal Rights Amendment which would guarantee equal treatment of men and women. The amendment failed when only 35 of a necessary 38 states approved it.

Environmental Movement

The environmental movement includes a wide variety of loosely networked groups and organizations. The movement is very diverse and lacks overarching goals because different environmental problems affect different industries and people. For example, the problem of water pollution in the Great Lakes has little to do with the problem of tropical deforestation. As a result of this diversity, success in the environmental movement usually requires groups to form complex coalitions with other groups. The affected groups pool their resources to achieve a specific goal. The fluid nature of these coalitions helps to distinguish the environmental movement from other social movements with long-lasting coalitions. The roots of this movement are found in American history. In all, there have been three periods in the environmental movement:

- *Exploitation period.* During the exploitation period, the ecosystem was viewed as either a vast storehouse of resources ripe for exploitation, or as a series of obstacles to be overcome. This included clear-cutting land and killing off the buffalo.

- *Conservation period.* The conservation period extended from the late 1800s through the end of World War II. During this time, the environment began to be a controversial issue, and two approaches emerged: preservation and conservation. The ultimate goal of preservationists was to protect the environment from economic exploitation. The conservationists believed in accommodating economic development whenever possible.

- *Ecological period.* After World War II the ecological period began. We are still in this period today. Currently, environmental organizations have their own separate goals, and they regularly lobby Congress about environmental matters. The environmental movement is now divided into three factions:

    - *Mainstream ecology.* these people work in formal organizations funded by independent financial contributions. They have professional staffs but depend heavily on volunteers.
    - *Populist ecology.* This faction emphasizes individual and corporate responsibility and generally ignores collective political action.
    - *Radical ecology.* This faction is the smallest of the three. Some radical ecologists follow *Gaia*, or the view that the earth's living matter--including the air, oceans, and land--are components of a self-regulating organism. Some are **eco-feminists** who believe that the oppression of nature is caused by the same male-dominated institutions that oppress women and minorities. Another branch is *social ecology*, which argues that the current environmental movement is not capable of solving the world's environmental problems because it is too closely linked with the status quo and only a new social order can provide a solution.

The environmental movement faces opposition from several powerful sources. Some politicians feel that it stands in the way of development. Many businesses are resistant to legislation that forces them to clean up after themselves. As the environmental movement grew, many racial and ethnic minorities came to realize that they are the groups most affected by pollution. This illustrates how two social movements can benefit by joining forces to achieve a common goal which was not initially foreseen by the founders of either movement.

Collective Social Action and Working for Change

Changing individuals

One way to affect change is to shape the knowledge, values, and attitudes of individuals through formal schooling, adult programs, classes, and workshops.

Changing organizations

Formal organizations are such an important part of our society that they are often the target of change. Several principles come into play when attempting to change organizations. First, organizations are more effectively changed when the rate of the members' participation is high. Second, those people working to bring about change need to be sensitive to the personal needs of the organization's members. Third, the expectations of people working for change are important. Fourth, those working for change must know the social structure and operations of the organization being changed.

Changing institutions

Mohandas Gandhi led the fight against political, legal, and economic oppression in South Africa and then in India. His strategy for non-violently affecting institutional change is as follows:
- Try to resolve conflicts and grievances through negotiation and arbitration without compromising the group's fundamental principles.
- Prepare the group for direct action, and prepare members to suffer the consequences of their actions.
- Engage in demonstrations and propaganda.
- Once again attempt to persuade the opponent to accept the group's demands, and explain that refusal will bring further actions.
- Invite strikes, boycotts, and similar types of action.
- Begin a program of non-cooperation with authorities.
- Engage in civil disobedience to laws related to objects of change.
- Take over some of the government's functions (if the government is the opponent).
- Establish a parallel organization to perform government functions that have been taken over.

Change in individuals, organizations, or institutions seldom occurs easily. People resist change because they accept the legitimacy of the existing system or because they make a rational calculation that they will lose something of value if change occurs.

Collective Social Action in the Twenty-First Century

Change in the future

Change is constant in human social life. Sociologist Gary Marx and Doug McAdam make the following predictions for the future:
- We will enter a period of heightened collective action.
- The growing gap between the rich and poor will stimulate collective action.
- As transportation and communication becomes easier and swifter, protest and terrorism will become easier and swifter as well.
- The issue of race will continue to divide people, and this will produce collective social action aimed at achieving social, political, and economic equality.
- Nationalistic ethnic movements will sweep the globe as more ethnic groups act on their own behalf.

Sociology may also change as some sociologists argue that we need to place more emphasis on *humanist sociology*, or on the "study of human freedom and of all the social obstacles that must be overcome in order to insure this freedom."

Critical Questions

CQ: (page411) Think about a time when you were part of a conventional, solidaristic, or expressive crowd. Did participation in this crowd evoke strong feelings in you? Did these feelings lead you to engage new or different behavior?

First define the key terms conventional, solidaristic, and expressive crowd. How did you come to be a part of this crowd? Did you intentionally join or were you simply in the right (or wrong) place at that time? Did membership in the crowd bring about strong emotions? If so, describe them. Were you surprised at your feelings? Had you experienced this before? Did you act on those feelings? If so, what did you do? What affect, if any, did your behavior have on those around you? Did you later regret your actions? Would you have done things differently? Have you ever observed crowd behavior from the outside? What did you think of the participants' behavior?

CQ: (page 425) At what point do you think a group committed to nonviolent change should rethink its commitment? Is violence ever justified in working for change?

Many movements begin as nonviolent movements but then have instances of violence or become violent. Take a few minutes to list some of the organizations and social movements that have made headlines in the past decade (for example Right to Life, Greenpeace, etc.) Did they have both violent and non-violent actions? Were there times when the organization and its members were non-violent but then others began the violence? No matter who started the violence, did it help the cause? Did it matter who started the violence? Violence can be against persons or against property – is one more justified than the other? The media shapes much of what we perceive about groups. Since quiet demonstrations are not "news worthy," do you think violence helps make headlines and therefore may be done to attract media attention? When there is violence, do you think it is a decision of the larger organization or a decision made by a few?

CQ: (page 421) This question refers to the story of Rachel Carson on pages 420-421. A new generation has come upon the scene since Carson alerted the public to the dangers to the environment caused by indiscriminate use of herbicides, pesticides, and other toxins. What about you? Do you worry much about the contaminants in your food? Do you think the government should continue its role of protecting the environment?

Review the account of Rachel Carson's work. At whose cost should the government regulate toxins? Taxpayers? Industries? Are you willing to pay higher prices for toxin-free goods? How much higher? Should the government require multinational corporations to abide by the same standards overseas that they do in the United States? Should the United Sates refuse to trade with countries that do not also follow strict environmental guidelines? Why or why not? Are developing countries in the position to implement environmental policies? Why or why not?

Self-Test Questions
Multiple Choice

1. What is the term for social interactions that are a response to unstructured, ambiguous, or unstable situations?
   - a. collective behavior
   - b. mobs
   - c. riots
   - d. social movements

2. According to Smelser, which is NOT a condition necessary for collective behavior to occur?
   - a. existing strains in the social structure
   - b. precipitating event
   - c. failure of social control
   - d. all of the above are necessary conditions

3. A group of people who are passive, have a low emotional engagement, and who move in and out without notice are called:
    a. expressive crowd
    b. casual crowd
    c. solidaristic crowd
    d. conventional crowd

4. The Million Man March was an expression of consensus among African-American men. Which type of crowd was it?
    a. solidaristic
    b. acting
    c. expressive
    d. conventional

5. Which type of crowd, including people gathered at a bus stop, is goal-directed and followed conventional norms of social behavior?
    a. expressive
    b. casual
    c. solidaristic
    d. conventional

6. According to Herbert Blumer, an acting crowd goes through five stages. Which of the following is NOT one of those stages?
    a. people share basic social characteristics
    b. people become restless, apprehensive, and susceptible to rumors
    c. something startling occurs and people become preoccupied with it
    d. people start milling around and discussing the event

7. In which type of crowd does violence occur?
    a. expressive
    b. solidaristic
    c. conventional
    d. acting

8. A collective but irrational reaction to a serious threat is called:
    a. mob
    b. panic
    c. riot
    d. fight

9. The tendency in a crowd for false information at one stage to be rapidly communicated to others in the crowd who then embellish the misinformation and communicate it to other crowd members is called:
    a. the rumor mill
    b. circular reaction
    c. mutual reinforcement
    d. self-fulfilling prophecy

10. Which theory of crowd behavior proposes that the crowd develops a collective mind that releases people's destructive tendencies?
    a. relative deprivation
    b. resource mobilization
    c. contagion
    d. emergent norm

11. Which theory of crowd behavior states that crowd unity forms from members who share similar views and attitudes?
    a. convergence
    b. relative deprivation
    c. emergent norm
    d. resource mobilization

12. Which type of social movement has the focused goal of changing society in a limited way?
    a. expressive
    b. revolutionary
    c. reform
    d. resistance

13. Which type of social movement has the goal of replacing the existing social order with a completely new order?
    a. reform
    b. revolutionary
    c. resistance
    d. expressive

14. The goal of the pro-life movement is to counter the work of the pro-choice movement. What type of movement is pro-life?
    a. repressive
    b. revolutionary
    c. reform
    d. resistance

15. Which theory states that social movements occur when people perceive an intolerable gap between what they feel their situation *should be* and what it *actually is*.
    a. resource mobilization
    b. relative deprivation
    c. emergent norm
    d. resistance

16. Which theory states that industrialization has led to anomie, alienation, and excessive rationalization which have, in turn, led to social movements?
    a. emergent norm
    b. mass society
    c. resource mobilization
    d. relative deprivation

Chapter 15 Collective Social Action

17. In which social period was the environment viewed as an obstacle to be overcome?
    a. conservationist
    b. preservationist
    c. exploitation
    d. ecological

18. Which present day social movement is divided into several factions making it difficult to define a single overarching goal?
    a. environmental
    b. women's
    c. civil rights
    d. none of the above

19. Which part of the environmental movement emphasizes individual and corporate responsibility and generally ignores collective political action?
    a. mainstream ecology
    b. populist ecology
    c. radical ecology
    d. feminist ecology

20. What is the term for the view that the earth's living matter, including the air, oceans, and land, are components of a self-regulating organism?
    a. Gaia
    b. human ecology
    c. web of life
    d. eco-feminism

21. When it comes to changing organizations, which of the following is true?
    a. organizations are more effectively changed when the rate of membership in the organization is high
    b. people working to bring about change need to be sensitive to the personal needs of the organization's members
    c. the expectations of the people working for change are important
    d. all of the above

22. Which of the following is NOT a reason people resist change?
    a. they accept the legitimacy of existing institutions
    b. they have a vested interest in the status quo
    c. social inertia
    d. they are concerned that others will be angry with them

True - False

T	F	1. Collective social action is the cooperative attempt to achieve a social goal.
T	T	2. Sociologists use the terms mob and crowd interchangeably.
T	F	3. Most people are frequently members of crowds but seldom members of mobs.
T	F	4. Riots, mobs, and acting crowds either are violent or have the potential for violence.
T	F	5. Many riots are started by rumors.
T	F	6. Most natural disasters result in panics.
T	F	7. People engage in collective social action when things are getting worse for them.

T	F	8. Reform movement theory argues that resources are the key ingredient for a successful social movement.
T	F	9. We are currently in the conservative period of the environmental movement.
T	F	10. Feminist social activists that claim that the oppression of nature is caused by the same male dominated institutions which oppress women and minorities are called eco-feminists.
T	F	11. Institutional ecology is that faction of the environmental movement that consists mainly of formal organizations funded by independent financial contributions with a combination of professional staffs and volunteer workers.
T	F	12. People resist change because they are afraid that they will lose something they value.
T	F	13. Organizations are most effectively changed when the rate of the members' participation in the organization is high.
T	F	14. One element of non-violent action is to engage in civil disobedience to laws related to the objects of change.

Self-Test Answers

Multiple Choice

1. a (404)	6. a (407)	11. a (410)	16. b (414)	21. d (423)
2. d (405)	7. d (406)	12. c (411)	17. c (418)	22. d (424)
3. b (406)	8. b (408)	13. b (411)	18. a (419)	
4. a (406)	9. b (409)	14. d (412)	19. b (419)	
5. d (406)	10. c (409)	15. b (412)	20. a (419)	

True - False

1. T (403)	4. T (407)	7. F (414)	10. T (420)	13. T (422)
2. F (405)	5. T (408)	8. F (414)	11. F (419)	14. T (424)
3. T (406)	6. F (408)	9. F (419)	12. T (424)	

NOTES FOR FUTURE STUDY AND REVIEW: